Dancing with the Devil

New Directions in Anthropological Writing
History, Poetics, Cultural Criticism

GEORGE E. MARCUS
Rice University

JAMES CLIFFORD
University of California, Santa Cruz

GENERAL EDITORS

Dancing with the Devil

SOCIETY AND CULTURAL POETICS IN

MEXICAN-AMERICAN SOUTH TEXAS

José E. Limón

THE UNIVERSITY OF WISCONSIN PRESS

The University of Wisconsin Press
114 North Murray Street
Madison, Wisconsin 53715

3 Henrietta Street
London WC2E 8LU, England

5 4 3 2

Printed in the United States of America

Library of Congress Cataloging-in-Publication Data
Limón, José Eduardo.
Dancing with the devil: society and cultural poetics in Mexican
American south Texas / José E. Limón.
256 p.   cm.—(New directions in anthropological writing)
Includes bibliographical references (p. 222) and index.
ISBN 0-299-14220-5 (cl)   ISBN 0-299-14224-8 (pb)
1. Mexican Americans—Texas—Social life and customs.
2. Devil—Folklore.   3. Folklore—Texas.
4. Texas—Social life and customs.
I. Title. II. Series.
F395.M5L56   1994

For Mr. Paredes,
and better times.
1967–1987

Contents

Preface

Before I became an anthropological folklorist, I had already spent a great deal of my life with the central concern of this book: inscribing in various ways the folklore of the people of Mexican descent of southern Texas—my folks—an inscription conditioned always by the lower-working-class existence in which I grew up. Necessarily, these inscriptions included also an order of social domination and war extending into the present, and this book is also about that.

To take only one major example: the Catholic Church first taught me about the existence of evil and, of course, introduced me to its ultimate personification, the Devil. But the Church's singular focus on personal conduct said nothing about the evident evil expressed in the social treatment of the *barrios* it ostensibly served. I was told only of a personal devil in church, and a very sexual devil at that; but on the streets of the Westwide of Corpus Christi, I was already learning what the folks in the *barrio* already knew and learned anew every day—the devil can take many forms.

The Church taught me other things as well, including something about cultural poetics. At about the same time I was learning about the devil, I became acutely conscious of the way this theological knowledge was represented to us in an enthralling Latinate ritual poetry whose rhythms, idioms, and metaphors, including, of course, the devil, remain with me to this day. Inadvertently, perhaps, the Church also taught me about the body other than in its prescribed sexual limits. The Church's Catholic Youth Organization sponsored dances, you see, where I first learned to dance—in limited fashion, since the Irish nuns did not permit gliding, turning, body-holding Mexican polkas, only slower American dancing and (strangely enough) noncontact rock 'n' roll. As with my sense of the devil, my dancing repertoire expanded elsewhere in our *barrio*. And so I learned of the inseparability of precursory traditions, politics, and cultural poetics and their often paradoxical relationship. In this extended essay on the politics and poetics of my scholarly precursors and of contemporary Mexican-American south Texas folklore, I must therefore first acknowledge the Church for its first basic instruction. Although of importance in the formation of this extended essay, these early lessons led to others, perhaps more important, that also require acknowledgment.

The key tenets of politically laden cultural authority inculcated in a south Texas Mexican boy coming of age in the late 1950s—the primacy of the Church; the "superstitious" character of Mexicans; the unquestioned rule of "Anglos"; the "natural" submissiveness of women; the monolithic character of Mexican culture itself—were further bedeviled for me at the University of Texas at Austin in the 1960s by a fine liberal arts education and a campus activism. As a fundamental part of this education and activism and largely through the work and example of the man to whom this book is dedicated, I also came to know my scholarly precursors and my people's capacity to culturally critique and bedevil those who have dominated the working-class Mexican people of the United States. I would like to think that this book continues in that critical tradition. I would, however, add a distinctive theme in these pages, and that is the capacity of my people to bedevil themselves, always under the constraining conditioning of the sociocultural Other. I will also speak here of how this community's self-questioning led to a greater sense of political and cultural freedom, with its cultural poetics as a primary form of interrogation.

Such are the general origins and themes of this book, a book about bedevilment that could not have come into specific existence without the assistance of various angels of mercy. I thank my good friend and colleague Juan Gomez-Quiñones, former Director of the UCLA Chicano Studies Center, for his assistance in securing a 1978–79 postdoctoral fellowship with the Center that made possible my initial theoretical reflections on these subjects. For good and bad reasons the project then went into a long hiatus, to be finally rescued by the generous assistance of the Stanford University Humanities Center, Blíss Carnochan, Director. A 1987–88 Ford Foundation Fellowship with the Center permitted the first substantial writing of the entire manuscript. I gratefully acknowledge this institutional support, and centrally that of Renato Rosaldo of the Stanford anthropology department. A George I. Sánchez Endowment Summer Fellowship from the College of Liberal Arts, University of Texas at Austin, permitted the final drafting of the manuscript. I thank the College and its former Dean, Standish Meacham, as well as Rodolfo O. de la Garza, former Director of the Center for Mexican American Studies.

Portions of the manuscript were drafted in the Mill Valley Public Library during holiday periods in California. I am grateful to them for the large table near the tall sunny window.

An invitation to join the School of American Research 1989 Advanced Seminar, "Recapturing Anthropology," and to present parts of this material led to invaluable supportive criticism. I especially thank Richard Fox, seminar director, and members Arjun Appadurai, Sherry Ortner, Paul Rabinow, and Michel-Rolph Trouillot. I also express my gratitude to other readers and audiences for versions and sections of the manuscript, principally Nathan Adler, Ruth Behar, Richard Flores, Douglas Foley, Don Graham, Michaele Haynes, the late Joan Lidoff, Teresa McKenna Joseph Porter, yet again Renato Rosaldo, José Saldívar, Ramón Saldívar, Suzanne Seriff, as well as colloquia at Stanford, Rice, and the Universities of California–Berkeley, Michigan–Ann Arbor, Texas–Austin, and Virginia. I am especially grateful to Professor Carey Wall and the College of Arts and Letters of San Diego State University for the opportunity to present most of this material during a week-long Faculty Development Seminar. Special thanks to seminar members Adelaida del Castillo, Emily Hicks, Eve Kornfeld, and most of all Bill Nericcio. Susan Tarcov greatly improved the manuscript with her skillful editing.

Earlier versions of some of these chapters appear as contributions to *Tonantzin: Chicano Arts in San Antonio,* ed. Juan Tejeda (San Antoñio: Guadalupe Arts Center, 1988); *Recapturing Anthropology: Working into the Present,* ed. Richard Fox (Santa Fe: School of American Research, 1991); *Criticism in the Borderlands: Studies in Chicano Literature, Culture, and Identity,* ed. Hector Calderón and José D. Saldívar (Durham: Duke University Press, 1991); and *Texas Studies in Language and Literature* (1994).

I also wish to thank the Guadalupe Cultural Arts Center of San Antoñio, Texas, for permission to reproduce as my book cover Douglas Jasso's poster "la noche cuando vino un diablito con accordion al baile grande" (the night a little devil with an accordion came to the big dance). Mr. Jasso, originally from San Antonio, but then a student at Kansas Art Institute, entered his original poster in the seventh annual Tejano Conjunto Festival Poster Contest and won first place. The Guadalupe Cultural Arts Center sponsors this musical festival and its accompanying poster contest. Mr. Jasso produced his artistic idea wholly independently of the present work, adding further testimony to the presence of the dancing devil in the popular imagination. Shortly after this very popular poster was sold and exhibited all over San Antoñio, conservative, predominantly Anglo Christian fundamentalist groups demonstrated at the Guadalupe Cultural Arts Center and wrote letters to the local newspapers accusing Mr. Jasso and this Chicano community arts group of consorting with the devil. Clearly, they were only dancing with him.

Finally, I am most indebted to my wife, Marianna Adler, for her own reading, her support, patience, and love, and to our *diablita,* our little daughter, Renata, for the sheer joy she has brought to my life as I've danced with the devil.

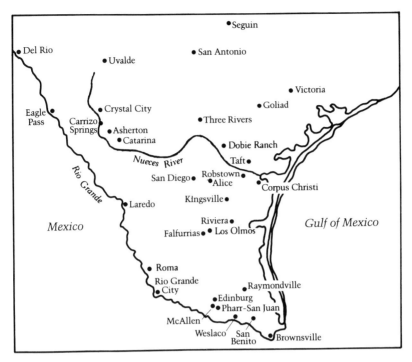

South Texas

Reprinted with additions, courtesy of the University of Texas Press, from *Anglos and Mexicans in the Making of Texas, 1836–1936* by David Montejano, 1987, University of Texas Press.

Dancing with the Devil

Hereby it is manifest, that during the time men live without a common Power to keep them all in awe, they are in that condition which is called Warre; and such a warre, as if of every man, against every man. For WARRE, *consisteth not in Battell onely, or the act of fighting; but in a tract of time, wherein the Will to contend by Battell is sufficiently known: and therefore the motion of* time *is to be considered in the nature of Warre; as it is in the nature of Weather. For as the nature of Foule weather, lyeth not in a showre or two of rain; but in an inclination thereto of many dayes together: So the nature of War, consisteth not in actuall fighting; but in the known disposition thereto, during all the time there is no assurance to the contrary. All other time is* PEACE.*
                                                    —Thomas Hobbes,* The Leviathan

To articulate the past historically does not mean to recognize it "the way it really was" (Ranke). It means to seize hold of a memory as it flashes up at a moment of danger. Historical materialism wishes to retain that image of the past which unexpectedly appears to man singled out by history at a moment of danger. The danger affects both the content of the tradition and its receivers. The same threat hangs over both: that of becoming a tool of the ruling classes. In every era the attempt must be made anew to wrest tradition away from a conformism that is about to overpower it. The Messiah comes not only as the redeemer, he comes as the subduer of Antichrist. Only that historian will have the gift of fanning the spark of hope in the past who is firmly convinced that even the dead will not be safe from the enemy if he wins. And this enemy has not ceased to be victorious.
                                                    —Walter Benjamin,* Illuminations

Among my Daily-Papers, which I bestow on the Public, there are some which are written with Regularity and Method, and others that run out into the Wildness of those Compositions, which go by the Name of Essays.
                                                    —Joseph Addison,* The Spectator

Mi hijito, si vas a decir algo de nosotros, dilo bíen. (My son, if you're going to say something about us, say it well.)
                                                    —My mother, the kitchen table*

3

Introduction

In the fall of 1950, some months after the beginning of the Korean War, a largely American United Nations Army had finally regained the initiative against the North Korean forces which had invaded South Korea in June. Now, in late October, under U.N. authorization, the Americans and their allies were counterattacking deep into North Korea and driving toward the Chinese border at the Yalu River; this, however, amidst rumors of a possible pro–North Korean intervention by the People's Republic of China. As one recent historian tells it, the U.N. supreme commander, General Douglas MacArthur, and his field general, Walton H. Walker "persisted in their conviction that their armies could drive with impunity to the Yalu. They continued to believe that the Chinese were either unwilling or unable to intervene effectively" (Hastings 1987:130). Yet, Chinese soldiers were already showing up among the North Korean casualties and prisoners. General Walker explained away this growing Chinese threat with recourse to a seemingly bizarre cultural simile. The number of Chinese didn't seem to matter: "After all," he said,

> a lot of Mexicans live in Texas. . . . (Hastings 1987:130)

In several respects—history, war, the political, the poetic, ethnographic constructions, and Mexicans in Texas—General Walker's commentary serves as a useful point of departure for this extended essay.

While terribly mistaken about Chinese intentions, "Bulldog" Walker, as he was poetically called by his troops, was and continues to be narrowly correct about the Mexicans: a lot of them do live in Texas. The general, you see, was a native Texan, born and raised in Belton close to San Antonio, a city which, as a military man, he would also come to know even better. You would think that as long as he was on the subject, and as a friendly gesture to a fellow Texan, he would have saved me a line or two in this introduction by noting further for us that most of the Mexicans live in

5

south Texas. There they constitute a large demographic majority, with San Antoñio, the region's dominant city, itself containing a population of over fifty percent Mexican descent. Walker was also narrowly correct on another point, but here also elaboration is required.

As a non-Mexican, he is correct, or at least consistent, in referring to these mostly U.S. citizens as "Mexicans," since this is what they are usually called by the "Anglo" demographic minority in South Texas; itself, of course, largely of English, Scottish, Irish, and German ancestry, mostly coming from the American South. Even with the recent appearance of new terms—"Chicano," on one end of a political spectrum, "Hispanic," on the other—"Mexican" remains the dominant operative term among "Anglos" in polite conversation. When the conversation is impolite—and, as we shall see, politeness has never been a strong suit for many "Anglos" when it comes to Mexicans—it might sound more like "Meskins," as in "We're going to need a whole bunch of Meskins for picking this year," or "Goddamn, honey, why the hell does the boy want to marry a Meskin gal?" Probably because of such more than occasional impoliteness, the "Mexicans" themselves rarely use the English term "Mexican" to refer to themselves, except in revealing jest, the way African Americans sometimes call each other "nigger." However, in everyday, predominantly Spanish-language conversation, they will almost invariably speak of themselves as "mexicanos"—Mexicans—but in Spanish.

The ancestors of some of these people entered the now south Texas area as part of the northward expansion of the Spanish from central New Spain in the mid-eighteenth century. The area, along with what is now the U.S. Southwest of course, then became part of the newly founded Republic of Mexico in 1821. This new national identity continued through the rest of the nineteenth century and was intensified by continuous immigration principally from neighboring northeastern Mexico, particularly in the early years of the twentieth century. Probably this is the reason my folks continue to identify themselves as *"mexicanos"* even though this south Texas ground violently became part of the United States in 1848. When an English self-referent is needed—and the population is now predominantly bilingual—they are likely to use "Mexican-American." I follow this usage (Limón 1981; J. Garcia 1981). Finally, my foregrounding of Anglo as "Anglo" is intended to suggest a political figuration and attitude, not a specific cultural reality. I have no quarrel with Anglos, only with "Anglos."

In addition to numbers and names, Walker was representatively "cor-

rect" on a more important matter. He subconsciously and correctly articulates the sociocultural domination that has characterized south Texas. It is
analogically instructive that this maker of war, this military representative
of U.S. foreign policy in the third world, even *thought* about Mexicans in
Texas as he and his Eighth Army were about to confront the Chinese near
the Yalu River in the late fall of 1950. This representative man, who had
also served as a young officer in the U.S. Army invasion of Veracruz, Mexico, in 1914, was fashioning a dualistic and racist cultural poetics, an "Orientalism" (Said 1979) reflected back upon a "Western" people in Texas. On
the one hand, there is a clear threatened sense of massive numbers of the
Other—"a lot," he says—a horde threatening to overwhelm. On the other,
there is an assured condescending conviction that these hordes—Chinese
or Mexican—are inert and passive, "unwilling or unable to intervene effectively" in war and society, to use Hastings' paraphrase.[1]

Fellow Texans that we are, Walker and I share a number of concerns:
Texas, of course, and Mexicans and "Anglos"; but also war, domination, colonialism, and cultural metaphors. Our understandings of these
questions—our respective poetics of culture and society—differ radically, but "Bulldog" and I would have mutually understood that, had we
talked; that's the way it's been in Texas at least since 1848. These are
also the themes of what follows in this book: an ethnographic essay,
historical and relatively contemporaneous, on a subaltern sector of
Mexican-American society in south Texas, an essay which examines a
range of expressive culture concerning this sector in relation to its socially dominated condition. As an ethnographic essay, it is a necessarily
partial vision, which is to say neither whole nor impartial. As an ethnographic essay on such matters, it is also necessarily involved in certain
ongoing political and intellectual discussions.

CULTURAL STUDIES, POETICS, AND THE
"EXPERIMENTAL MOMENT" IN ANTHROPOLOGY

Centered to some degree on dancing, the essay attempts to dance to the
music of certain trends in cultural studies, but, like a good south Texas
Mexican-American dancer, it proposes its own distinctive rhythm and
style. Permit me a brief review of these matters as a context for setting
forth my argument.

One such trend is what Marcus and Fischer have called "an experimental moment in the human sciences" (1987), a moment marked by at least

three tendencies or characteristics. First, its largely anthropological participants display an intense reflexive awareness of the textual and ideological character of inquiry and writing, again, principally in anthropology. Here we note a "blurring," to evoke a now famous phrase (Geertz 1980), of the textual genres of "ethnography," "literature," "criticism," and "history," and cross-disciplinary appropriation such as the literary-critical use of anthropology and vice versa.

This concern blurs into our second characteristic of the "moment." Here we note a decided shift away from the "traditional" objects of anthropology—values, social structure, myth texts, systems of rules and meaning, etc.—toward social process but, quite often, aesthetically salient social process. As James Peacock notes, the anthropologist typically has tended

> to pay too little heed to the dynamics of cultural performances, to
> report from the performances only those tidbits of content which
> lend support to his portrait of the values and organization of the
> society in which the performances are found . . . this kind of analysis
> which fails to grasp the essence of symbolic performances can yield
> no full appreciation of social dynamics. (1968:256)

Peacock spoke of symbolic "performances" in 1968. Today, we almost take for granted the ubiquitous construction of social process as "text," "drama," "symbolic action," etc. (Geertz 1980).

Finally, always aware of the uncomfortable proximity of anthropology to Western colonialism, the "experimental moment" is deeply concerned with the status of the usually socially dominated Other in its textualizations and the critical (mis)uses of those textualizations. The issue of the rhetorical strategies appropriate to give substantial voice to the Other in ethnographic discourse emerges here (Clifford 1980:50–54). Here too there is recognition of the ethnography as a persuasive and political rhetoric in *our* culture as well as a deconstructive rethinking of the history of anthropology as cultural discourse (Manganaro 1990). More closely related to this last issue but implicit in the first two and throughout my own writing are two other questions: the political significance of "ethnography" in the present moment and the question of the "native" investigator. In the first case, I largely share the idea that "ethnography is written representation of a culture (or selected aspects of a culture)" (Van Maanen 1988:1). But, as Van Maanen argues, between the culture and its written representation lies fieldwork. Beyond requiring a continuous exposure to a culture "in the field" and its subsequent written representation, Van Maanen is careful not to fix the temporal and practical features of this fieldwork or the stylistic forms this written representation may take, particularly the latter. Indeed, it is his task to explore the varieties of representation based on fieldwork. As for "native" ethnography, the experimental moment largely has not broached the issue, nor will I in any sustained way, although the entire book implicitly addresses this question.

From these general issues, we can best move toward my practice by considering a specific encounter between the experimental moment and an ethnography not that distant from my own. In a review of Willis' *Learning to Labour* (1981), Marcus (1986) makes three specific critical recommendations concerning the ethnographic rendering of culture and domination, recommendations that eventually turn into a larger subsuming suggestion for the ethnographic treatment of this question.

First, Marcus points to the positivistic fallacy of conceiving of ethnographic exposition only as "descriptive" method as Willis does, description which will then be elucidated by the authoritative voice of high theory in a follow-up section. Second, he cautions against assuming or describing only in linear terms the world of the dominant, thus reifying rather than rendering it ethnographically as well. Finally, he takes Willis to task for the latter's too insistent attempt to find positive meaning—socially resistive critical meaning—in the lives of his English working-class youth. Here there are two specific subcomplaints: first, that the everyday cultural data on which to base such a reading of resistance are "thin," leading Marcus to critically wonder why Willis did not make interpretive use of these youths' rich popular culture; second, that Willis too easily converts the culture of these young men into a seamless form of resistance, ignoring or textually diminishing internal contradictions such as the male chauvinism and sexism on which this culture of "resistance" is founded (Marcus 1986:173–88).

For Marcus, however, Willis' work and its limitations are conditioned by a more fundamental problem of ethnographic form, namely, Willis' investment in a realist ethnography whose very commitment to a linear rendering does not allow him to capture the flux and contradiction that are culture as Marcus conceives it.

In the spirit of the "moment," Marcus suggests an ethnographic textual mode that will presumably overcome the difficulties in such work as that of Willis. This is a mode articulated as a mixed genre to evoke different perspectives and modeled after what Marcus calls "the modern essay." Presumably and specifically, this form eschews "realist" descriptive repre-

sentation followed by theoretical exposition but rather brings these textually together; finally, it recognizes and textually renders the disorderly
contradictions that often prevail in the world of the dominated rather than
ordering them into a 1960s-influenced seamless narrative of resistance
(Bruner 1986). What Marcus leaves unclear and highly programmatic is
precisely how all of this is to be done in this mixed-genre, modernist form.
Partial anticipatory examples are offered, but it is clear that this is ethnography yet to be born.

Let us listen to Marcus as he recommends what he calls the modernist
form of the essay. The modern essay, he tells us,

> opposes conventional systematic analysis, absolves the writer from
> having to develop the broader implications of his thought (while
> nonetheless indicating that there are such implications) or of having
> to tie loose ends together. The essayist can mystify the world, leave
> his subjects' actions open-ended as to their global implications, from
> a rhetorical posture of profound half-understanding, half-
> bewilderment with the world in which the ethnographic subject and
> the ethnographer live. This is thus a form well suited to a time such
> as the present, when paradigms are in disarray, problems intractable,
> and phenomena only partly understood . . . A sustained tolerance of
> incompleteness and indeterminateness about the order in the world
> that lies beyond the experience of ethnographic subjects, intensely
> focused upon, seems to be a key rhetorical marker in modernist eth-
> nography. (1986:191–92)

In somewhat similar though independent fashion, Shirley Brice
Heath has also pointed to the formal virtues of the essay for capturing
cultural contradiction. Drawing masterfully on a large body of critical
commentary on the essay, often by its best practitioners, she recommends the essay to ethnographers but in a way that makes it more germane to the present effort. She first makes us aware of the essay's critical open-ended quality, a quality intimately related to oral traditions.
For like the latter and often by their literal inclusion in its form, the
essay features "brevity, self-reflexiveness, variety, conservational quality, and opposition to any strict ordering or predictable and methodical
system of prose presentation . . ." (1990:8). Building on this first insight, she then notes the cultural homology between the essay form and
the social situation of the disempowered. Yet, as she critically notes,
even the essay form itself has come under domination in the twentieth
century as the educational system turned it into a linear form reproduc-

ing the prevailing social order. Heath revives for us an older yet more critical sense of the essay to argue brilliantly for this form as a politically appropriate way of providing accounts of dominated people. Like such people, the essay is or should be "a form made up of migrations, alterations and the refusal to let categories dictate or predestine its size, scope, content or manner" (Heath 1990:15).

Such essayistic explorations and experimentations should be adopted cautiously for epistemological but also for political reasons, for the modern essay, if not conscious of its own stance in the world, can soon blur into a kind of negative "postmodern." The potential difficulty is that in an unchecked indeterminacy, reflexivity, and the kind of genre blurring that Jameson calls "pastiche" (1984), such essaying may uncritically reproduce the socially fragmenting effects of late capitalism (Rabinow 1986:247–51). For Rabinow, postmodern experimentation has much to recommend it, but always in the interest of a socially grounded critique, rather than one sustained only textually through formalistic pastiche. We can no longer return to "earlier modes of unselfconscious representation," Rabinow argues, yet we cannot ignore "the relations of representational forms and social practices either" (1986:250–51). Rabinow offers one example—a feminist example—of an anthropology that, while sensitive to a decentering postmodernism, is nonetheless acutely concerned with politics and social practice. As distinct from what Rabinow calls "textual radicalism," which seeks "to work toward establishing relationships," "to demonstrate the possibilities of sharing and mutual understanding, while being fuzzy about power and the realities of socio-economic constraints," Strathern's (1987) feminist practice "insists upon not losing sight of fundamental differences, power relationships, hierarchical domination" (Rabinow 1986:255–56). Both in its concern for an appropriate balance between textual and social practice and later for the question of women, Strathern's example could be taken as a partial charter for this essay.

These pages are also offered as an invitation to the field of folklore scholarship, as I sense the neglect of folklore in general within the cultural studies enterprise, a neglect in favor of written literature and mass media cultural production. The present work is informed by Gramsci's observation:

> Folklore must not be considered an eccentricity, an oddity or a picturesque element but as something which is very serious and is to be taken seriously. Only in this way will the teaching of folklore be more efficient and really bring about the birth of a new culture

among the broad popular masses, so that the separation between
modern culture and popular culture of folklore will disappear.
(Gramsci 1988:362)

As a special case of this neglect, I am also addressing the particular
situation of Chicano cultural studies. Here, again, I see developing a field
of inquiry that, while claiming the rubric "cultural studies," nonetheless
focuses its attention principally on elite written literary forms or film (R.
Saldivar 1990; Calderon and Saldivar, 1991; J. Saldivar 1991; Noriega
1992;). What I don't see often in either the general or the particular case
are integrated works addressing folkloric popular forms, scholarly discursive practices, mass media, and written literary forms in one interpretive
universe always with a close attention to political economy. Rosaldo
(1989) and Gilroy (1991) do take us in this desirable direction.

ON WAR, DANCING, DEVILS, AND DOMINATION

This extended ethnographic essay is an attempted response to the forego-
ing issues, a response that begins with and is subsumed by its general
construction as an essay. Through this form, I propose to examine several
distinct though interrelated spheres of folkloric symbolic action concerning the working classes of Mexican-American south Texas.

In Part I, I will appear to be concerned on the surface of things with
"reviewing the literature" in some academically obligatory way, that is,
with examining past efforts beginning in the 1890s to write ethnographies—written representations—of the expressive culture of this population after periods of fieldwork largely in rural settings. These principal
precursors are John Gregory Bourke, J. Frank Dobie, Jovita Gonzalez,
and Américo Paredes.[2] But, in the spirit of the "experimental moment,"
I wish to construct and deconstruct their written representation as symbolic action, as cultural practices in themselves, as expressive culture
about expressive culture. As part of the "experimental moment," which
includes a growing deconstructive understanding of the history of ethnography, Part I is a kind of historical ethnography of a writing (adjective)
culture about south Texas Mexican-Americans. Interpreting this writerly
culture in its historical moments, as we are bound to do, requires that I
set out in Part I a simultaneous, if condensed, historical narrative of this
place and people. This should also be particularly useful for readers
wholly unfamiliar with the area and serve as "background" to the rest of

the book. A section that I call an Interchapter follows, where I set out an interpretive sociocultural context for Part II.

In Part II, I turn to a somewhat more traditional stance for an ethnographer of expressive culture, which is that of offering my own ethnographic, interpretive account of expressive activity "in the field." In more experimental fashion, I offer a rendition of working-class Mexican-American popular culture in Texas, based on experiential fieldwork conducted in that area from the mid-1970s to early 1980s. Here I shall be concerned with male humor and meat consumption (Chapter 6); popular dancing (Chapter 7); a women's devil legend (Chapter 8), and finally, in Chapter 9, a concluding discussion of ethnographic authority, folk healing, gender, and the fiction of Tomás Rivera.

What do I mean to say about the worlds I have chosen and that have chosen me, these situated expressive worlds unified by their relationship to the lower-class Mexican people of south Texas? It should be noted that in choosing these discourses and their authors, those of my precursors and of present-day south Texas, I have already engaged in my first act of interpretation. Why these choices? Here, we may cite yet revise Stephen Greenblatt in his choice of Thomas More, Spenser, Marlowe, Shakespeare, William Tyndale, and Wyatt for his study of the English Renaissance:

> In attempting to glimpse the formation of identity in the English Renaissance, we cannot rest content with statistical tables, nor are we patient enough to tell over a thousand stories, each with its slight variants. The problem is not only lack of patience but a sense of hopelessness: after a thousand, there would be another thousand, then another, and it is not clear that we would be closer to the understanding we seek. So from the thousands, we seize upon a handful of arresting figures who seem to contain within themselves most of what we need, who both reward intense, individual attention and promise access to large cultural patterns. (1980:6)

A received canonical tradition and Greenblatt's impressive scholarly experience in his field manifestly condition his choices. I have less of the former to draw upon, although my now nearly twenty years in the "field"—in the sense of both field of scholarship and site of ethnographic research—convince me that my particular choices of figures and figurations also "reward intense, individual attention and promise access to large cultural patterns." I shall try to demonstrate the basis of this conviction in subsequent chapters.

From Greenblatt I also borrow and now address a key interpretive

concept in my subtitle—"cultural poetics" or the "poetics of culture"—
referring to acts of cultural interpretation focused on aesthetically salient,
culturally imbedded textualities and enactments, or as Greenblatt defines
it, the "study of the collective making of distinct cultural practices and
inquiry into the relations among these practices" (1988:5). The scholarship I will interpret and, indeed, it might be argued, the "folk" practices
are themselves a cultural poetics, so that what I propose to offer in these
pages is a cultural poetics of cultural poetics. And what is that—my cultural poetics? My interpretive position with regard to these several
worlds?

My unifying concern and most general thesis is that in and through
these situated renderings of expressive culture, whether scholarly or
"popular," we can "see displayed," as with that famous Balinese cockfight, certain cultural preoccupations (Geertz 1973a). Here, however, I
veer from an idealist wing in symbolic-interpretive anthropology toward
that of culture as practice, grounded in but not reducible to the "material"
conditions of social domination and speaking to essentially political interests (Ortner 1984). The question of culture and domination recalls the
third characteristic of the "experimental moment": its concern with politics as well as poetics, to invoke the title of another landmark contribution
to the "moment" (Clifford and Marcus 1986). And it is here, on the question of power and domination, that this study dances away a bit from the
"experimental moment." My own political cultural formation and the particular and not personally separable history I will be addressing require
(of me) a greater emphasis on this issue beyond that seemingly offered by
the "moment." For critical to our writing of culture are the often socially
dominated conditions of those we write about, our own ideological
stances as ethno/writers, and a general failing to bring together political
economy and cultural criticism. To this end also I draw on the Marxist
cultural theory of Fredric Jameson.[3]

In this essay I propose to explore what Jameson has termed the "political unconscious" (1981): the socially produced, narratively mediated, and
relatively unconscious ideological responses of people—scholars and
"folk"—to a history of race and class domination. In the first phase of this
study, I shall be employing the concept of the political unconscious as
defined above, but in a less strict and more simple fashion than Jameson
proposes in his complex system of reading at three levels. Later in the
essay I will address this greater complexity but in such a way as to bring
Jameson into a more equitable and reflexive conversation with the sub-

jects of this study. I also draw on Jameson's work on postmodernism (1992), but also in a revisionary manner, in my Interchapter.

As I think through my various expressive discourses, scholarly and "folk" alike, what I shall presume to discover at the level of the political unconscious are not seamless narratives of domination *or* resistance relative to this working-class sector. Rather, in varying historical moments, these expressive discourses give evidence, yes, of "resistance" and "domination" but also of seduction, anxiety, internal conflict and contradiction in race, class, and especially gender dimensions conditioned always, as always, by a changing "Anglo" capitalist political economy.

The political unconscious—the largely repressed cultural poetics, if you will—of these subjects, ethnographers and working-class folk alike, is to be discussed in a field of two sociocultural processes, dialectically literal and metaphorical, derived from the experience of these subjects.

The first of these processes in this field of interpretation is war. Here I again take my lead from Antonio Gramsci who in his commentary on the state and society closely pursues the connections between warfare and society in an incisive extended fashion (1971:210–76). In what is really a rich elaboration of Marx and Engel's concept of the class struggle, Gramsci shows us that war, sometimes literal, sometimes only thinly metaphorical, always political and cultural, is the fundamental relationship between antagonistic, fundamentally class forces in modern societies. Within this organizing concept, Gramsci then makes a number of more specific theoretical, semimetaphorical subcontributions germane to this study. Among these are the distinction between the war of "maneuver" and the war of "position;" here, at least implicitly, I also take up the battlefield leadership of the intellectuals, and the tactics of mass formations and small groups.[4]

General Walker made a ghastly error in underestimating the Chinese that dreadful Korean winter of 1950–51. Ironically, he might have avoided this bloodletting underestimation had he but recalled, in his comparative metaphor, a more accurate, less stereotypic, historical sense of Mexicans in Texas. Had he done so, he might have more accurately sensed the Chinese willingness to go to war in defense of *their* border against what they saw as American imperialism. For it is a basic premise and organizing metaphor for this essay that since the 1830s, the Mexicans of south Texas have been in a state of social war with the "Anglo" dominant Other and their class allies. This has been at times a war of overt, massive proportions; at others, covert and sporadic; at still other moments, repressed and internalized as a war within the psyche, but always conditioned by an ongoing social struggle fought out of different battle-fields. Earlier I spoke of a Mexican-American subaltern working-class sector. What I would now emphasize is that it is this lowest socio-economic class sector which has historically waged the most intense war-fare and suffered the most intense defeats, including, now, the imposition of what I shall describe as a racial and class-inflected postmodernity. It is this sector, present in Part I and further defined in my Interchapter and Part II, that chiefly concerns me.[5]

The second metaphorical process related to the lives of this sector and their written representation is the devil. "He" appears in various forms and meanings in these lives and this writing, most centrally and dramatically in Chapter 8. Who is the devil? By his very nature I shall have no final answer, but here are two distinct perspectives explored in what follows.

> Through the archetype of the Devil mankind has said something about the psychological forces, inside man himself, sustaining the economic activity which ultimately flowered into capitalism. The Devil is the lineal descendant of the Trickster and Culture-hero type in primitive mythologies. The Trickster is a projection of the psychological forces sustaining the economic activity of primitive peoples; and the evolution of the Trickster, through such intermediary figures as the classical Hermes, into the Christian Devil, paralleled the changing forms of human economic (especially commercial) activity. Hence when Baudelaíre and Blake declare the essentially Satanic character of commerce, they exploit a great mythological tradition to say something which has not yet been said in any other way. (Brown 1959:220)

And,

> Mephistopheles, like *Faust* itself, is as varied as the world. On even the most superficial level his nature is left unclear, for he sometimes appears to be Satan or Satan's equivalent and at other times only a minor demon . . . In fact, Mephistopheles is much too complex, diverse and ambiguous to be identified with the Christian Devil . . . Goethe kept the ambiguity pronounced, as part of Mephisto's function is to deny any dichotomy in nature, moral or otherwise . . . He is an invitation to the reader to face the multiplicity of reality . . . Mephistopheles is partly a Christian devil, partly an ironic commentator on society . . . (Russell 1986:158–89)

For all of this, the devil is an apt, if shifting, signifier to capture my subjects' contradictions under capitalism. And, if hell is the devil's traditional site of power and war is hell, then General Sherman's infamous equation brings together my two working metaphors, accentuated always by the nearly year-round oppressive heat of southern Texas.

Let us begin with a literal warrior turned anthropologist who met the devil in southern Texas.

Part I

Politics, Poetics, Precursors

Chapter One

John Gregory Bourke

Hence, the [military] professional is caught in a world of means and
instruments, himself among others. He makes war a means for further-
ing political ends, and his preoccupation, like his occupation, is seldom
with things for their own sake. This is the abiding curse of the military
profession. The total human being has no chance to break through the
consciousness because there is no official interest in the whole human
being. So the professional image of the enemy is a consequence of the
pattern of life imposed on those who serve as instruments and not ends.
The abstraction of the image is more or less inevitable.
　　　　—J. Glenn Gray, *The Warriors: Reflections on Men in Battle*

¿Que calor, no? he says to me and anyone else who would hear him. He
pushes and pulls his rake gathering up the very few dead leaves and some
tourist trash on this terribly hot August day in 1979 in Rio Grande City,
Texas. Yes, it is, indeed, hot, I reply in Spanish completing yet another
formulaic exchange about the oppressive south Texas weather repeated a
thousandfold today from here to San Antonio, to Corpus Christi, and
downriver to Brownsville. The label above his shirt pocket announces his
name to be Solís, and today he is the custodian at, and in some ways, of,
Fort Ringold in Rio Grande City. I am here this Friday on a kind of break
from my fieldwork activities some thirty miles upriver in the community I
shall fictitiously call *Límonada* (I have many relatives there). In Límonada I have continued a dance with the devil, a dance begun at other
places including here at Fort Ringold.

　　Rio Grande City and nearby Roma are famous in south Texas for their
delicious *cabrito* (kid goat), so on this weekend I drove down to indulge. I
tell him this. *Si, señor, aqui nomas hay cabrito y cabrones,* Solís replies
(Yes sir, here there are only kid goats and he-goats).[1] We both laugh as he
goes about his raking, slowly; in southern Texas the idea is not to fight the

21

heat. Life is already enough. After the *cabrito,* washed down with cold
Lone Star, I drive out to the fort. Its military functions ceased long ago.
Now, it is a small museum; its buildings, once instrumental to killing, are
now used by the local school system as it wages its own war to better the
lives of the predominantly Mexican-American children of this often most
impoverished of American regions. I came for *cabrito* and to the fort,
because I once again wanted to see a key place where the dance with the
devil had begun, the devil that dances among these my folks and those
who have studied them; for it is here that the first of my precursors literally walked and often rode.

Forts like Ringold are important historical features of the south Texas
sociocultural landscape. Downriver there is Fort Brown; upriver one
finds Fort McIntosh at Laredo and Duncan in Eagle Pass (now a country
club for the Eagle Pass wealthy, anglo and *mexicano* alike); and of course
Fort Sam Houston in San Antoñio, one hundred fifty miles north. Before
they become museums, country clubs, school buildings, or ruins, military
forts are about only one thing: war. So now, having read about my fellow
Texan General Walker in Korea, I am puzzled. Why didn't he know?
And, if he knew, why did he stop caring? For surely he knew and cared to
forget that it was in this south Texas area that, in 1846, the United States
initiated the successful campaign under the command of Zachary Taylor
that eventually resulted in the American incorporation of the Southwest,
including the south Texas area and its resident *mexicanos.*

For my historical ethnographic purposes, it is important to note certain
local effects of this initiating instance of political domination at gunpoint,
this first American construction of the "third world."

As Taylor's army left Corpus Christi intent on reaching and crossing its
Yalu—the Rio Grande—it immediately met armed resistance from local
mexicano settlers now turned guerrillas, even before it met the main Mexican army at Palo Alto and Resaca de la Palma on the northern side of the
river (Lavender 1966:61). "Rancheros" (ranchers) Johannsen tells us,

> . . . led by Ramón Falcon, were involved in the early skirmishes
> with American soldiers along the Rio Grande, and later several hun-
> dred of them, under Antoñio Canales, served as irregular cavalry at
> the battles of Palo Alto and Resaca de la Palma. Canales, whose
> very name inspired fear . . . later led his irregulars in guerrilla activ-
> ity against American supply trains. (1985:24)

As with indigenous guerrillas everywhere, these irregulars were
promptly labeled "bandits" and, like today's "terrorists," inspired both

fear and fascination in their American foes, resulting in still another Orientalist expressive construction, one remarkably close to Edward Said's regional concerns.

> Descriptions abounded, in the soldiers' accounts, the press reports, the histories and the novels, until a stereotype emerged that may or may not have borne a relation to reality. Half Indian and half Spanish, gaunt, dark, and of swarthy visage, with ferocious-looking brows and menacing mustaches, they were the "Arabs of the American continent." Feared by their own people as much as by the Americans, they exhibited "but little advance in civilization." They spent their lives in the saddle, and their expert horsemanship aroused the admiration of their enemies. Tough hide leggings, a blanket with a hole in the center and a straw sombrero constituted their costume. Add to this a lance ornamented with red bunting, a horse "as savage and unmanageable as himself," a belt plentifully supplied with pistols and knives, and a lasso hanging from the saddle, and "you have the *Ranchero* as a member of a troop of banditti, or a soldier in a body of cavalry." (Johannsen 1985:24)

Lurid descriptions circulated of the tactics and military conduct of these south Texas *rancheros,* charges that would seem untenable and uncharacteristic of settled subsistence agriculturalists, Catholic, with families, defending their land from invasion. Indeed, by all accounts, including American, these allegations are more likely psychological projections—displacements—of the outrageous conduct of the American force as it crossed then Mexican south Texas and into Mexico. This total warfare included the wanton killing of civilians, raping, plundering, and desecrating churches (Dufour 1968:98–99; Lavender 1966:89–90; Oates 1973; Weems 1974:210). The Texas Rangers, a paramilitary unit created by the new Republic of Texas, played a leading role in these atrocities. Such was the nature of the first sustained encounter between the *mexicanos* of south Texas and northeastern Mexico and American society.

This first military step in the colonial project was, as I have noted, consolidated and institutionalized by the long-term establishment of several military forts in the area. Ostensibly protecting the newly acquired territory against any future military reprisals from now national Mexico, these forts also militarily guaranteed the coming imposition of a new political economy and hegemonic sociocultural order.

But here too expressive culture played its role as four of the forts located in deep south Texas—Duncan, McIntosh, Ringold, and Brown—

were named after American soldiers killed in action on south Texas soil or in Mexico. The fifth, Fort Sam Houston in San Antoñio, was, of course, named after the Texas leader who defeated the Mexican army at San Jacinto in the War for Texas Independence. For years to come, and one suspects even now, the political poetics of these names would serve to reinforce for everyone in the area the identities of victors and vanquished. Hand in hand with the military institutionalization in this area, in the latter half of the nineteenth and into the early twentieth century, we see the continuation of such political nomenclature in civilian society. New bustling Anglo-American towns with names like McAllen, Edinburg, Harlingen were created, eradicating or marginalizing the established *mexicano* ranching settlements with their family-based Spanish-language names: Ramireño for Ramirez, Salineño for Salinas, etc.

As Russell Berman reminds us,

> Geographical designations, even the apparently most objective, are never neutral. Names, distances, and directions not only locate points but also establish conceptualizations of power relations. The nomenclature of space functions as a political medium. (1986:3)

The new political nomenclature, of course, signified the creation of a new sociocultural order as capitalized Americans came to a new environment to create a new politically and militarily sanctioned culture and economy. The latter would be based on commercializing south Texas into a major agribusiness sector responsive to the demand for food in industrializing America. Based on the "appropriation" of *mexicano* land, more often by foul than fair means, this impoverishing social imposition on *mexicano* society continued to be ideologically sanctioned by the same continuing racism, religious prejudice, and linguistic xenophobia that had been introduced with the war (de Leon 1982, 1983; Montejano 1987).

Here we need to note a theme that will continue to reappear in these pages: the emergence of gender and class as a crosscutting dimension to these otherwise racial-cultural asymmetrical social relationships. In occasional and partial collusion with these new largely Anglo interests, we find a small racially distinct *mexicano* "upper class" whose alliance, often through marriage, with these new interests was ambivalent, tenuous, and carried its own internal contradictions (Montejano 1987:36–37).

As this new order materialized, war—literal, flesh-ripping war—did not cease, as fresh blood continued to irrigate the parched soil of south Texas. It was a warfare in which the Texas Rangers, again, played a leading role as a counterinsurgency unit. Anglo observers report scenes from the 1870s reminiscent enough of the aftershock on civilians of those fascist armies that rolled across Europe, especially Eastern Europe, in the Second World War. This report is from an R. C. Barfield, described as a "thoroughly reliable man."

> Not long after the Nuecestown raid he saw, so he says, many little ranches in the lower country deserted by their Mexican inhabitants; he saw too the remains of various Mexicans hanging from trees. Captain King had built a bridge across the Agua Dulce Creek between his Santa Gertrudis Ranch and Corpus Christi, and this bridge became notable for the number of Mexicans that were there picked off by Texas men. Mexicans were shot on sight and pitched into Clark Lake, into the Oso, into the Agua Dulce. (Dobie 1981:62)

And, in a report which also speaks to the class dimension noted earlier, we hear from another Anglo observer:

> Walter Billingsley, of San Antoñio, is responsible for the following account. One time during these troublous days a group of Texans were riding ten or fifteen miles out from Corpus Christi when they met a well dressed Mexican followed by his *mozo* (servant). The *caballero* had no "pass" and could not satisfactorily establish his identity. The more hot-headed of the Texans began to prepare a rope, but J. N. Garner and another man protested, saying they felt sure the Mexicans were innocent travelers. The crowd voted Garner and the other protestant down, however, and the two rode away. A few days after the Mexicans were hanged, it was learned that the *caballero* was a merchant of Laredo and a good citizen of the state. (Dobie 1981:62)

We shall learn more about the author of these passages, J. Frank Dobie, in the next chapter. For the moment, let us simply note the affirmation, that of an Anglo by way of other Anglos, of a warlike state of affairs in south Texas keyed on racist premises, massive wanton killing, and the appropriation of land.

This particular set of killings occurred as a massive retaliation for the Nuecestown raid, a guerrilla attack by *mexicanos* defending their interests. It was still another, and not the last, instance of a "war of maneuver," as Gramsci would say. This is the kind of warfare, always inseparable from political interests, in which there is "more extensive use of patrols, and particularly the art of organizing sorties and surprise attacks with picked men," and in which victory is still undecided (1971:232). Whether literal or metaphorical, such warfare must always be seen in every act of aggressive and counteraggressive political/economic interest in either incipient or formed class societies. For, "to fix one's mind on the military model is the mark of a fool: politics, here, too must have priority over its military aspect, and only politics creates the possibility for maneuver and movement" (1971:232). Thus the war of maneuver in which clear victory is still an open question is perhaps centered on literal warfare but can and often does include other weaponry. The Nuecestown raid by *mexicanos,* one of many during this period, needs to be seen in the context of other forms of fighting over contested terrain, forms that in south Texas included journalism, labor unions, organized "nonviolent" politics, everyday cultural poetics, and intellectual discourse (Limón 1973, 1974; Nelson-Cisneros 1975; de Leon 1982; Zamora 1992).

It is in this social context that we undertake an interpretive appreciation of the first of my predecessors in the construction of a cultural poetics of Mexican-American south Texas.

JOHN GREGORY BOURKE: WAR AND THE ORGANIC INTELLECTUAL

I refer to John Gregory Bourke—Captain John Gregory Bourke, United States Army—Captain John Gregory Bourke, major American ethnologist and folklorist of the late nineteenth century, a friend and colleague of Franz Boas.[2]

His long-term relevance to the *mexicanos* of South Texas was oddly enough established with his first military experience fighting as an enlisted Union cavalryman in the Civil War. He received the Congressional Medal of Honor for heroism at the Battle of Stones River, where he rallied his company into a charge against the Confederate lines after all their officers had been killed. Ironically, as we shall see later, his principal adversaries on the Southern side of this battle were Terry's Texas Rangers who, after their "service" against Mexicans, had joined the Confederacy as a special unit. According to Joseph Porter, his biographer (1986), from this war service, Bourke, an Irish-American Catholic, acquired a deep prejudice against the Protestant South and its slavery as well as a horror of insurrection. He also decided to make war one of his two professions.

Commissioned as a second lieutenant at West Point in 1869, Bourke was posted west to the Arizona, Wyoming, and Montana territories, where he spent the early 1870s fighting the Apache, the Cheyenne, and

the Lakota tribes. At West Point, Bourke excelled in the study of languages, and this no doubt facilitated to some degree his ability to learn at
least something of the languages of those Indian peoples, who by the late
1880s were largely defeated, no longer his active enemies and readily available on reservations. This same facility for languages as well as his strong
Catholicism also explain why he was attracted to the Mexican-descent
population that he encountered in southern Arizona and to learning Spanish. Porter also notes that Bourke's father had a strong interest in Gaelic
folklore but otherwise does not explain Bourke's early interest and education in anthropology, yet this interest was surely there, as he learned not
only languages but also wrote voluminous ethnographic fieldnotes on
these "new" cultures.

Publications and intellectual recognition followed, both illustrated by
his book *Scatologic Rites of All Nations,* a comparative work which drew
on his Indian materials and whose German edition included a complimen-
tary foreword by Sigmund Freud. He then came to the attention of scholars like Franz Boas and the influential Major John Wesley Powell, an
army officer assigned to be director of the Bureau of Ethnology at the
Smithsonian Institution in Washington.

Under Powell's direction he broadened his reading in anthropology
and learned as much as there was to learn of this science in that day. At a
theoretical level, he wholly absorbed and unquestioningly accepted the
contemporary dominant anthropological paradigm of the day, that of
English evolutionary anthropology with its central idea that different
societies represent different degrees of a progressive evolution. Modern
Western societies represented the apogee of development, while other
societies and their cultural traits were viewed as less evolved and developed, as survivals in the present world of periods in history that modern
Western societies had long ago left behind (Stocking 1987). From Powell
and others, Bourke acquired both discourse and power, for as Porter
reminds us, "The Bureau of Ethnology and the Anthropological Society
of Washington, under Powell's control, set the standards that governed
American Anthropology during the Victorian era" (1986:73). Working
out of the bureau but always also for the army, Bourke conducted extensive and intensive fieldwork among various Indian groups, principally
the Oglala.

As an evolutionary anthropologist focused on survivals, Bourke was
interested in studying and recording cultures before they "vanished" under evolutionary pressure. However, in far more synchronic and applied

fashion, he did not wholly separate the practice of anthropology from military considerations. He wanted to maintain his position as an army officer assigned to fieldwork and based in the Bureau of Ethnology, and therefore he argued that there was military value to his studies of "the people whom we so often had to fight and always to manage" (Porter 1986:280). Yet, on the other hand, it is clear that Bourke, against strong opposition, continually advocated a humane and respectful policy toward "pacified" Indian peoples, always within the constraints of his evolutionary outlook.

With the waning of the Indian Wars and the development of harsher policies toward reservation Indians, higher authorities no longer saw the need for this linkage between the military and anthropology, and pressure mounted for his reassignment as a field officer. A dispute ensued which Bourke lost and for which he was punished by assignment to the military district of southern Texas. As if to emphasize the punishment, the assignment was to begin in the early summer of 1891, when daytime temperatures in the area would already be constantly above one hundred degrees. As he prepared to leave Washington, Bourke recalled that his friend, General Philip Sheridan, had once said that if he owned hell and Texas, he'd rent Texas and live in hell (Porter 1986:284).

After reporting to the district headquarters in San Antoñio, Bourke was ordered to Fort McIntosh in Laredo, from which he then assumed command of Fort Ringold in Rio Grande City some fifty miles downriver. From Fort Ringold, Captain Bourke—his disfavor in Washington kept him a captain until his death after some thirty years of military service— continued his twin professions of making war and making anthropology. In both cases the Other was the *mexicano* population of south Texas.

In south Texas, however, anthropology and war were conjoined in a different way. Here, the native population was not exactly on reservations. Here anthropology and war proceeded more or less simultaneously, both conceived as "duty." Listen to Bourke on exactly this point in the opening paragraph to one of the five articles he published on this regional culture.

> The following material, collected by me during the time I was in
> command of the post of Fort Ringold, Texas, may be of interest
> from the light it throws upon the character of the Mexican popula-
> tion of our extreme southern border . . . As many of these Mexicans
> were engaged in armed attacks upon Mexican territory, and in
> armed resistance to the American troops sent to suppress them, it

became my duty to make as earnest a study of their character and
condition as means would permit. (1894b:119)

Bourke is referring to the activities of a local *mexicano* journalist,
intellectual, and guerrilla leader, Catarino Garza, and his followers. As
Bourke suggests, Garza was, from his base in south Texas, attempting to
bring down the U.S.-supported autocratic dictatorship of Mexico's
Porfirio Diaz in 1891, the first sustained attempt prior to the Mexican
Revolution. One of the first consequences of the U.S. acquisition of a
southern rim was the development of a practice supporting those Latin
American dictatorships which are friendly to American investments.
Part of such support always seems to involve military assistance in the
suppression of local populist guerrilla movements. This is what Bourke
was ordered to do against Garza, who, though a south Texan, saw it as
his internationalist revolutionary duty to cross the river and bring down
Diaz. Garza provided the United States with a technical excuse—
violation of neutrality laws—for ordering Bourke into action against
him. (Yet it must be noted that Bourke himself had no use for the Diaz
regime [Porter 1986:285–86]. In pursuing Garza he was carrying out his
orders.) Garza, of course, fought back, and his movement took on an
anti-American dimension as well, not a difficult thing to do given the
increasingly obvious Anglo domination of *mexicanos.*

According to Porter, in one particular engagement, "Bourke sent patrols into the chaparral where there was a brief, vicious skirmish that included hand-to-hand encounters between the soldiers and the *insur-
rectos* . . . the Garzistas rallied with the cry 'Kill the d___d Gringos,' "
quoting Bourke. Porter continues, specifying warfare reminiscent of reports from Vietnam: "These fights in the chaparral were ugly and brutal; a
testament to this is that some soldiers carried shotguns loaded with buck-
shot rather than army issue carbines or rifles" (1986:286–87). And, also
anticipating Vietnam, Bourke entered a *mexicano* village, Uña de Gato
(Cat's Claw), and "delivered a bombastic and threatening speech in Spanish telling the 'assembled . . . that I intended to come out and burn their
huts to the ground if I learned that they were harboring or aiding any of
the Mexican revolutionists . . .' " (Porter 1986:285). Eventually assisted
by his old enemies, the Texas Rangers, Bourke and his troops succeeded
in violently suppressing the Garzistas but never captured Garza himself.

Yet even as he made war on the south Texas *mexicanos,* he, quite literally in his spare time from war, simultaneously carried out his other
"duty"—the study of their culture, principally their folklore. His two

Captain John Gregory Bourke in the 1890s. Courtesy Nebraska State Historical Society.

careers—war and anthropology—were not always separate endeavors, however. At the heart of warfare and anthropology is good intelligence.

> Because of his fluency in Spanish, Bourke often gathered his own intelligence. He visited Hispanic festivals, parties, theaters and circuses. Dressing in nondescript civilian clothes, he drank the "fiercest of mescal and the vilest of whiskey" as he eavesdropped on conversations in saloons and restaurants . . . (Porter 1986:285)

As I suggested earlier, there is no evidence that Bourke felt any personal, racial, or cultural animosity toward those Indian peoples he had fought and studied. Indeed, there is evidence of affection, respect, and admiration. At times, according to Porter, one detects Bourke's gnawing suspicion that these Indian cultures were humanly better than what he was simultaneously witnessing in his own white, industrializing, expansive America. Yet, even though these Indian tribes had inflicted many more casualties upon his troops than the Garzistas, his manifest attitude toward the *mexicanos* is often markedly ethnocentric and racist. Why? Why, toward a people culturally closer to him than Indians?

His most extended and general ethnographic description of the area begins by comparing the Rio Grande to the Nile. Like the latter, the Rio Grande has its origins in "snow-clad sierras far away" and "made its way to the sea unswelled by any affluent of importance" (1894a:591). But he changes his metaphor as the river enters southern Texas, an anthropologically "unknown region."

> Through the centre of this unknown region, fully as large as New England, courses the Rio Grande which can more correctly be compared to the Congo than to the Nile the moment that the degraded, turbulent, ignorant, and superstitious character of its population comes under examination (1894a:594).

He is not content with the double racist thrust to the peoples of the Congo and the Rio Grande. He makes it more explicit, if that is possible, and compounds it with a highly revealing further comparison even as he also introduces class into his commentary.

> To the Congo, therefore, I compare it, and I am confident that all who peruse these lines to a conclusion will concur in the correctness of the comparison, although stress cannot be too pointedly laid upon the existence within this Dark Belt of thriving, intelligent communities, such as Brownsville, Matamoros, Corpus Christi, Laredo, San Diego, and others, in which are to be found people of as much re-

finement and good breeding as anywhere else in the world, but exert-
ing about as much influence upon the *indigenès* around them as did
the Saxon or Danish invaders upon the Celts of Ireland. (1894a:594)

Within this Dark Belt can be found people of "refinement and good breeding," principally in the towns. Clearly Bourke is referring to the small
upper-class *mexicano* society and the rapidly expanding Anglo entrepre-
neurial class in the 1890s. However, the national-character metaphor that
he uses to make his point is striking, revealing a latent psychological-
political contradiction in Bourke's consciousness. This refined, well-bred
class, Bourke tells us, exerts very little cultural influence "upon the
indigenès around them," as little influence "as did the Saxon or Danish
invaders upon the Celts of Ireland." But why this particular European
comparison now after the earlier African racism?[3]

I submit that we are witnessing a not too unconscious projection of
Bourke's own uneasy and ambivalent ethnic identity onto the *mexicanos.*
His deep-rooted tension and ambivalence are expressed stylistically by
the *single* long, unbounded sentence which constitutes this statement; the
style, perhaps, of an analysand's outpouring to an analyst at a critical
point of self-revelation, a sentence style suggesting a man caught up in a
psychological contradiction which can be handled only by an unmeasured
flow of words, an agitated formal expression reflecting his anxiety. There
are traces in Bourke's personal and social biography to support such a
reading.

Bourke was born on June 23, 1846, even as Zachary Taylor's regiments
were crossing the Rio Grande into interior Mexico. Porter tells us little
about his early childhood and family, but what he does say is succinctly
instructive. His father was a solid, stalwart Irish Catholic immigrant who
had brought his family to Philadelphia in the early 1840s, but his mother
was of both Irish and English antecedents and had been reared an Angli-
can, becoming a Catholic upon her marriage to Edward Bourke. As noted
earlier, the elder Bourke "was a student of the Gaelic folktales of western
Ireland," and "he passed his love of this lore to his children." But, of his
mother, "in later years her son remarked that he has never met a woman
better grounded in English literature, history, and belles lettres" (Porter
1986:1).

Although the Bourkes were better off than most Irish immigrants, to
be Irish and Catholic in the northeastern United States in the mid-
nineteenth century was no inconsequential matter. The Bourkes were ex-
posed to such strong prejudice, articulated principally by the Know-

Nothing party which "bitterly resented Roman Catholic immigrants," that, on occasion. "Edward Bourke took his rifle to defend his parish church against mobs bent on destroying it" (Porter 1986:1). This reinforced a strong sense of his Catholicism in the younger Bourke. On the other hand, one has to wonder what ambivalencies might be stirred in a young upper-middle-class American Irish boy who sensed the non-Irish world's contempt for those they stigmatized as, in Bourke's words about *mexicanos,* "degraded, turbulent, ignorant and superstitious . . ." Porter offers no clue in his book, but consider what a well-educated Irish-American young man in his impressionable twenties would feel if he had read Matthew Arnold's 1867 essay "On the Study of Celtic Literature." Arnold speaks of the Celt's sensuality, of his love for "bright colours, company and pleasure," but also of his "failure to reach any material civilization sound and satisfying, and not out at elbows, poor, slovenly, and half-barbarous." Arnold continues: "as in material civilization he has been ineffectual, so has the Celt been ineffectual in politics . . . The Celt, undisciplinable, anarchical, and turbulent by nature, but out of affection and admiration giving himself body and soul to some leader, that is not a promising political temperament . . ." (1962:345–47).

Substitute "Mexican" for Celt in this stereotypic formulation, as American popular culture has indeed done, and we can surmise the possibility that in construing *mexicanos,* Bourke was also coping with his own repudiated and projected self-ambivalencies. For even as he though of *mexicanos* as degraded, he seems at least subconsciously and critically aware that they, like his Irish forbears, also were the victims of an unjust conquest and domination. He recalls the conquest of south Texas.

> Two waves of North American aggression have swept across this region, bearing down all in its path . . . the first of these ethnic storms was the advent of the army of General Zachary Taylor . . . this war . . . although it undoubtedly resulted in the development of immense areas of most productive country, the necessity for beginning it or continuing it has been doubted by no less an authority than the late President Grant. (1894a:592)

Yet Bourke speaks of a *second* "North American aggression," a second "ethnic storm." And what is this? It is, for Bourke, precisely the resulting economic "development" that he recognizes as a "storm," an "aggression." That he was now an intrinsic military agent of this continuing domination could not have escaped so well-educated and perceptive a man.

His ambivalence and the unconscious analogy are also registered in the following, where he locates most *mexicanos* at a lower stage of evolution. Yet one detects almost a note of admiration for what he says of these Mexicans, he might well have said of his own Irish vis-à-vis the English.

> If we enter into the homes of these people and mingle among them, it soon becomes evident that we have encountered a most interesting study in ethnology and anthropology; they constitute a distinct class, resisting all attempts at amalgamation. There are to this rule, as to all rules, notable exceptions, and there are on the river some few representatives of a higher stage of evolution; but, in general terms, the Rio Grande Mexican resists to-day, as he has always resisted, the encroachments of the Gringo, and the domination of his own Mexico. (1894a:606)

According to Gramsci, intellectuals play key roles in social warfare. I suggest that John Gregory Bourke, U.S. military officer and ethnologist, is a partial specimen of what Gramsci calls the "organic intellectual." Gramsci recognizes that in moments of class warfare, "traditional" intellectuals are subject to the pressures of this warfare, and take sides. Under "normal" circumstances, such intellectuals are defined by and ostensibly committed to a universal mission of learning and the transmission of high culture. However, under the exigencies of struggle, contending groups attempt "to assimilate and to conquer 'ideologically' the traditional intellectuals . . . ," but, Gramsci continues, "this assimilation and conquest is made quicker and more efficacious the more the group in question succeeds in simultaneously elaborating its own organic intellectuals . . ." (1971:10), "the latter defined by their function in directing the ideas and aspirations of the class to which they organically belong" (1971:3).

Writing from the perspective of the twentieth century, Gramsci clearly sees a quite conscious and specialized functioning for such intellectuals, but here greater flexibility is required of Gramsci. Bourke does, in effect, direct the stereotypic ideas of his class and culture. His published attitudes toward *mexicanos* must have had their large reinforcing ideological effect on his Anglo-American audiences, especially if one keeps in mind the semipopular circulation of intellectual discourses in his day. This ideological circulation was supported by the most legitimizing kind of "I was there . . ." ethnographic authority possible in late-nineteenth-century imperialist America, that of a fighting soldier who had seen the "savages" close up (Clifford 1988a). However, and in revision of Gramsci's too tight sociological categories, the development of organic intellectuals surely cannot be an ideologically seamless, coherent affair. As a later Gramscian, the late Raymond Williams, reminds us, cultural formations of any kind are never without their disruptions, discontinuities, and internal contradictions. The dominant culture is not fully comprehensive in its domination even within itself and always excludes, and what it excludes "may often be seen as the personal or the private or as the natural or even the metaphysical." Usually "it is . . . in one or another of these terms that the excluded area is expressed" (1977:125). It is so, I think, with this Irish-American soldier anthropologist whose unconscious ethnic identification with the Rio Grande *mexicanos* produces an ideological discontinuity and ambivalence in his work.[4] But thus far I have considered only Bourke's more manifest and general appraisal of culture, although I have begun to point to its unconscious political dimensions. We can also see this ideological discontinuity registered in his cultural poetics of *mexicano* folklore and society.

THE POLITICAL POETICS OF ROMANCE

There is a kind of redemption that he finds in south Texas Mexicans, in the same way that so many thinkers, Matthew Arnold and Bourke's middle-class father included, Irish or not, have located a redemptive Irish "genius" in that people's folklore in similar sociological contexts, although this is always an ambivalent identification. Bourke never attributes "genius" to *mexicanos*, but he uses two closely interrelated scholarly strategies that, if seen in social context, have a redemptive ideological effect, even if that effect is not consciously intended. The first is the representation of sheer folkloric abundance among the people, and the second, the historical displacement of meaning through his evolutionary theory of survivals.

A reader today may be struck with the thickness of the description in Bourke's account of those people whom he also fought. An early article is offered with the proviso that "it is not to be accepted as exhausting the subject of the folklore of that region which is simply interminable. Other notes, equally extensive, were gathered . . . but it is not possible on account of their bulk to present them here" (1894b:119).

What he offers, however, is not a thick description of culture as Geertz would have it (1973b), but rather a seemingly more conventional dense cataloging of alphabetically arranged descriptive observations in evolutionary anthropological style. In this catalogue style, Bourke offers relatively brief but dense itemizations of folk foods (1985), language (1896), and a folk play (1893) from the *mexicano* south Texas border country. In

one such botanical description in which his contradictory outlook reappears, he notes the *mexicano's* fondness for fruits and flowers: On the
southern side of the river,

> I noted pinks, roses, bananas, geraniums, jasmines, oranges, lilies,
> mignonettes, lemons, peaches, grapes, forget-me-nots, tulipans, mag-
> nolias, heliotropes, carnations, and such exquisite flowers, all at
> their best.
>   In that part of Texas where the Mexicans once had settlements
> the same rule holds good, although I am far from attributing it to
> former occupancy alone. (1895:70)

From a "modern" perspective the sheer hyperdescriptiveness of such nota-
tion may already have ideological significance, indicating the manifest
presence of culture; and this claim may be true not only for Bourke but for
all who practiced ethnography in this manner in the nineteenth century.
As Stocking suggests, such dense descriptive activity has its theoretical
place in "the actual contact between nineteenth-century Europeans and
the 'savages' whose origin, status, and fate social evolutionism would attempt both to explain and justify." He continues: "From this broadly contextual point of view, as well as from the narrower perspective of the role
of ethnographic data in a major theoretical reorientation, these rather
concretely descriptive vignettes may carry substantial exemplary weight"
(1987:80–81).

     It is as if, even while imputing a backward, degraded character to the
mexicanos, his dense textual rendition of their rich abundance of such
"interesting" cultural poetics absolves them of some portion of stigmatiza-
tion. Even this unconscious textual compensation is not always carried
out without racist overtones. Even as he notes and renders this creative
lushness he is "far from attributing it to former occupancy alone." We
should note the politically critical admission that he is discussing a place
"where the Mexicans once had settlements." He cannot always sustain his
redemptive description and reverts to the role of an organic intellectual of
his class. The new rulers of this land are also engaged in botanical cultural
poetics: of all the gardens he sees in south Texas, "most interesting of
all . . . was the cactus garden of Mrs. Miller, near the Havana Ranch . . .
in Starr County, Texas" (1895:70–71).

     The element of political unconscious in textual abundance takes on
greater saliency in the context of Bourke's evolutionary anthropology
everywhere evident in his writings. In this evolutionary view, these abun-

dant folkloric practices acquire part of their interest and fascination because they are to be seen as "survivals."

Applied here and perhaps everywhere in nineteenth-century evolutionary studies, the construct of "survivals," for all of its ethnocentric bias, may
participate in a redemptive mission. For Bourke, much of what he is observing in south Texas has historical meaning beyond itself, and once again we
find ourselves in a rhetorical poetics of Orientalism. As one of his subtitles
succinctly proposes, Bourke wants to think of many of these practices not
as present-day inherently Mexican (which is to say, degraded) but as traces
of an older, higher, even more interestingly exotic, though still barbaric,
civilization—not Aztec, but Arabic via Spain—survivals which in a sense
continue to valorize the present culture (1896). I offer only two of many of
his "examples," selecting these largely because of their pertinence later in
this study in Chapters 6 and 9. Bourke comments on a famous folk healer of
south Texas, whom he identifies as "San Pedro of Los Olmos," and notes
him as a survival: "Such prophets, semi-prophets, and inspired healers cor-
respond closely to the Mahdes who, since A.D. 685 have arisen periodically
among the Moslems . . ." (1896:114). And, on a more profane level, he
"explains" the local custom of eating with one's fingers from a common dish
as also ancient Arabic (1896:88).

The abundance and longevity of their folklore are the principal specific
figurations through which Bourke unconsciously offers his readers and
himself this redemptive sense of the otherwise socially "degraded" *mexicanos*. These specific strategies are also in the service of a larger authorial
narrative strategy, also subconscious, through which Bourke articulates
his ambivalence on a larger scale. Here, we need to think of Bourke's
entire career and writings as a continuous narrative discourse in which
ideological meaning is articulated formally as well as manifestly.

Hayden White has offered a complex scheme for grasping the ideological underpinnings of historical narrative discourse (1973). To make my
case for this anthropological discourse, let me loosely draw on White's
most pertinent critical concept in this scheme—the emplotment or narrative organization of intellectual discourse. "If, in the course of narrating
his story," White tells us,

> . . . the historian provides it with the plot structure of a Tragedy, he
> has "explained" it one way; if he has structured it as a Comedy, he
> has "explained" it another way. Emplotment is the way by which a
> sequence of events fashioned into a story is gradually revealed to be
> a story of a particular kind. (1973:7)

Of a particular kind here refers not only to the generic style—Tragedy, Comedy—but also to the different explanatory and ideological effects achieved by each of these as well as two more possible choices, Satire and Romance.

To a large degree, Bourke's life narrative was cast in the form of Romance which, for White, is "fundamentally a drama of self-identification symbolized by the hero's transcendence of the world of experience, his victory over it, and his final liberation from it . . ." (1973:8). Here is an anthropologist who starts out from a specific problematic world of Irish experience and English authority to some degree represented respectively by his father and mother. It can be argued that his simultaneous careers of anthropology and war both respond to these primary influences and transcend them but always in tension and ambivalence. He becomes an anthropologist, a professional student of socially marginalized cultures, and a soldier of an imperial power, representing the source of that marginalization. In both cases he lives up to and indeed transcends his parent's expectations and those that society ascribed to the Irish.

The archetypal Romance is the knightly quest, against all adversity, for the Holy Grail (White 1973:8–9). For Bourke, the adversity may be the socially problematic side of his Irish identity, itself already a product of a nineteenth-century Irish political economy dominated by England. This was an identity which might have been projected unto Southern Protestant Confederates or American Indians were they not so Other to his experience. Of greater service to his ambivalence were those semi-Others: those darkish, non-English-speaking Catholics along the Rio Grande against whom, by the logic of an American political economy, he came to make war. Yet even as they were adversaries, for this Irish-American anthropologist, they also possessed a Holy Grail, a rich treasure trove of folklore which he claimed, ostensibly in the service of scholarship, but more fundamentally to redeem them and himself.[5]

Bourke's redemptive ambivalence is evident in two major folklore encounters he had with informants in south Texas, although viewed from another angle these might actually belie my thus far romantic reading of Bourke. For there is in these more than a hint of another Bourke, a pre-postmodernist anthropologist before his time, sensitive to domination, to the dialogic, to irony, and to a nonunitary sense of culture. The first of these—in two examples—is compelling, for here, unlike the rest of my precursors, this very masculine captain, this nineteenth-century officer and gentleman, works closely with a female informant, Maria Antoñia Cavazos de Garza, a *curandera* (healer). Their first interactively generated and inscribed subject broaches questions of gender and sexuality that recall Bourke's affiliation to Freud.

> Señora Cavazos de Garza informed Bourke about the difficulties facing women on their wedding nights and during pregnancy. She described the mythical but feared *axolotl* (lizard) that could enter a woman's vagina during menstruation. The victim swelled as if pregnant, and the *axolotl* sucked the blood from the woman until she turned deathly pale. The *curandera* knew two remedies. In one the afflicted woman crouched over a bowl of hot goat milk, and the vapors killed the lizard. Bourke termed the second method "the heroic remedy" because it required a courageous man to have sexual intercourse with the victim. The infuriated *axolotl* will seize the penis, and [quoting Bourke] "unless its fangs can be withdrawn, amputation must be performed."

But for its completion the "heroic remedy" depends, it would seem, on male disciplinary medical authority.

> "But if there be a skillful Doctor present, he can remain in the room with the young couple, holding a lighted blessed candle in his hand," Bourke learned. "When the lizard emerges, the flame of the candle burning its eyes causes it [to] precipitately let go its hold." (Porter 1986:294)

Bourke and this *curandera* also pursue subjects of race, class, and women again by way of witching, and we also get a glimpse of the devil.

> Maria Antoñia was emphatic in her expression of belief that there were lots of "brujas" (witches) around . . . There were not only witches in the world, but a class of people whom she styles "gente de chusma" [low-class folk] who seem to be allied to our fairies. They fly about from place to place on the winds.

And, "they have sold their souls to the Devil and must never think of God when they die" (1894b:142–43).

Thinking perhaps of Irish "fairies" and Irish *chusma,* this Irish-"Americano" discovers from Señora Cavazos de Garza that

> everyone believed in witches; there might be some fool "Americanos" who would say they did not . . . However, what the "Americanos" did concerned her but little. She had been told that many "Americanos" were not "Christianos." "Don't you believe in brujas, mí capitan?" "Why surely, comadrecíta,—do you not see that *I am different* from those fool Gringos who come down here pretending to know more than their grandparents did? [emphasis mine] What I am anxious to learn is,

what is the cure, or the best preventative, so that I may run no danger
of being 'malificiado' [sickened] myself." (1894b:142)

Perhaps nowhere in all of Bourke's ethnographic reportage are all of
his contradictions better captured for my purpose than in his report of yet
another south Texas–Mexican folk custom—the miracle pastoral folk
drama. "As Christmas approaches," our Catholic soldier anthropologist
tells us,

> all the villagers take their several parts in the Miracle Play of the
> *Nacimiento* in which the incidents of the child-life of our Saviour are
> delineated . . . These incidents and characters include . . . the wrath
> of Lucifer when his minions hurry down to Hell to apprise him that
> the Babe has been born in Bethlehem, the visit of the Magi, the
> adoration of the Shepherds and the joy of men and dumb beasts to
> know that at last the chains of sin were broken. (1894a:609)

But in this ancient play, Lucifer then mounts an attack upon this scene of
emergent freedom, only to meet resistance, for

> there is an old Hermit who announces the birth of the Redeemer
> and puts Satan to flight he being all the time armed with a crucifix,
> before which the Enemy of Souls recoils in abject fear. (1894a: 609)

And then, in very next paragraph about this quite traditional play, our
keenly intelligent, Catholic, anthropologist army captain startles us with
either his incredible naiveté or his witty sophisticated irony which gleans
life's contradictions.

> Through some distortion of the intellectual faculties the managers of
> the play desire to have the Devil represented as a cavalry officer.
> Just what the origin of this quaint fancy has been, I have never been
> able to discover, but I know that it exists, because in Rio Grande
> City, I was once asked to lend a cavalry uniform for the purpose,
> and when I offered to secure one of the infantry, the offer was de-
> clined. (1894a:609)

Bourke says no more on the subject and moves on to a catalogue of folk
food customs.

In 1893 Captain John G. Bourke was reassigned out of south Texas
where he had come to make war and anthropology and ended up meeting
the devil. A year later, as the first of his south Texas fieldwork was being
published, he was to be found leading troops in attack against the Pullman
railway labor strike in Chicago. " 'All were hostile,' reported Bourke,

'and greeted us with obscene and profane epithets in the use of which the women seemed to be more proficient than the men.' He prescribed going 'after the rioters and licking them into obedience,' " rioters in Chicago whom he described as " 'composed of all nationalities, saving perhaps the Irish . . .' " (Porter 1986:298).

WAR OF MANEUVER, WAR OF POSITION

In 1897 shortly after Bourke's U.S. Army and the Texas Rangers had subdued the rebellious forces of Catarino Garza, the new Anglo-American citizens of Laredo, Texas, joined by a few upper-class *mexi-canos,* decided to establish a city holiday and celebration on George Washington's Birthday. According to a highly commendable history, these "city fathers" felt that a proper *American* festival was needed to counter the influence of *las fiestas patrias* among the *mexicanos* of the city (Hinojosa 1983:120). These were the annual celebrations of the cry of Mexican Independence from Spain first uttered in 1810, an event still celebrated by Mexican-Americans today. Along with Bourke's troop from Ringold, soldiers from McIntosh, the fort at Laredo, had also pursued Garza. So it is not at all improbable that the quite recent war against the Garzistas influenced these individuals as they planned a new image for a city and region opening up to Anglo-American "development." What more patriotic means than a celebration of the birthday of the "father of our country"?

The war of position had begun in south Texas. In Gramsci's terms, such a phase of struggle begins when one side has achieved nearly complete dominance, making open maneuver nearly impossible. In this new phase, the dominant

> organise permanently the "impossibility" of internal disintegration—with controls of every kind, political, administrative, *etc.,* reinforcement of the hegemonic "positions" of the dominant group, *etc.*
> (1971:239)

It is with the war of position in mind that we can understand also the efforts to incorporate and win over not only the upper *mexicano* classes (already won) but the middle and lower classes as well. Public "Anglo" celebrations such as that in Laredo began to foster this incorporating process, as did other, more utilitarian, pragmatic means. After reassignment from Fort Ringold, and in his report to the secretary of war on his experience in south Texas, Bourke recommended

that the government raise a battalion of Mexican-Americans to deal
with affairs such as the Garza movement. He believed that more
Spanish-speaking persons should be employed by the federal government as customs collectors, marshals, inspectors, and in other of-
fices. He insisted that the federal government should try to attract
the Mexican-Americans to its own interests and away from those of
local Texas politicians or groups in Mexico. (Porter 1986:289)

The dominated also carry out a war of position, and here ethnicity and
class formations become the continuation of war by other means, to paraphrase Clausewitz. Journalism, labor unions, nonviolent civil rights activity, education became and continue to be points of positional warfare in
south Texas (Limón 1973, 1974; Nelson-Cisneros 1975; de Leon 1982;
Zamora 1992; Montejano 1987).

The more salient emergence of the war of position did not mean a total
end to the war of maneuver, even it its most literal aspects. In 1915,
armed, organized Mexican-Americans rode once again in open rebellion
against domination, always with some *mexicanos* on the other side. These
rebellious forces, known as *los sediciosos* (the seditionists), attacked U.S.
Army and Texas Ranger installations and large ranches such as the famous King Ranch. They were, of course, answered by a massive force of
cavalry and Rangers which, true to their style of warfare, did not discrimi-
nate between combatants and noncombatants (Harris and Sadler 1978).
The eminent historian Walter Prescott Webb, an ardent partisan of the
Rangers, was forced to conclude that as many as five thousand *mexicanos,*
mostly noncombatants, may have died at the hands of the counterinsurgency (1935). This phase of the war of maneuver went hand in
hand with the growing political-economic hegemony over the area, the
other "aggression" Bourke had noted. Another of our later precursors
comments:

> Texas Rangers and sheriff's deputies took out their frustration at not
> being able to catch the *sediciosos* by slaughtering as many innocent
> Mexican farm workers as they could lay their hands on. Hundreds
> were summarily "executed" without trial, and many hundreds more
> fled to Mexico to escape the *rinche* terror. The results were that
> more land in south Texas was cleared of Mexicans so it could be
> "developed" by Anglo newcomers in the 1920s. (Paredes 1976:33)

Chapter Two

J. Frank Dobie

Now, as this odd
Discoverer walked through the harbor streets
Inspecting the cabildo, the facade
Of the cathedral, making notes, he heard
a rumbling, west of Mexico, it seemed,
Approaching like a gasconade of drums.
The white cabildo darkened, the facade,
As sullen as the sky, was swallowed up
In swift, successive shadows, dolefully.
The rumbling broadened as it fell. The wind,
Tempestuous clarion, with heavy cry,
Came bluntly thundering, more terrible
Than the revenge of music on bassoons.
Gesticulating lightning, mystical,
Made pallid flitter. Crispin, here, took flight.
An annotator has his scruples, too.
—Wallace Stevens, from "The Comedian as the Letter C"

While the war of maneuver thus raged across south Texas along with the war of position, a few hundred miles north a new phase in the ethnographic war of position was developing. A young instructor joined the English department at the University of Texas at Austin. His name was J. Frank Dobie, and between 1921 and 1958 he became the principal figure to engage south Texas Mexican-American culture and my next precursor.

The cultural poetics of his ethnographic treatment is my subject in this chapter, a poetics already embodied in Dobie's very choice of names: no, not his names for those whom he studied and inscribed—he had few problems here; they were all "Mexicans," occasionally, "Meskin." I mean the name he chose for himself, for use by his friends and colleagues—Pancho—the Mexican nickname translation of his given English name,

43

Frank. In this primal act of seeming affection and cultural appropriation—a cultural poetics that also characterizes the studied maintenance of Spanish-language place-names in the Southwest by those who rule—in this act of self-naming, we see minutely expressed the cultural contradiction dominating Dobie's ethnographic work, the bedevilment of his writing. So, to facilitate my writing, to lend it, let us say, a certain native touch, and because I am sure he would have wished it so, let me call him "Pancho."

When I arrived at the University of Texas campus in Austin in early September of 1964 for my first year at the university, our paths almost crossed. He died a few days later at his home not far from campus. Wouldn't he have recognized this young fellow south Texan who had swum and fished in the rivers and creeks that he knew so well, those boundaries where his people and mine met, where "Mexicans were shot on sight and pitched into . . . Agua Dulce" (Sweet Water) Creek, one of the Nueces' tributaries (Dobie 1981:62)? And, if this common heritage were not enough, could we not have been colleagues had he lived longer? After all, I now teach in the same English department, the continuing site of much debate concerning the canonical and the minor, a debate that he arguably anticipated in his desire to teach folklore, popular culture, cowboys and Mexicans. And, there is more. Do I not now teach English 342, *Life and Literature of the Southwest,* the course he started in the 1930s against much opposition? Yes, I think this is enough. I shall call him Pancho where appropriate. He certainly did not ask our permission to take this name, and I now reclaim it to my purpose, to begin literally to name upon this ethnographer, this second of my precursors, the cultural contradiction that I explore in what follows. I take as my principal texts Dobie's *A Vaquero of the Brush Country* (1929) and *Tongues of the Monte* (1935), although his autobiography, *Some Part of Myself* (1964), will be brought to bear along with James McNutt's excellent study of Dobie (1982).[1]

ALLA EN EL RANCHO GRANDE, ALLA DONDE VIVIA

Of Southern heritage, Dobie's ancestors—pioneers, he called them—came to settle in Texas in the great colonization of the 1830s, his parents eventually becoming ranchers in south Texas in the 1870s. Dobie himself was born in 1888, a few years before Bourke fought Catarino Garza not far from the Dobie ranch. Indeed, three of Dobie's uncles had served with the Texas Rangers, and his grandfather had actually met Garza (McNutt 1982:200). A child of the war of maneuver, Dobie grew up in the cusp between outright violence and what would replace it—the war of position. With Mexican labor increasingly under control (Montejano 1987:198–219), Dobie was permitted to play with the children of his father's Mexican *vaqueros,* although aware always of their segregated status, especially in matters of schooling. As a teenager, he worked side by side with his dad's *vaqueros,* yet always knowing that "white ranch hands . . . drew six bits a day. Mexican hands drew four bits a day," but also knowing "there weren't any better cowhands than some of the four-bits-a-day *vaqueros,*" no doubt like my maternal great-grandfather who worked as a *vaquero* close to Dobie's ranch (1980a:86). It was, of course, permitted, indeed necessary, to *speak* to this Mexican labor, but his father disapproved "of our acquiring much Spanish." As a teenager coming of sexual age, Dobie also soon met his parents' injunction "that their sons never debase themselves by living which Mexican women" (1980a:86–89).

Above all—a motif that recurs in his writing—Dobie was aware of "the one romantic feature of our ranch,"

> . . . what we called Fort Ramirez. It was never a fort, but it was called a fortified ranch house built by a Mexican named Ramirez before Texas became a republic. Not within the memory of the oldest resident of the county had the fort been inhabited. (1980a:31)

But where the Ramirez family went, leaving land and fortified stone ranch house behind, and *why* they went, Pancho does not say.

Dobie also learned more conventional things as well that, nonetheless, left their mark on his later treatment of Mexicans and their folklore. From his father, he acquired a particular work ethic, a deep love/hate relationship to ranch work; indeed a Protestant work ethic reinforced by and fostering a parallel love/hate relationship to his father's strong-voiced nightly readings from the Bible, a strong voice, however, that also sang cowboy worksongs across the ranch (1980a:57–70). Before marrying, his mother was a schoolteacher, and from her Dobie acquired a substantial attraction to the classics of English and American literature (1980a:71–82). As Dobie came of age in 1906, his mother's influence initially prevailed but not for long.

Although he had been away from his parental south Texas ranch before—to work on his BA at Southwestern University in Georgetown near Austin; to teach high school in West Texas; to receive an MA in English at Columbia in New York—in 1914 Dobie revisited and left the ranch in a more definitive way to move more or less permanently to Austin to join the English faculty at the University of Texas. From this academic base, the brief though telling exceptions, he forged an unorthodox academic and public career.

This career was uncertain and fraught with anxiety as Dobie sought to resolve a cultural and psychological contradiction rooted in his upbringing. Although obviously attracted to the literary life, and the teaching of English literature in a deeply impressionistic way, he found himself put off by the pedantic demands of literary scholarship. Against these he experienced a great desire to take up the adventure of a world journalist—he had worked on an interim basis on local newspapers—or to return to the life of a cowboy on the open range. This difficult choice also encapsulated his worrisome concern that the denial of the latter, masculinized world, and the persistence in the life of an English department and the teaching of canonical English and American literature, could make him effeminate (McNutt 1982: 180). For a moment, though not finally, he swerved to his father's side, a momentary swerve that served to recall the Mexicans of his youth and the continuing war; a swerve reflecting the paradoxical role of Mexicans in his earlier life and marking his later ethnographic treatment of them.

The occasion was the complex of political events occurring between 1914 and 1917 as the United States contemplated military intervention in Mexico as a result of the Pancho Villa raid in New Mexico, even as it prepared to enter the war in Europe. The infamous Zimmerman note served to bring the two events together. On the one hand, Dobie initially and paternalistically opposed military intervention, in his own words, in "childish, ignorant Mexico" when the real target should be "brutal and bigoted" Germany. On the other hand, and as McNutt notes, "inexplicably" Dobie was soon infected with the war fever concerning Mexico and offered his services to the government. His letter to the federal authorities is worth quoting at length for what it tells us about Dobie and Mexicans at that moment, even as it demonstrates a rhetorical overcompensation for Dobie's anxieties about his manhood in an English department.

> I was born and reared in Southwest Texas among Mexicans, on a ranch. I can *speak Mexican* fluently and read Spanish easily, though I am tardy in writing Spanish. However, with a very little effort I could handle the Spanish language in any capacity. I know the Mexican genius. I am an expert rider and a good shot. I am a graduate of Southwestern University (Texas); and I have done graduate work in the University of Chicago and in Columbia, from which latter institution I hold the A.M. degree. I have been reporter on two newspapers. At present, I am instructor in English in the university of

Texas. I have had considerable business experience, and have managed good sized bodies of workmen, Mexicans especially.
    I am twenty-eight years old, am five feet, eight inches high, and
weight 145 pounds. I am in excellent health and have remarkable
powers of endurance. By nature, I am an adventurer, and a virile
and sincerely passionate personality makes it easy for me to lead
men. If authorized by the government, I can and will raise a company of one hundred men out of the ranch countries of Southwest
Texas, which region I know and in which I am known, being, as I
am, a son of two pioneer families of wide and honorable reputation
as "cow people." These men would be hard of physique, efficient as
to riding and shooting, and knowing as to Mexican territory and genius. They would be well mounted. (McNutt 1982:186)

    Dobie's services were not deemed necessary for war with Mexico, but
he did volunteer for service in France in a capacity as close to a now almost
militarily obsolete cavalry as he could get. He rode a horse guiding others
pulling artillery caissons. The war was over by the time his unit arrived in
France, and after the war he returned to his old job in the Texas English
department.[2]
    Soon, however, his old problems and anxieties recurred, aggravated by
pressure from the department to get a Ph.D., which he though unneces-
sary for the teaching of literature, a demand Dobie soon came to loathe
and refuse, at the cost of salary promotion. Later in his career, this institutional conflict would become even more serious. In 1920 he chose yet
again in his father's direction by resigning from the university to return to
south Texas as a manager of one of his uncles' ranches. As Dobie was
resigning from academia and preparing to return to his father's world, the
elder Dobie died in June of 1920.
    Dobie spent only a year on the ranch. Falling cattle prices, as he said,
certainly contributed to his decision to return to the University of Texas,
but there were now other reasons as well. On the ranch, still imbued with
his mother's way, the way of literature, and with his father now physically
absent, Dobie had a kind of intellectual conversion experience that re-
solved much of his anxious contradiction and allowed him to return to
academia as a literary intellectual and as a "man." On the ranch one night
he found a fit scholarly subject that would allow him to overcome the
demands of his department while fulfilling his own deeply impressionistic
love of the literary; that would allow him to close the gap between the
cultured city life of the university and the open range he equally loved;
that would permit a reconciliation of his mother's and father's traditions

while relieving him of his gender anxieties. Finally, this subject would permit Dobie to resolve the history of Anglos and Mexicans in Texas. As Dobie's own wife, Bertha, put it: "The wells of English literature and childhood on a ranch, with Mexicans for playmates and mentors are for Frank, deep, deep wells" (Tinkle 1978:145).

Dobie best describes the event and the motives leading to his major work on Mexicans, *Tongues of the Monte* (1935).

> I recall the night on which the first dim intimation of such a book to be written came to me. After the first World War was over and I had been in the army going on two years, I returned to the University of Texas as an instructor in English. I was very restless leading such a pallid life, and was not drawing enough salary to support my wife and myself. I resigned to manage a large ranch for my uncle, J. M. Dobie, on the Nueces River, in the brush country. All the labor was Mexican. (1980b:x)

"One of the Mexicans at the ranch was named Santos Cortez" according to Dobie; an older man who, in the evenings, would come up to Dobie's room craving "conversation on higher things." This conversation consisted largely of Cortez telling Dobie folktales, mostly legends, from Mexican tradition. "In the course of time," Dobie tells us, "Santos told me many other things that I set store by. And that night, Dobie continues, "I had the idea of a book made up of people like Santos and of their stories" (1980b:x–xi).

I shall return to this book and this story later. As I've already suggested, Santos Cortez did a great deal more for Dobie than furnish the stories for one book. Beyond and subsuming what I've already noted, he launched Dobie into a lifelong career as the foremost, best-known ethnographer of the Mexican people of Texas and the southwest for the first half of the twentieth century. Dobie always acknowledged the significance of this older Mexican man from south Texas, this fount of folkloric wisdom who must have recalled for him another old Mexican man from his childhood, Genardo del Bosque, whom Dobie venerated:

> I have often fancied that if I were doomed to the everlasting fires of a traditional hell, could be redeemed by a substitute, and were such a churl as to call another man to take my place, Genardo, of all men I know, would without a quiver of hesitation plunge into the furnace. (1980a:25)

That excludes a lot of men, including those family men closest to Dobie— his father and his uncles—as does Dobie's additional superlative comment that Genardo, whose "people once had land in Texas," was "the best trailer I have ever known," a Mexican *vaquero* whose "intelligence, energy, cow sense and responsibility would have made him a first-class manager of a big outfit"—but didn't (1980a:24).

A war was taking place in Dobie's soul, reflecting the continuing war in society. For, that same year, having just met the venerable Santos Cortez, having found an attractive "masculine" career in a folkloristic ethnography indebted to Mexicans, and just a few days before resuming his teaching position at the University of Texas—a position that henceforth would mean considerable teaching and research about Mexicans—Dobie, our Pancho, now so indebted to Mexicans, "accompanied a group of Texas Rangers, led by Captain Will Wright, on a raid of a Mexican bootleggers' camp. One bootlegger was killed, six others captured and a load of tequila confiscated." With evident glee, he wrote his wife: "Mexicans in the county are literally afraid of sticking their heads out of houses . . . I've never enjoyed two days so much in my life" (McNutt 1982:188). As McNutt perceptively notes:

> After hearing about hard rides and daring raids all his life, Dobie finally got into action . . . and could return to civilization with conspicuous virility. His raider experience . . . complemented his long-standing fascination with Mexico with a cowboy adventure he could think worthy of a rancher's son. (1982:188)

His father absent and his manhood fortified with war and Mexican folklore, Dobie resumed his position in the Texas English department and launched his newfound career based essentially on this folklore.

This new career opened on a telling note. Though Santos Cortez had told him ghost and devil legends, Dobie chose the Mexican balladry of south Texas, the *corridos,* as the topic of his first published work. It was not a fortuitous or aesthetic choice but one conditioned by the state of war and his own participation in it. With the help of his brother, a foreman on the well-known King Ranch in south Texas, Dobie collected and wrote about a *corrido* he identified by the title *Versos de los Bandidos* (Verses concerning the Bandits), citing no native authority for this title. Indeed, he admits that "sometimes the Mexicans refer to it as Versos del Rancho de las Norias . . ." (Verses concerning the Norias Ranch) (1925:31).[3] This *corrido,* which Dobie labels a bandit *corrido,* deals with the Mexican uprising of 1915–16 noted in the previous chapter, although it is narrated from the point of view of one of the Mexican cowboys who worked for the King Ranch—the "bandits' " principal objective in their raid—and who then, with other King Ranch Mexicans, joined the Texas Rangers in pursuit of the raiders. Most *corridos* spoke from the point of view of the dispossessed, to be sung among them and not to the race/class enemy. As a statement from the vanquished side in this war, the *corrido* Dobie chose is unreliable, but in the politics of fieldwork, it was one of the few accessible to him, coming as it did from Mexicans tied to the King Ranch and working for his brother. Our Pancho could appropriate a Mexican name but not Mexican songs of combat, as he ultimately discovered. In this same article, he recounts his participation in the Texas Ranger killing of Mexican smugglers.

> I am told that a very long song was composed on the subject, in which certain *gringos,* including myself, are not very well spoken of. (1925:30)

And, in a supreme colonialist gesture of hubris, he confesses, "Much to my disappointment, I have been unable to hear the song or to secure a copy of it" (1925:30). Faced with these obstacles in addition to a definite language barrier, Dobie found that "other folklore genres . . . were easier to handle than songs" (McNutt 1982:194), and it was to those usually more politically benign forms that he turned for the rest of his work on Mexicans.[4] But before getting there, he offered another kind of necessary work as a preliminary step.

In 1929 he published *A Vaquero of the Brush Country* based on an extended narrative he had collected from one John Young, an ex-cowboy and ex-Texas Ranger from south Texas. Why this stop after the overwhelming inspiration of Santos Cortez? In McNutt's words, *Vaqueros of the Brush Country* "is an apology for Anglo border violence" (1982:200). Indeed, the longest and central chapter of the book is entitled "The Bloody Border" and details the many, often wanton killings of Mexicans in south Texas, often with John Young's participation in the nineteenth and into the twentieth century. But as McNutt correctly notes, Dobie represents and rewrites Young's account in such a way as to rhetorically exculpate this colonial violence.

Dobie constructs his rhetorical apologia with two principal devices. First, in rewriting whatever Young told him about the bloody border, Dobie editorially distinguishes between "good" and "bad" Mexicans and makes the symbolic, logical deduction that all the dead Mexicans were "bad." But Dobie also presses his newfound academic interest in folklore to his rhetorical service in the construction of this apologia. Notwithstanding Dobie's effort to speak of good and bad Mexicans, Young's account of raw violence was so overwhelming that, left alone, it makes "Vaquero sound more like an indictment than a celebration of brush country Anglo cowboys" (McNutt 1982:202). But this blanket indictment Dobie could not permit. To do so was to indict not only his own general community, the Anglo "cow people" who overran south Texas, but his specific male parental lineage, heirs by power to "Fort" Ramirez, and, ultimately, himself, the young English instructor seeking his manhood by participating in the killing of Mexican smugglers. Again, McNutt is of the greatest assistance as he notes the way in which Dobie's general folkloristic ethnographic methodology was pressed into political service. For in his treatment of folklore—Anglo and Mexican—Dobie became an example of the romantic regionalist folkloristic ethnographer, he or she (and we will soon meet a "she") who collects folklore from a community (usually his or her own) and then represents it in publication. This representation is done in an embellished, stylized form usually translated into a standard literary language (English in this case), so as to make the original text sound more like "high" literature, fit for a dominant literate reading public. Through such treatment, the romantic regionalist believes, a better appreciation can be had of the "authentic" genius and spirit of the "folk." This methodology guided not only Dobie's management of his own collected materials but that of other collectors who came under his influence when he became the long-term editor of the Publications of the Texas Folklore Society (McNutt 1982:215–67).

In 1929, the method served to construct an aesthetic character for John Young and his Texas cowboys. Dobie was faced with a skeletal narrative of raw violence from a rather candid ex-Texas Ranger; his "solution to this problem was to embellish the narrative with an overlay of romantic idioms, cowboy songs and tales not directly connected with Young" (McNutt 1982:202). The method relieved their narrative of violence of its rawness: but such a folklorized transformation of the narrative frame had a more telling effect: it also allowed Dobie "to ignore the continuation of the bloody border into his own time such as . . . the events of 1915, and beyond" (McNutt 1982:202).

After this apologia for the violent Anglo-American colonization of south Texas, Dobie returned to Mexican folklore to produce two principal books on the subject: *Coronado's Children* (1930) and *Tongues of the Monte* (1935). The former takes as its general subject legends about lost mines and buried treasure throughout the Southwest and was well received nationally. The latter, an account of a folkloristic journey into Mexico that Dobie took in 1932, was not a success, yet, in telling fashion, it continued to be Dobie's favorite book.

There are conscious and unconscious reasons why *Tongues of the Monte* had this special meaning for Dobie. Although a product of fieldwork in Mexico, it takes us back to Mexican south Texas and the continuing war. For, if *A Vaquero of the Brush Country* was an effort to folklorically exculpate Anglo violence, *Tongues of the Monte* is a folkloristic effort to overcome the memory and meaning of that violence at another symbolic level.

Tongues of the Monte, this book about Mexico, actually opens in south Texas with this sentence:

> I cannot remember my first association with Mexicans, for I was born and reared in a part of Texas—the brush country towards the border below San Antonio—where Mexicans were, and still are, more numerous than people of English-speaking ancestry. At that time few of them spoke English, though many of them were native born. (1980b: vii)

For the next few pages, in this travel tale of Mexico, Dobie will insistently continue to talk about south Texas:

> I must have been about grown before I came to know that "cowboy" is not a literary word. Most of the Cowhands I knew were Mexicans, and all of them were called vaqueros. My father was a stockman, having driven horses up the trail to Kansas with Mexican vaqueros, then turning to cattle. All that country used to be grazed by herds of wild horses. My father also rented fields to Mexicans, and several families lived on the ranch, which, as ranches go, was small. (1980b: vii)

I note several key elements in this revealing paragraph: a time when Anglo and Mexican worked together in something of a democratic fashion bound through the common symbolic action of the *vaquero*—the cowboy; a time identified centrally with his father; a time when the country is conceived of as a place "grazed by herds of wild horses"; and, finally, a time of small ranches. Yet, there is more than a hint here of some form, benign, perhaps, of social inequality, for his father is clearly the proprietor who rents fields to the Mexicans. The third paragraph amplifies this latter relationship:

My father and mother were *patrón* and *patrona* to these people, looked to for medicine and medical advice when they were sick, for assurance of credit at the store during droughts and dearth of crops, and for advice and help on many matters. When my father and two other ranchmen built a schoolhouse, located on our place, he saw to it that the Mexican children were allowed to attend. Not many did attend, and in not knowing English, they were at such a disadvantage that they learned little. Along in December each year, my father would go to the town of Beeville, thirty miles away, and bring back, along with our Christmas, blankets, apples and candy as gifts to the Mexicans. He was resourceful and could carpenter, and when a Mexican child died he would be called upon to make the coffin, sawing it out of pine boards and lining it with cotton sheeting. (1980b: viii)

Such death is accompanied by others as we further learn of older Mexicans dying of tuberculosis, their only medical resource being Mexican folk healers (1980b: viii)

Then, and somewhat abruptly, Dobie recalls the folklore of these ranch Mexicans, and, in a tone of admiring pleasure, we are briefly told of treasure legends, house building, the transformation of horse mane and tail into fancy ropes, quirts, and riatas, and of singing—south Texas Mexican singing, wild and eerie, "like the sounds of accompanying coyotes in the brush (1980b: x), and we are moved into an aesthetic universe that relieves the marked oppression of these, my people.

"I tell these few things of my childhood," Dobie continues, "as a kind of warrant for my right in years long afterward to write a book about the Mexican people" (1980b: x).We are then moved to the recollection I noted earlier: the meeting with Santos Cortez, after a "pallid" life in academia, and the beginning of Dobie's folkloristic career. But now we may add more, for, given Dobie's free hand in the edited production of his folkloric books, it is instructive that the single story Dobie chooses to put into this man's mouth, this representative of those who are unequal on Dobie's south Texas ranch, is a story of the devil, here cast in the local idiom as the *bulto,* a hulk that appears in the night to oppress people. Santos tells us, in Dobie's stylized English, how one night, as he slept out in the open with his goats and the coyotes he tells, he

awoke drawing my breath in quick pants, like this. There was *un bulto*—a bulk—on my chest so heavy that it was smothering me. I always kept my rifle at my side. I started to reach for it but could not move a finger. It was as if I were tied down with a wet raw-

hide rope. Tight, man tight! I could not raise my body to pitch the
bulto off. I tried to yell. I had no breath to make a sound with,
and my mouth, it was dry like lime. Look, my tongue would not
moisten my lips. I was pinned back flat so that I could not bend
my neck to see the *bulto* there in the dark. *Pues,* what could I do?
(Dobie 1980b: xii)

Santos thinks hard of God and the Holy Virgin, according to Dobie, and
the devil goes away. "The night that Santos made me believe in the *bulto*
that sat on his chest," Dobie tells us, "I had the idea of a book made up of
people like Santos and of their stories" (1980b: xiii).

Yet Dobie does not follow through. He does not write about Santos or
the south Texas Mexicans and their abundant folklore, their songs, material practices, stories. Instead and without any explanation, he chooses to
overlook the folkloric culture of the south Texas Mexicans and under-
takes a folkloric quest into deep internal Mexico.

During this year [1921] and during years that immediately followed,
I made various trips on horseback or muleback, with pack outfit and
mozo (combination guide and servant) wandering through the vast,
unpopulated mountains of Mexico, lingering at ranches and mining
camps, living the freest times of my life. The written result was this
book. (1980b: xiii)

And he did find freedom in Mexico as so many other Americans have.
It included the freedom to produce *Tongues of the Monte,* a folkloric
quasi-fiction populated with various and assorted semifictional characters
including himself, thinly disguised as a "Don Federico"; a rambling discourse whose principal common thread of development is a series of encounters with various Mexicans, mostly men, who unfailingly provide
Don Federico with folkloric experiences. Mostly benign relative to social
warfare, these experiences seem to lead Dobie to a greater awareness of
his humanity and his love for the common man. Or, at least, that is the
general way he rewrites whatever it was he experienced, for *Tongues* is the
consummate example of the romantic folkloristic ethnography. Our
Pancho is candid on this point:

Anyone who reads the present book will make a mistake if he takes
everything literally . . . I invented a slight string of experiences on
which to thread tales and people. (1980b: xiv)

McNutt correctly notes the book's commercial and artistic failure: "the
persona of the narrator was too inconsistent, the action too disconnected"

(1982:206), but there is some telling unity to the book in addition to that provided by the narrator's quest. Accompanying Dobie/Federico for most of this journey, almost from the moment he crosses the Rio Grande from south Texas, is an elderly Mexican guide and servant named Inocencio, a figure reminiscent of Dobie's south Texas elderly Mexican companions Genardo del Bosque and Santos Cortez. "Inocencio, my old *mozo* [servant] and friend had a prototype, but he combines several *mozos* in himself and arrogates to himself a great deal of the wisdom common to the Mexican *gente* [people]" (Dobie 1980b: xiv). Inocencio, of course, too obviously symbolizes the wisdom and innocence that Dobie is encountering *and* gaining in his quest into Mexico always away from south Texas.

But all is not innocence on this field trip. Inocencio and our Pancho meet another Pancho, at least indirectly, via a character they encounter— "White Mustache"—a former member of the feared *dorados,* the golden ones, Pancho Villa's personal guard. Loyal always to *his* Pancho, White Mustache does not like Federico nor his Inocencio, a former Porfirista who longs for the calm days of the dictatorship and politics soon spills over into sex, or is it the other way around? Our questing protagonist, né Dobie, nom de guerre Pancho, nom de plume Federico, meets and falls in love with a "lovely being" named Dolores temporarily and novelistically overcoming his parents' racial/sexual prohibitions. But it is only tempo-rary; for as the affair develops, Federico recalls his past, reins in his "senses and emotions," and realizes "that a wall higher and broader than the great wall of China prevented my ever taking this lovely being for my wife" (1980b:123). *Race,* as Dobie had experienced it in south Texas, is, of course, the great wall here. *Class,* however, prevents even a casual affair, for "she was the charge of my dear friend and host," the fictive owner of the *hacienda* where our Anglo-Texan and our ex-Porfirista have taken up temporary residence on their journey, *hacienda* at that moment actually owned by the Transcontinental Rubber Company which made it available for Dobie's use.

This professional sexual courtesy among the ruling class, and Federico's "great wall," did not extend to the Mexican female help on the *hacienda.* Even as he wards off Dolores, Don Federico carries on with his chambermaid, Lupita, who "had ripened into firm lushness beyond the soft milk-corn age at which Mexican girls of her class usually marry" (1980b:126). Our Federico tries again to *remember* his racial past, but "the healthy fresh body of a ripe woman makes him forget" (1980b:135). But "White Mustache," the Villista who has his own appreciation of

Lupita's firm lushness, will have none of this and attacks Don Federico, only to be stabbed himself by none other than the faithful Inocencio. The Anglo-Texan, who once wanted to go to war with Mexico, and the Porfirista emerge triumphant over the representation of Villa's revolutionary Mexico and are able to continue their folkloric quest for innocence and humanistic wisdom that will climax in a final parting scene in the closing chapter.

Of course, this book was not written in the field. We must now imagine Pancho back in Austin, probably sometime in the early thirties, rewriting his experiences, arranging and composing chapters, moving as writer toward this final scene of innocence and insight that I shall attend to shortly. But just before he gets there, in the penultimate chapter he lends another kind of unity—not chronologically linear but cyclical—to his work, and this too momentarily disturbs the book's structure of innocence. In this chapter, Don Federico and Inocencio meet an old goatherd named Toribio. From him they hear a devil narrative, and just as our narrator is preparing to return to Texas, we are reminded of his journey's beginning when Santos told Dobie of the *bulto*/devil's visitation as he slept among the coyotes.

From Toribio, Dobie and Inocencio hear of a competition between God cast as a sheepherder and the devil, a goatherd. They contest over which one can move his respective animals faster toward a distant source of water. They agree that he who gets there first shall win the contest and receive the other's animals as a prize along with an additional prize: the devil will get the shepherd dogs that assist God; God will get the coyotes that help the devil herd his goats. God wins, but the devil is unable to keep his full bargain because his coyotes have a mind of their own and refuse to serve God, so that

> instead of running as guardians they became the most depredating beasts of prey the goats knew. And the men whom Dios put on earth saw that these coyotes were enemies and they have always pursued them and killed them. (Dobie 1980b:274)

However, Dobie, Inocencio, and the goatherd all agree that the coyote— that animal of the south Texas brush country who, like Mexican singers, sings in a wild eerie voice—is "next to God . . . the most astute animal in the world" and "as cunning as an eagle" (1980b:274), and in this case he is the devil's animal.

Do I imagine too much? Do I give Dobie too much credit by thinking his political unconscious to be at work here? For it is as if, before ending his folkloristic journey of innocence, before his narrative persona begins his return to the continuing war in Texas, Dobie must acknowledge and anticipate this continuing war that he left, if only through metaphysical and unconscious indirection. The "wild and eerie" Mexicans of south Texas—not the innocent pastoralists of central Mexico—those south Texans who depredated among, which is to say fought against, Dobie's kind require an unconscious acknowledgment as Dobie's narrator prepares to return to Texas. At the other end of this folkloristic journey of innocence, a devil waits.

This final disruption of innocence, like all emerging repressions, must be contained, and Dobie's folkloristic journey ends in a final chapter with Inocencio in which the old Mexican recounts one last Mexican legend dealing with the difficulty of acquiring wisdom even in old age. Federico is moved to ask, "Inocencio, do you think I shall ever be wise?" and Inocencio—not so innocent after all—offers an ambivalent "Pues [well], you are strong." Then in the morning, after serving him coffee, Inocencio gives Federico his favorite knife, but before the narrator leaves at the train station, Inocencio uses it to make a small cut on his wrist, places a drop of his blood on Federico's palm. From the departing train, Federico looks back and sees Inocencio "touching his breast with the fingers of his hand and then extending his arms and holding them stretched wide apart." Federico remembers a quote "from some writer of Mexico" which closes the book: "Just as all plant life springs from the soil, so from it come also the souls of men" (1980b:301).

The novelist and critic Larry McMurtry, for whom Dobie is also a precursor, astutely noted in 1968 that "the South Texas that Dobie knew was dominated, then as now, by very ambitious men and it is not surprising that he should have to cross the Rio Grande to find his figure of innocence" (1968:50). For, of course, Dobie did know of domination, as *Vaquero of the Brush Country* makes clear and as *Tongues of the Monte* suggests in its too revealing preface. As we saw, in this preface, he acknowledges division in the social world, between Anglo dominance and Mexican subservience. This world continued forcefully into the 1930s, for as Dobie was writing this book in Austin, in San Antonio, seventy miles away, Mexican female strikers—another kind of Lupita and Dolores—in the cigar, garment, and pecan-shelling industries were being violently suppressed (Nelson-Cisneros 1975)

We have also seen how Dobie quickly moves us from this world of social alienation to an acknowledgment of Santos Cortez and the rich folklore of the south Texas Mexicans. For all of his insistence that he grew up among these, my people, and knew them well, Dobie evades the opportunity for fieldwork among them and instead crosses the river into Mexico to construct *Tongues of the Monte.* I have suggested that Dobie did not— could not—hear this folklore. Like the *corridos* he quickly abandoned or Santos' oppressive devil *bulto,* it would have told him more than he wanted to hear or than he wanted his audience to know about social alienation. Instead he constructed another Mexican world, far from southern Texas but a displacing commentary on it nonetheless.

"*Vaquero of the Brush Country* was an apology for Anglo oppression," says McNutt, while "*Tongues of the Monte* was a romance across the border" (1982:205) True enough, but not enough. For I submit that *Tongues of the Monte,* with its telling beginnings and endings with reference to south Texas, is also a commentary albeit a displacing commentary about south Texas and Dobie's life in relation to that place. And, if it is so, McNutt's formal definition of it as a romance, which it is, does not capture its social function as a *comedy.* I appeal here to Hayden White's dramatic form of comedy, whose plot structures hold out "for the temporary triumph of man over his world by the prospect of occasional reconciliations of the forces at play in the social and natural worlds" (1973:9). *Tongues of the Monte* was Dobie's way of attempting a reconciliation of certain contradictions in his life and society. These ranged from the seemingly more "personal"—his parental relationships, his manhood and sexuality, his disciplinary vocation—to his largest contradiction, his relationship and that of his people to the Mexicans of south Texas, none of these really separate from each other. Dobie had to have a way of coming to terms both with his clear admiration for the folklore of the Mexicans of south Texas and with his certain knowledge that *his* people were largely responsible for their social misfortune. Dobie reconciles this tension in an easier setting—innocent Mexico.

Displaced to internal Mexico, Pancho's discourse, like his nickname, is his unconscious comedic attempt to reconcile and overcome the social alienation in southern Texas through an ethnographic rendering of innocence that momentarily, and only textually, erases this conflict. For Pancho and his readers—and he was enormously popular—the ideological effect of this erasure is an absolution from complicity and guilt and a continuing ratification of social domination. We see here yet another intellectual seemingly organic to his class and culture, playing his part in forming and directing the ideas of that class and culture in relation to the continuing war of position. But, as with Bourke, such dominant, organic intellectuals are not thinking, linear, ideological machines, free from internal contradiction, doubt, anxiety, and possibility.

J. Frank Dobie's ideological construction of Mexicans served comedically to mask their social treatment in Texas, but it may have served another paradoxical purpose as well. Since his early conflicts with the institutional demands of the Texas English department, Dobie had developed yet another paradoxical relationship with the University of Texas as a representative institution in a changing Texas culture. Deeply attached to the University of Texas—like a wayward lover, he had left it and returned thrice—he valued it as a small-scale site (then) of liberal learning, including his own multicultural curriculum of cowboys, cattle, and Mexicans. By the 1940s he became defined as a progressive liberal, for some a Communist, for his strident opposition to the growing corporate control of the university. In the end, the board of regents took advantage of a technicality in the leave of absence policy and dismissed Dobie, a full professor who was then lecturing at Cambridge University (Tinkle 1978: 153–204).

Supported by powerful and aggressive oil, insurance, and real estate interests—Texas advanced capitalism—these forces threatened not only Dobie's academic pastoral sense of the university but also the brush country of Mexican *vaqueros* and Anglo cowboys that he loved, a threat captured vividly by Larry McMurtry in *Horseman, Pass By,* later made into the film *Hud.* In this particular alignment of forces—this other Texas war—it may be argued that Dobie's pastorally overwrought ethnographic sense of the Mexicans, whatever its masking effect, was also and simultaneously a symbolic defense against those who truly dominate Texas, for Dobie always fundamentally a land of *inocencia. Inocencia*—up to a point—also characterizes the work of Dobie's most interesting student and protegé and our next precursor.

Chapter Three

Jovita Gonzalez

Experience is a crucial *product* and *means* of women's movement; we must struggle over the terms of its articulation. Women do not find "experience" ready to hand any more than they/we find "nature" or the "body" performed, always innocent and waiting outside the violations of language and culture. Just as nature is one of culture's most startling and non-innocent products, so is experience one of the least innocent, least self-evident aspects of historical embodied movement.
> —Donna J. Haraway, *Simians, Cyborgs, and Women:*
> *The Reinvention of Nature*

"Amigo mio Don Pancho," she writes, in a letter circa 1935, "the material is excellent and true to the people it portrays and the presentation is just like Don Pancho would do it." She is referring to his editing of *Puro Mexicano* (1935), a collection of essays on Mexican folklore by various contributors, mostly Anglo, mostly amateurs, all written in the Dobie style, "just like Don Pancho would do it," as she says. The collection included a typically recast Mexican folk story, "Catorce" (Fourteen) by Don Pancho himself, material very similar to his *Tongues of the Monte*. "Your *Catorce*," she continues in particular approval, "has that spirit of *el mexicano* . . ." Modestly, she does not mention her own contribution to the collection, a story called *Traga-Balas* (The Bullet-Swallower). Another letter, circa later 1935: The salutation "Amigo mio Don Pancho" gives way to "Muy amigo mio de mi mayor aprecio y estimacion" (Most appreciable and esteemed friend of mine) as she offers praise—high effusive praise—for *Tongues of the Monte*. She read it for her Don Pancho in manuscript form, and "in my *humilde* estimation, it is a masterpiece of its kind and superior to *Coronado's Children* and that is hard to best." But this is yet not enough praise for her Don Pancho: "I cannot help but puff up with pride when telling people that I have read the manuscript." In turn, she has sent him a portion of her own book-length manuscript, a

60

novel called then *Dew on the Thorn*. She is quite dissatisfied with it but promises to continue working on it so that "when it is properly done, it will be something that will make you proud that you were my *padrino* . . . your good opinion has always meant much to me." Of course it was not always "Don Pancho" and "muy amigo mio," this relationship of Jovita Gonzalez (later de Mireles) to J. Frank Dobie. When they met and first corresponded in the mid-1920s, "Mr. Dobie" and "Miss Gonzalez" were proper form. But it quickly changed and never faltered as long as the relationship lasted.[1]

   She came to know him at the University of Texas as a graduate student in history in the 1920s, because, like him, she too was from southern Texas and keenly interested in Mexican folklore. Over the next twenty years he nurtured and mentored her, soliciting and editing her manuscripts, engaging her in sustained evening discussions of the subject in his home, underwriting bank loans for her field trips, promoting her organizational participation in the Texas Folklore Society so that she eventually became its president, an unusual thing for a group dominated by white male Texans then as now.[2] Under his guidance she became, in effect, one of the first professional native scholars of Mexican-American culture and very probably the first woman.[3]

   But, to a considerable degree, she also took in Dobie's ethnographic style, his ideological vision, and something of his cultural contradictions, because, to a considerable degree, they suited or were not that far removed from her own race- and class-derived inclinations. To a considerable degree, but not entirely, for within the body of her work—the work often of a disorganicized intellectual won over to the side of domination, perhaps won over from the very beginning—we nonetheless find some key instances of a counter-competing vision on questions of race, class, and gender domination, a bedeviled consciousness that ultimately finds the devil for its best articulation.

   We might begin our analytical sense of this work and its double consciousness, as W. E. B. Du Bois might say, with some necessary element of curiosity about its primary institutional context—the University of Texas at Austin. From here we can work backward, forward, and outward. That a son of race and class privilege like Dobie was at Texas is no particular surprise, but what was a young Mexican-American woman fresh from the battlefield of southern Texas—she would have been eleven during the wars of 1915—even *doing* in graduate school at this university in the 1920s? Race would not have barred the admission of Mexican-Americans—unlike African-Americans—in the 1920s or even earlier, but lack of class/

academic preparation and other cultural resources would have precluded the presence of most, with the exception of individuals like Jovita Gonzalez who ultimately shared more background with Dobie than seems initially evident.

She was born in 1904 into a landed—as part of the Spanish settlement— upper-class Mexican-American family in Roma, Texas, next door to Captain Bourke's ethnographic and killing field. Indeed, although I cannot prove it, it is possible that our captain *knew* her family. As an officer and a gentleman he as well as his brother officers did socialize and sometimes intermarried with Gonzalez's class, with that class Bourke, you will recall, referred to as people of "refinement" and "good breeding" living in an otherwise "Dark Belt" in southern Texas. In a brief but important sociological historical work on the area, Gonzalez herself notes this class and cultural affiliation, one also consistent with *racial* distinctions between her class and those below, those also of darker skin such as the *vaquero*, the mestizo, or the *peones* "of Indian blood" (1930b:48–64). It is an affiliation continued in her relationship with her Pancho and appears as a theme in her work, though not free of repressed contradictory elements.

Perhaps the most encompassing form of this contradiction is that she dedicates most of her work to the ethnographic rendering of just these lower classes. In this case, however, she is a near native, and in one article she can speak of being "Among My People" (1932). For the most part as she writes of the lower classes of her people—the laboring *vaqueros* and *peones*—she does so with a superior, often condescending and stereotyping colonialist tone resembling Bourke's and Dobie's. Yet, like Bourke's, it is an idiom that at times appears to be repressing a certain sense of admiration for these classes and an acknowledgment of the state of war. From the beginning this contradiction is evident in her work.

Her first paper—"The Folklore of the Texas-Mexican Vaquero"—was supervised by Dobie, read before his Texas Folklore Society, and published in one of his edited volumes (1927), as was most of the rest of her work. Indeed, *he* wrote her instructive author's blurb. "Her great-grandfather was the richest land owner of the Texas border," Dobie tells us, and with no intended irony, he continues: "Thus she has an unusual heritage of intimacy with her subject" (1927:241). Her subject, she tells Dobie in their correspondence about the paper in progress, is, indeed, not *her* class; she "is not dealing with the landed proprietor who, in my part of the state, forms the better class" (1926). Rather, she tells us in an introductory footnote to the published article, she will deal with "the wandering

Jovita Gonzalez and J. Frank Dobie at the 1930 Texas Folklore Society meetings in San Antonio. Courtesy E. E. Mireles and Jovita Gonzalez Mireles Papers, Special Collections and Archives Department, Corpus Christi State University.

cowboy whose only possessions are his horse, an unlimited store of legends and traditions and the love for his *chata* [girlfriend] . . ." (1927:7).
Yet as she writes of this not better class she begins by noting the social
alienation of the *vaquero*, "unknown to the vast majority of Texans"
though "Texas born and Texas bred"; to "Anglo Americans of a few years'
stay in the state he is an outcast" (1927:7). But we are disappointed if we
expected to be then taken into a discussion of the *vaquero's* folklore
keyed on this social alienation, this state of war. What then follows is a
discussion of the *vaquero's* essential *racial* traits inherited from his Indian
and Spanish parentage:

> From his Indian ancestor he has inherited a love for freedom and
> the open prairie, a dislike for law and restraint, a plaintive melan-
> choly that permeates all his actions, and a fatalistic tendency that
> makes him see the hand of fate guiding and mastering all his efforts
> when misfortune assails him, the only answer to his problem is a
> shrug of the shoulder and "Si es mi suerte, que le voy a hacer (If it
> is my fate: what can I do about it?).

Let us imagine her standing there at the podium on a stage, by all
accounts a small and, at that moment, young woman of twenty-three,
reading these words to the Texas Folklore Society. An unidentified newspaper account of the actual reading tells us that "the stage was delightfully
set to represent the great open places with cactus, prickly pear bushes and
a campfire," and the *Dallas Morning-News* of April 25, 1927, adds that
"about the fire were Mexican rifles, blankets, canteens, moorals and cow
saddles." The setting is aural as well as visual. Just before Gonzalez
spoke,

> three Mexican vaqueros sang songs of the trail in Spanish. José,
> dressed in his vaquero costume, was the hit of the evening. Two
> young women from the university sang the ballad of "Harachio Ber-
> nal" [*sic*].

Other newspaper accounts of the event tell us a bit more about the folksong repertoire; we discover that "José" sang a particular song, one the
newspaper identifies as the ballad of "Gregaria Certes" [*sic*]. From her
news clippings we learn that "Miss Jovita Gonzalez" then read her paper
"with a delightful accent."⁴
    In southern Texas, in 1927, the war continues as Mexican agricultural
strikes are violently suppressed (Zamora 1992), but here, at this academic
meeting, do not her delightfully accented words flow like soothing balm

to the gathered company of mostly white men—some of them rich, powerful men? In his customary cowboy boots, his Stetson hat politely in his lap,
does her Don Pancho sit there also, probably in the first row? Dare we
hope that as she read her paper, she at least *thought* to herself of the
"fatalistic" Catarino Garza who shot it out with Captain Bourke? Of the
1915 revolutionaries whose answer to the domination of south Texas was
not a "shrug of the shoulder" but war? Of the song "Gregaria Certes" [*sic*]
just sung by "José," which most of the audience could not tell was a war
song? Of a history that she knew full well whose continuation in the form
of those agricultural strikes was going on at that very moment? For this
future teacher of Spanish, is it a mistake, a typo, a choice, or Pancho's
long editorial hand, that her translation of "Si es mi suerte, que le voy a
hacer" into "It is my fate: what can I do about it" *deletes* the politically
loaded conditional "Si"—"*if it* is my fate."

We dare hope, but it is only hope. She continues with little in this paper
of 1927 to sustain hope as she reports on an assortment of benign
folklore—birdcalls, love songs, plant knowledge—of the *vaqueros* rendered, of course, in a pastoralized and pasteurized literary English. But a
bit does slip through the repression.

> An old *vaquero* told me once of what to him was paradise: the open
> prairies with no fences to hinder the roaming of the cattle and the
> wanderings of the cowboys.

But for this *vaquero,* the coming of the fences, synonymous with the advent of Anglo capitalist ranching, is no mere impediment to an idealized
pastoral freedom. In her narrative, he follows up immediately with a specific sociological observation by way of a proverb: "Cuando vino el
alambre, vino el hambre." This time there is no translation lapse as she
renders it perfectly: "With the coming of the wire, hunger came." But
immediately the *vaquero's* political sociology is, in her narrative, awash in
Pancho pastoralism, and the balm flows out once more. "In spite of his
pessimism," she continues, "the vaquero is a poet at heart. He sees the
beauty of the sage-brush in bloom, the singing of the mocking bird on
clear moonlight nights invites him to sing." And she continues in this vein
to the end.

However, three years later, in another article, this one not read to the
Texas Folklore Society, we hear a somewhat different voice. In this far
more sociological piece derived from her master's thesis, we are immediately confronted by the war metaphor clearly embedded in her title,
"America Invades the Border Towns" (1930). What follows, however,

does not sustain the metaphor as it attempts an evenhanded approach that belies our known history of the area. What has happened in south Texas between 1848 and 1930, she tells us, "is a racial struggle, a fight between an aggressive, conquering and materialistic people on the one hand, and a volatile but passive and easily satisfied race on the other" (1930a:472). The aggressive conquering aspects of the former are left wholly undiscussed, while the clear implication left for the latter—the Texas-Mexicans—is that, although they have suffered some injustice (left largely unspecified), it is they who must adopt American values if racial relations are to improve (1930a:476–77).

A second article of this same year is a continuation of the earlier "Folklore of the Texas-Mexican Vaquero." This one, "Tales and Songs of the Texas-Mexicans," speaks in its introduction of its author's having collected this lore from *vaqueros* and *peones,* all classified in her phrase as "half-breeds" (1930c:86). What follows is, for the most part, another assortment of folklore on birds and plant life, once again rendered in a literary English with little analytical commentary. But then, and interrupting the thus far pastoral thematic, she offers three sketches concerning the appearance of the devil in southern Texas. Earlier that same year of 1930 *she* excerpted these stories for a reading before the Texas Folklore Society, and I invite you to imagine *this* reading to Dobie and his colleagues.

The longest of these stories begins with "an abnormally hot day in hell" as the devils feed their fires awaiting the arrival of a barber, a student, and a banker. They come to hell terrified at what awaits them. Among them, however, a fourth and unexpected character appears, who "with the coolness and nonchalance of one accustomed to such things" is not "a bit impressed by the fiery reception awarded them." He is described as "an athletic sort of a man" who "wore a five gallon hat, chivarras and spurs and played with a lariat he held in his hands." Ignoring the heat, this man immediately gets to work shoveling coals into the fires. Quite impressed by all of this, his "Satanic majesty" demands to know who this odd fellow is. He identifies himself as that most famous of Spanish and Latin American picaresque figures, Pedro de Urdemañas, and tells Satan that he is a world traveler with hell his latest stop. "Where was your home before you came here?" Satan asks.

> Oh in the most wonderful land of all. I am sure you would love it. Have you ever been in Texas? The devil shook his head.

Pedro then describes Texas as a marvelous country with many cows, "and what's more," he tells Satan, "there is plenty of work for you down there." Satan is anxious to visit Texas with the promise of more people for hell, but he is a bit anxious about the cows. Pedro tries to calm his anxieties, for "there is a marked similarity between you and a cow," he tells him; "both have horns and a tail." He leaves for Texas, but since Satan's "most productive work had been done in the cities and he knew nothing of ranch life," he "left for Texas gaily appareled in the latest New York style."

Unfortunately he arrives in August "on a little prairie surrounded by thorny bush, near the lower Rio Grande," on a very hot day. The Texas heat "burned the Devil's face and scorched his throat. His tongue was swollen; his temples throbbed with the force of hammer beat." But then he sights what he thinks are some refreshing red berries growing on a bush and swallows a handful, only to be introduced to red-hot Texas wild chile peppers.

"The fire that he was used to was nothing compared to the fire from chile peppers that now devoured him." He then finds and tries what he thinks are fresh figs, although he thinks it strange that they are not growing on a fig tree. But "at first bite he threw it away with a cry of pain. His mouth and tongue were full of thorns. With an oath and a groan, he turned from the prickly pear and continued his journey."

This takes him to a south Texas ranch where he finds a group of men dressed like Pedro de Urdemañas herding cows—those creatures that Pedro said looked just like Satan, a blow to his vanity as he sees "those insipid creatures, devoid of all character and expression." He promises himself to send Pedro to the hottest part of hell when he returns there. He watches the *vaqueros* on horseback taking down cows by flipping them by their tails. Asking to try the trick, Satan walks up to a cow, *squeezes* its tail as instructed by a sly *vaquero,* only to be kicked "whirling through the air." The story ends:

> Very much upset and chagrined, he got up. But what hurt more were the yells of derision that greeted him. Without even looking back, he ran hell-bound, and did not stop until he got home. The first thing he did when he got home was to expel Pedro from the infernal region. He would have nothing to do with one who had been the cause of his humiliation. And since then Satan has never been in Texas, and Pedro de Urdemañas still wanders through the Texas ranches always in the shape of some fun-loving *vaquero.*

Let us imagine her again as she reads this jocular story she has rewritten from folk tradition. What does her audience think, these collectors of

Texana folklore and Texana privilege? Pedro de Urdemañas' Texas-Mexican picaresque and subversive *vaquero* identity is only too clear, but who is the devil who has come as an alien to south Texas? Once narratively in place, the devil is closely identified with cows for this cowboy-invested audience, cattle then and perhaps even now a Texas metonym, cows said to be "insipid creatures, devoid of all character and expression." Gonzalez's only and slight rhetorical concession to her audience is her geographical displacement of the devil as dressed in the "New York style," inviting them, in delusion, to think of him as a "Yankee" rather than as a representation of their own Southern forebears.

JOVITA GONZALEZ: AMBIVALENCE AND REPRESSION

She finishes to polite applause no doubt, and takes questions. What did they ask? What did she say? Unfortunately we have no record. The questioning period concludes, more applause perhaps; she sits down, perhaps next to her Pancho. What is she thinking, this young Texas-Mexican woman in a roomful of largely male Anglos in 1930? Dare we hope? McNutt has a clear and less charitable answer than I am offering. As one of only two previous students of this woman's career, McNutt concludes:

> Dobie's paternalistic attitude met agreement in Miss Gonzalez's own conservatism. She viewed herself as a member of the Mexican American upper class, a descendant of Spanish aristocrats. She and Dobie were sharing information about mestizo peons when they collected and discussed folklore. (1982:252)

McNutt's chief concern is Dobie's career and not Jovita's, so he offers no close reading of her texts that would complicate his opinion. But from other sources he adduces data that clearly signal this career's contradictions. For it turns out the Pancho and Gonzalez had reached an interesting agreement. McNutt quotes her:

> You see, it was an agreement that we made, that I would not go into one of his classes because I would be mad at many things. He would take the Anglo-Saxon side naturally. I would take the Spanish and the Mexican side. (McNutt 1982:251)

We learn more about the war waged pedagogically at the University of Texas. Future teachers, she told McNutt,

> couldn't afford to get involved in a controversy between Mexico and the University of Texas . . . but if the history of Texas were written

the way it actually was . . . because things, some of those things that happened on both sides were very bitter. So we just didn't mention them. You just forgot about it. (McNutt 1982:251).[5]

Notwithstanding this repressed conflict, McNutt concludes that overall, "such relationships as that between Dobie and Miss Gonzalez reinforced the patterns of ethnic conflict in the Southwest, particularly in the way it made class distinctions the basis for agreement about the nature of 'the folk' " (1982:252).

The second scholar of Jovita Gonzalez's work is at once more charitable and more politically hopeful, even as her treatment undercuts her argument. Velasquez-Treviño is concerned with reading Gonzalez in two dimensions: as a potential critic of patriarchy and as a critic of Anglo-American dominance. Gonzalez largely fails the first test as she

> devotes little attention to the description of female experience. In her prose fiction, the female characters do not appear as protagonists and are assigned very little space within the narrative discourse. When women do appear, they are confined to traditional roles within their ethnic culture while male experience is foregrounded. (Velasquez-Treviño 1985:101)

Gonzalez fares better, though actually not much better, on the second test as Velasquez-Treviño argues a thesis of "cultural ambivalence" (1985:69). Here,

> the intermediary social position of Jovita Gonzalez, which reflects an attitude of both resistance and assimilation to the dominant culture, produces specific ideological contradictions which are imbedded in her narrative. (1985:80)

Drawing on the evidence adduced here, I would make a distinctive argument for Jovita Gonzalez that follows but also departs from my two predecessors in the study of this woman. As I've suggested throughout, in substantial agreement with McNutt, there is a clearly dominant line to Gonzalez's ethnographic rendering and to her discursive statements. She articulates a class/race paternalism and colonialist attitude consistent with that of her *padrino*, Dobie, thereby reinforcing Anglo-American capitalist dominance in Texas as a whole. Yet, with respect to Velasquez-Treviño, I do not sense here "ambivalence" in an ordinary understanding of the term, as a synonym for "uncertainty." Gonzalez seemed quite certain most of the time of her allegiances in the war of position.

Yet Velasquez-Treviño is right in first having noted the "specific ideo-

logical contradictions which are embedded in her narrative." I would insist, however, pursuing Velasquez's own metaphor, that these are indeed
imbedded and have to be excavated to yield any sense of resistance, as I
have tried to do with Jovita's devil story. Because they are imbedded, I
would suggest that the problematic with Gonzalez is not ambivalence but
repression, as she herself put it to McNutt: "you just forgot about it." But
the repressed returns, as it did when she uttered, then published, her devil
story for her Anglo-American audience. It would return at least twice
before her ethnographic career came to a close and in ways that point us
toward a future cultural poetics.[6]

In the same "Tales and Songs of the Texas-Mexicans" where the devil
appears, Jovita Gonzalez takes note of songs as her title promised. This
time, however, it is not pastoral love song that interests her but rather the
politically laden *corrido,* also called *tragedia* (tragedy). Even here, we
clearly sense repression as she soothingly shapes her reassuring discursive
flow to the audience's expectations and probably her own. Yet once again
more than enough slips through as she discusses one *corrido* about one
man.

We learn immediately of the *corrido's* formal character, "the most rudi-
mentary type of song" (1930c:109), as befits its social milieu, the lower
classes, as she represents them: "a motley crowd, *vaqueros,* goat herders,
smugglers and not seldom bandits escaping from justice" (1930c:110).
"Of the latter type" she continues,

> . . . was Remigio Treviño, a soldier stationed at Camargo, who in
> the early sixties made up his mind to kill and expel the few Ameri-
> cans living along the border. With a band of men he swept across
> the river when least expected killing the settlers and burning their
> homes. His one boast was that altogether he had killed ten Ameri-
> cans. But in 1863 while making a raid on Rio Grande City he was
> captured and received the one punishment meted out to all outlaws.
> He was hanged. (1930c:110)

Clearly the state of war is rhetorically before us and her audience, and,
contrasted to the earlier pastoralism, we learn much politically by what is
implied but not said. What motivates Treviño, presumably a soldier in the
Mexican army stationed in Camargo across the border, to enter south
Texas on his raids at the risk of his life? Or is it *reenter?* Who was Remigio
Treviño before he joined the Mexican army? Perhaps a Texas-Mexican?
Why did he leave? Why does he return to kill settlers and burn their
homes rather than, let us say, rob banks or loot towns? She offers her

audience a few verses of the *corrido* that he allegedly composed but which say nothing on this and only express a general lament at being captured. However, her closing commentary on this folksong strains to reveal more as it undercuts the theme of "banditry" and "outlaw" and replaces it with political resistance.

> This is the earliest Mexican ballad composed on Texas soil that I have found. The turbulent period following the independence of Texas was one of resistance to the Americans who came as far south as the border. I have been told that many *tragedias* originated then, but the above is the only one I have been able to collect. (1930:111)[7]

The male Texas-Mexican resistance fighter is also a central motif in the penultimate article of her career. In 1935 and no longer at the university, she submitted the story "The Bullet-Swallower" to Dobie's collection *Puro Mexicano,* a story that, if understood as political resistance, was ironically appropriate for the collection, for it is indeed "pure Mexican." According to the narrator, the story's central protagonist, named Bullet-Swallower, or in Spanish, *Traga-Balas,* is "a landowner by inheritance, a trail driver by necessity, and a smuggler and gambler by choice," who "had given up the traditions of his family to be and do that which pleased him most" (1935:107). This man, who willingly disowns his south Texas class privilege to join the lower social orders—is there repressed desire here, displaced unto a man?—is "a tireless horseman, a man of *pelo en pecho* (hair on the chest) as he braggingly called himself, he was afraid of nothing" (1935:107). In an opening narrative within the narrative, Traga-Balas tells how he got his name. The story is worth repeating in full. Through it and as with the devil story, we gain purchase on what Jovita would more often choose to "forget," that "bitter" history which made her "mad" and which she was not permitted to utter in Pancho's classes. Bracketed within the permissive narrative frame of a "folk" story; perhaps, pointedly directed at her Don Pancho who, let us recall, had been complicit in the killing of Mexican smugglers, her words flowed out—perhaps this time like acid—when she read this as a paper to the Texas Folklore Society gathered in Dallas on April 19, 1935. Continuing the war by other repressed means, she has Traga-Balas say:

> "People call me Traga-Balas, Bullet-Swallower—Antonio Traga-Balas, to be more exact. *Ay,* were I as young as I was when the incident that gave me this name happened!
> "We were bringing several cartloads of smuggled goods to be delivered at once and in safety to the owner. Oh, no, the freight was

not ours but we would have fought for it with our life's blood. We
had dodged the Mexican officials, and now we had to deal with the
Texas Rangers. They must have been tipped, because they knew the
exact hour we were to cross the river. We swam in safety. The pack
mules, loaded with packages wrapped in tanned hides, we led by the
bridle. We hid the mules in a clump of tules and were just beginning
to dress when the Rangers fell upon us. Of course, we did not have
a stitch of clothes on; did you think we swam fully dressed? Had we
but had our guns in readiness, there might have been a different
story to tell. We would have fought like wild-cats to keep the smug-
gled goods from falling into their hands. It was not ethical among
smugglers to lose the property of Mexicans to Americans, and as to
falling ourselves into their hands, we preferred death a thousand
times. It's no disgrace and dishonor to die like a man, but it is to die
like a rat. Only canaries sing; men never tell, however tortured they
may be. I have seen the Rangers pumping water into the mouth of
an innocent man because he would not confess to something he had
not done. But that is another story.

"I ran to where the pack mules were to get my gun. Like a fool
that I was, I kept yelling at the top of my voice, 'You so, so and so
gringo cowards, why don't you attack men like men? Why do you
wait until they're undressed and unarmed?' I must have said some
very insulting things, for one of them shot at me right in the mouth.
The bullet knocked all of my front teeth out, grazed my tongue and
went right through the back of my neck. Didn't kill me, though. It
takes more than bullets to kill Antonio Traga-Balas. The next thing I
knew I found myself in a shepherd's hut. I had been left for dead,
no doubt, and I had been found by the goatherd. The others were
sent to the penitentiary. After I recoverd, I remained in hiding for a
year or so; and when I showed myself all thought it a miracle that I
had lived through. That's how I was rechristened Traga-Balas. That
confounded bullet did leave my neck a little stiff; I can't turn around
as easily as I should, but outside of that I am as fit as though the
accident—I like to call it that—had never happened. It takes a lot
to kill a man, at least one who can swallow bullets." (1935:102–3)

The story then goes on to develop a further adventure—the Bullet-
Swallower's confrontation with Death which proves him a courageous,
worthy man.

We close where we began. "Amigo mio Don Pancho," she writes about
Dobie's *Puro Mexicano,* including her *Traga-Balas,* "the material is excel-
lent and true to the people it portrays and the presentation is just like Don
Pancho would do it." Given the critical edge of *Traga-Balas,* do we now

Jovita Gonzalez ca. 1935. Courtesy E. E. Mireles and Jovita Gonzalez Mireles Papers, Special Collections and Archives Department, Corpus Christi State University.

hear fawning praise, or, in critical counterpoint to her generally shared comedic outlook with Dobie, do we really hear the tone of an ironic trope, affirming "tacitly the negative of what is on the literal level affirmed positively . . ." (White 1973:37)? She was Dobie's collaborator in Webster's first definitional sense of the term, i.e., "to work jointly with others especially in an intellectual endeavor," but was she also a collaborator in a second sense: "to cooperate with or willingly assist an enemy of one's country and especially an occupying force"?[8]

Whatever the prevailing culture poetics of her brief ethnographic career, I have suggested that in her final essays, largely written after she returned to south Texas to teach Spanish, Jovita Gonzalez reveals more or her narratively unrepressed critical political unconscious.

Yet this increasing revelation puts her in another kind of paradoxical and repressive position, this one keyed on gender politics. We recall Velasquez-Treviño's admonition concerning Gonzalez's nearly complete exclusion of women and her nearly exclusive devotion to the description of male experience. We have certainly seen this disparity in these final essays. Indeed, in these essays, the articulation of this woman's critical political unconscious takes her, not just to a world of men, but specifically to that of the mythic male hero, a sphere of super-enhanced masculinity and a concomitant repression of women. Though she was a woman, was this male heroic world her best historically available alternative to respond critically to the powerful, white, largely masculine world in which she chose to work, a world exemplified by J. Frank Dobie? Whatever her motives, it was the world she chose, the world of the *vaquero,* often rendered pastoral but, at times, heroically politically potent.

In a section of her *Women, Native, Other* called "The Triple Bind," Trinh T. Minh-ha says of the third world woman writer:

> Today, the growing ethnic-feminist consciousness has made it increasingly difficult for her to turn a blind eye not only to the specification of the writer as historical subject (who writes? and in what context?) but also to writing itself as a practice located at the intersection of subject and history . . . (1989:6)

But if the case of Jovita Gonzalez shows us anything, it reveals a woman before "today," at another historical moment, unsupported by the luxury of a "growing ethnic-feminist consciousness," who perhaps only appears "to turn a blind eye" on her role as a historical writing subject with respect to her native community. As a specific intellectual entangled between the sites of power represented by Dobie, her own race/class affiliations, and her larger community, she often repressed the better part of her political consciousness and became like those "women writers" who

> are both prompt to hide in (their) writing(s) and feel prompted to do so. As language-stealers, they must yet learn to steal without being seen, and with no pretense of being a stealer, for fear of "exposing the father." Such a reluctance to say aloud that the emperor has no clothes and therefore to betray or admit of an evidence comes perhaps less from a subjection to man than from an acute awareness of emptiness—emptiness through (his) power, through (his) language, through (his) disguises. (Minh-ha 1989:19)

But Jovita Gonzalez was not wholly empty of native resources when she dealt with her "father," J. Frank Dobie, and his politically constructed male academic authority. Within her cultural consciousness, she, as woman, paradoxically located a tradition of Texas-Mexican male heroic resistance which, in her moment, she specifically and narratively spoke to power even as she anticipated the later full development of this important trope in our next and final precursor, he who would authoritatively inscribe that ballad sung at Jovita Gonzalez's first public reading in 1927, reported by the newspapers as the ballad of "Gregaria Certes" [sic].

Chapter Four

Américo Paredes

Is it anything more than a well-known habit of using the past, the "good old days," as a stick to beat the present? It is clearly something of that, but there are still difficulties. The apparent resting places, the successive Old Englands to which we are confidently referred but which then start to move and recede, have some actual significance, when they are looked at in their own terms. Of course we notice their location in the childhoods of their authors, and this must be relevant. Nostalgia, it can be said, is universal and persistent; only other men's nostalgias offend. A memory of childhood can be said, persuasively, to have some permanent significance. But again, what seemed a single escalator, a perpetual recession into history, turns out, on reflection, to be a more complicated movement: Old England, settlement, the rural virtues—all these, in fact, mean different things at different times, and quite different values are being brought to question. We shall need precise analysis of each kind of retrospect, as it comes. We shall see successive stages of the criticism which the retrospect supports: religious, humanist, political, cultural. Each of these stages is worth examination in itself. And then, within each of these questions, but returning us finally to a formidable and central question, there is a different consideration.
    —Raymond Williams, *The Country and the City*

In 1958, a new scholar appeared to offer an analytically advanced, comprehensive, and compelling elaboration of the Texas-Mexican male heroic tradition and its *corridos*. Celebrated in folksong and legend, such a hero defends his rights and those of his people "with his pistol in his hand," the *corrido* line and title of the most important ethnographic work of this new intellectual figure, Américo Paredes.

At the beginning of *With His Pistol in His Hand* (1958), we find a dedication, in itself a conventional and not surprising beginning to any

76

book. But immediately the *form* of this dedication subverts convention,
for it is cast as a poem:

> To the memory of my father
> who rode a raid or two with
> Catarino Garza;
> and to all those old men
> who sat around on summer nights,
> in the days when there was
> a chaparral, smoking their
> cornhusk cigarettes and talking
> in low, gentle voices about
> violent things;
> while I listened.

We read these words with memory at our service, and if we read with
such memory, this already formal surprising poetic dedication now startles. Out of time the name of Catarino Garza, Bourke's antagonist, returns in 1958 to provide us immediately with the most fascinating of link-
ages in the south Texas war of maneuver and position. As we read and
remember, it dawns on us that Captain Bourke, our first precursor, was
trying to kill, not only Garza, but Paredes' own father, riding "a raid or
two" with Garza against Bourke. And, as further connection, is it unrea-
sonable to assume that after the week's search-and-destroy, perhaps on a
Saturday evening, the good captain, an officer and a gentleman—his wife
back in Philadelphia—might have politely danced with Jovita's future
mother at an upper-class *fiesta* in town? "The dances were held in what is
now the old court-house," an older upper-class informant tells Jovita,
"the officers from Fort Ringold and their wives were our honor guests.
There were neither racial nor social distinctions between Americans and
Mexicans" (1930b:63). No distinctions, indeed; but as they danced, out
there in the chaparral, around a campfire, Catarino Garza and the elder
Paredes may have waited for the opportunity to dance with Bourke as
well. We read these words and recognize the direct linkage between my
most distant and most immediate precursors through memory and oral
tradition. As a young boy Américo Paredes listens to the "low, gentle
voices" of his father and other older men talking "about violent things"
and they do so "in the days when there was a chaparral." We complete our
reading of the poem now fully conscious that this is no conventional dedication, and what follows is no conventional book.

J. Frank Dobie had just left the English department at the University of Texas at Austin a few years before our fourth major precursor, Américo Paredes, entered that department as a graduate student in the early fifties. Like Dobie, he had been born and raised in south Texas, but unlike Dobie, and more like Jovita Gonzalez, not just *in* south Texas but *of* the *mexicano* community. The year of his birth was 1915, the war of maneuver and death was all about, and he would grow up amidst the continuing positional warfare of race and class that Dobie's Comedy sought to repress and Gonzalez's irony had begun to reveal.

After high school, Mr. Paredes worked as a newspaperman in his hometown of Brownsville, Texas; then, like many men of his generation, he was called into the army during the Second World War. Mr. Paredes did not fight in World War II. His prewar career as a journalist in south Texas led to an assignment as a Pacific correspondent and editor for *Stars and Stripes,* the U.S. military newspaper. In this capacity he covered the postwar trials of Japanese generals accused of atrocities and became convinced of their innocence and suspicious of American racist motives, which he had known in his south Texas past. He developed a deep affection for Japan and particularly for one of its women, marrying her and remaining in that country after the war. Employed as a journalist for the American Red Cross, he, like General Walker, also visited Korea but in the late 1940s before the Korean War. Unlike the general and his Eighth Army, Mr. Paredes did make it to China to witness the revolutionary triumph of Mao Tse-tung's people's armies in the late forties. And, unlike the general and most Americans, he developed an attachment to these Asian peoples and a conviction that racism had played a key role in the extension of American military power in that part of the world. This conviction was reinforced when he and his wife decided to return to the United States and encountered racist immigration quotas for Japanese designed to discourage marriages such as his. These barriers were eventually overcome and they came to Austin, Texas, where he pursued graduate work in English with interests in folklore and creative writing. He was also to publish fiction and poetry as well as scholarship.

Less like Dobie and more like Bourke, Mr. Paredes has dedicated a substantial portion of his professional life to the study of *mexicano* folklore in south Texas. Given his native experience and his formal academic training, he takes a very different critical orientation, one that in its broadest formulation, I call critical, modern tragedy. It is a perspective constituting the political unconscious of the major scholarly work he has published since attaining his Ph.D. in 1956 and assuming a position as a faculty member in English and Anthropology at the Austin campus from 1957 to his present emeritus status.

With His Pistol in His Hand: A Border Ballad and Its Hero and some articles, chiefly on joking behavior, shall be my major texts. It is a corpus of work offering an unrepressed critique of past and present Anglo social domination. Yet it is also a narrative whose tragic sentiment, as Unamuno would say, is already being articulated in the line of the dedication which tells us that all of this heroism happened "in the days when there was a chaparral." It is a tragic sentiment that eventually leads us to detect a tragic flaw in this work.

With His Pistol in His Hand is a study of the life, legend, and corpus of ballads generated by the activities of one individual, Gregorio Cortez (yes, "Gregaria Certes" of Anglo newspaper fame). Until June 12, 1901, Cortez was a rather ordinary Mexican-American in Texas, an agricultural laborer like so many others, who, from his own perspective, was witnessing the intensification of Anglo-American and capitalist domination of Texas, including the predominantly Mexican-American region of south Texas. As we have already noted, this domination of the native and increasingly immigrant Mexican population took the form of class and racial subordination, the latter evidenced in part in the rough and ready lynching "justice" often administered to Mexican-Americans accused of crimes.

Such was the fate that Cortez undoubtedly expected on June 12 in the moments after he killed Sheriff W. T. Morris in Karnes County in central Texas in an exchange of pistol fire which also left Cortez's brother, Romaldo, seriously wounded. In his last official act, Sheriff Morris, an ex-Texas Ranger, had come to the farm where the Cortezes, migrants from the border, were sharecropping. The sheriff was looking for reported horse thieves. Because neither he nor his accompanying deputy spoke Spanish well, if at all, they mistakenly accused the Cortezes of the thievery, and the sheriff drew his gun. Probably thinking they were about to be gunned down in cold blood, Romaldo charged the sheriff not knowing that his brother had a gun hidden behind his back. Morris shot Romaldo but in the next instant was himself cut down by Gregorio with his pistol in his hand even as the deputy ran for his life and help.

With the sheriff lying dead before him, Cortez knew that he faced certain Texas justice. Entrusting his brother to his family, Gregorio began a long horseback ride of escape to south Texas and the Mexican border. Along the way he evaded numerous posses through skillful riding and help from local Mexican-Americans. He also killed a second sheriff. Eventually Cortez learned that the authorities had jailed his wife and children and were carrying out reprisals against those who had helped him. He turned himself in to the authorities near Laredo, Texas, where Mexican-Americans still had some measure of political control. Nonetheless he was returned to Karnes County, where under constant threat of lynching he was tried and convicted, although in one of those paradoxes that has characterized Texas he was eventually pardoned by a liberal Anglo Texan governor.

By 1901 the Mexican-Americans of Texas had experienced half a century of domination, and Cortez's encounter with this domination and his largely successful adventurous ride to freedom stirred to folk imagination of this community. Its folksingers turned to a traditional musical form— the *corrido*—to speak of these events. As a song narrative the *corrido* had as its ancestral form the medieval Spanish *romances* such as those of *El Cid*. The, as now, it served communities well in recording important historical events and artistically rendering their perspectives on these events (Limón 1992). Soon after or perhaps even during Cortez's ride, they began to compose the legend and balladry of Gregorio Cortez, as Mr. Paredes says, "in the *cantinas* and the country stores, in the ranches when men gather at night to talk in the cool dark, sitting in a circle, smoking and listening to the old songs and the tales of other days" (1971:33).

They tell of Gregorio Cortez and his heroic exploits and they make him one of them.

> He was a man, a Border man. What did he look like? Well that is
> hard to tell. Some say he was short and some say he was tall; some
> say he was Indian brown and some say he was blond like a newborn
> cockroach. But I'd say he was not too dark and not too fair, not too
> thin and not too fat, not too short and not too tall; and he looked
> just a little bit like me. (Paredes 1958: 34)

They also sang *corridos* telling of this man and his exploits in the traditional octosyllabic meter with rhyming quatrains of *a b c b* and in duets of two guitars. This is one of the better versions of the ballad which Mr. Paredes translates and offers as a representative text in his book.

El Corrido de Gregorio Cortez

In the country of El Carmen
A great misfortune befell;
The Major Sheriff is dead;
Who killed him no one can tell

Who killed him no one can tell
At two in the afternoon,
In half an hour or less,
They knew that the man who
    killed him
Had been Gregorio Cortez.

They let loose the bloodhound
    dogs;
They followed him from afar.
But trying to catch Cortez
Was like following a star.

All the rangers of the county
Were flying, they rode so hard;
What they wanted to get
The thousand-dollar reward.

And in the country of Kiansis
They cornered him after all;
Though they were more than
    three hundred
He leaped out of the corral.

Then the Major Sheriff said,
As if he was going to cry,
"Cortez, hand over your weapons;
We want to take you alive."

Then said Gregorio Cortez,
And his voice was like a bell,
"You will never get my weapons
Till you put me in a cell."

Then said Gregorio Cortez,
With his pistol in his hand,
"Ah, so many mounted Rangers
Just to take one Mexican!"

    In part I of the book, Paredes offers a compelling dramatic narrative of
a compelling dramatic narrative. As a representative of the underdog
dominated, the hero faces unjust and immoral superior odds. He initially
defeats them with superior skills in horsemanship and shooting, and even

in the end scores a moral triumph by surrendering only to spare the lives
of his family and his community. More significant for our purposes, the
balladry and legend also construct Cortez as a Christlike figure. Such a
construction has to leave the clear narrative implication that on the other
side are the forces of evil, the Texas Rangers. Indeed, de Leon quotes one
Anglo observer describing the Texas Rangers as a "reckless, devil-may-
care looking set [which] would be impossible to find this side of the Infer-
nal Regions" (de Leon 1983:76), and the *mexicano* community referred to
the Rangers as "los diablos tejanos" (Oates 1973).

Incident and balladry occur in the early 1900s, so that the song and its
associated legends symbolically reverse the dominated condition of *mexicanos,* even as they symbolically reproduce and enhance the willingness
of the community to continue the actual war of maneuver. After all, the
bloodletting of 1915 was yet to come. As directly experienced by Bourke,
denied by Dobie, and anticipated by Gonzalez, this communal resistance,
we must remember, is singularly embodied in the idiom of heroic male
resistance fighter—a warrior hero, in Paredes' phrase. Yet as the legend
recounts it, he is a man of the people who looked "not too dark and not
too fair, not too thin and not too fat, not too short and not too tall; and he
looked just a little bit like me" (Paredes 1971:34)

Indeed, elsewhere I have argued that, as an ethnography, *With His Pistol in His Hand* is influenced formally by the Mexican ballad (Limón 1992),
and that as a new *"corrido"* in the form of postmodern ethnography it also
does political work as a text of positional warfare in two directions. First, it
directly attacks the degrading, or comedic, visions of *mexicanos* that were
then promoted in intellectual discourse by two intellectuals organic to the
dominant class of Texas. We have already noted the comedic discourse of J.
Frank Dobie with its internal contradictions. A more seamless discourse of
dominating power with no such contradictions is to be found in the eminent
historian Walter Prescott Webb's writings on *mexicanos,* who he said
lacked fighting qualities: although the Mexican has a "cruel streak" in him,
when it comes to fighting, his blood is as "ditch-water" (1931:125–26), and
"the whine of the leaden slugs stirred in him an irresistible impulse to travel
with rather than against the music" (1935:14). Second, in offering Cortez as
a refutation of such racist characterizations, in standing up as an assistant
professor to his powerful senior Anglo colleagues at Texas in the late fifties
and early sixties, not to mention the Texas Rangers, Mr. Paredes and his
book become like a *corrido* and its hero for a new generation of Chicano
social activists of the sixties, who recognized the legendary fighting qualities of the two men, Cortez and Paredes.[1]

Professor Américo Paredes ca. 1990. Courtesy University of Texas News and Information
Service.

In this respect, one can also note a third line of attack, for this book also appears at a moment when critical political discourse among the *mexicano* intelligentsia of south Texas had practically ceased in favor of an ascending, pro-American, assimilationist rhetoric, a process reflecting a growing class division within *mexicano* society that had intensified in the thirties and forties (Garcia 1978). For it is also the case that in the positional warfare for hegemony, the dominant side will also try to win over the other side's organic intellectuals. They succeeded (and continue to succeed) with many, but not with Américo Paredes who in this period of time stands practically alone, face to face with those who wield power in Texas.

THE BEDEVILMENT OF "COMMUNITY"

Few intelligent cultural texts are without internal contradiction when viewed from the perspective of the political unconscious. We have seen it already in Bourke, Dobie, and Gonzalez; it is present also in Mr. Paredes' anthropological discourse.

The *corrido* world Mr. Paredes describes so vividly and poetically, the world that exerts such a deep influence on his own poetics, is the one that existed, as noted earlier, "in the days when there was a chaparral"; when the brush in south Texas "was so heavy that herds of stolen beef or horses could be hidden a few miles from town in perfect secrecy" (1971:10). Described in chapter 1, "The Country," of *With His Pistol in His Hand,* in this pre-twentieth-century world, "social conduct was regulated and formal, and men lived under a patriarchal system that made them conscious of degree." And, in community life,

> decisions were made, arguments were settled, and sanctions were decided upon by the old men of the group, with the leader usually being a patriarch, the eldest son of the eldest son, so that primogeniture played its part in social organization though it did not often do so in the inheritance of property. (1971:11–12)

Certainly the *corrido* male warrior hero such as Cortez is perfectly consonant with this patriarchal world. Yet though it presents this deeply masculinist resistance to the world of the devil, this community itself is bedeviled from within. Renato Rosaldo asks of *With His Pistol in His Hand:* "How could any human society . . . function without inconsistencies and contradictions? Did patriarchal authority engender neither resentment nor dissent?" (1989:151), a question also implicitly posed by Ramón Saldivar (1990:38). In this world of patriarchy there also existed a socio-economic hierarchy of those who owned land and those who did not (the latter were peones), although in an agricultural economy which was largely self-sufficient, the gap between these two was not that great and, Mr. Paredes suggests, open to mobility. There was self-subsistence in other ways, for in this closely knit community that was south Texas up to the late nineteenth century, "most tasks and amusements were engaged in communally" (1971:13). But at the turn of the century, this seemingly communal world experiences a severe accentuation of its latent cultural contradictions.

As we have been noting throughout, the beginning of the end of this world lay in the war of 1846–47, but severely intensifies during the period roughly 1870 to 1930 with a nearly total transformation after the 1930s. We have taken ample account of one of the national sources of this change and transformation, the coming of a rapidly advancing Anglo-American capitalist political economy and culture to the area during this period. In Paredes' cultural poetics this Anglo-American capitalism is chief antagonist to a protagonist which is this community, a protagonist, however, articulated with what I have already called a modern tragic sentiment, a sentiment that broaches the questions of immigration, class, and Americanization and is missed in current treatments of Paredes' work which focus only on the attractive, overpowering *With His Pistol in His Hand* or his fiction (Limón 1992; Rosaldo 1987, 1989; Saldívar, R. 1990; Salvídar, J. 1991).

This social drama of transformation takes on classical tragic form beginning with a flawed protagonist in a world which ultimately demands "the resignations of men to the conditions under which they must labor in the world" (White 1973:9). For even as he identifies and critiques the Anglo antagonist who disrupted this world, who with his control of *mexicano* labor "cut down the chaparral to make way for agri-business," Paredes at times and somewhat unconsciously articulates a contradiction—a flaw— *within* the greater *mexicano* protagonist community. "The Rio Grande people," he tells us, "lived in tight little groups—usually straddling the river—surrounded by an alien world." But this alien world had two geographical origins: "From the north came the gringo, which term meant foreigner"; but, often missed in political readings of Paredes' book, "From the south came the *fuereño*, outsider, as the Mexican of the interior was called" (1971:13).

The implication of Paredes' construction is that *fuereños* are a *different* kind of *mexicano*. They have no ties to the land of south Texas and its local tradition of resistance. They leave Mexico between 1876 and the 1930s as

a result of Diaz's autocratic dictatorship and the subsequent socially disruptive revolution. Accustomed for generations to work for *patrones*, this
refugee peasantry comes to south Texas escaping with their lives, few
belongings, and looking for work, any work at any price or social cost;
they join Jovita Gonzalez's *peones* already resident in south Texas. These
new immigrants and the local *peones* became a perfect match for a developing Anglo agribusiness sector in great need of labor, preferably an ac-
quiescent labor force. What Mr. Paredes specifically says about the southern side of the Rio Grande is just as true for the northern side during this
period.

> The brush disappeared, and the character of land and people
> changes. The country became a flat, dusty expanse of cotton land,
> and *the people a diverse conglomeration from many parts of Mexico.*
> [emphasis mine]

More specifically on the Texas side of the border, "New people had settled
in most of the country; grapefruit orchards and truck farms replaced the
chaparral." But then he adds a new element for "with the advent of World
War II greater numbers of north-bank Borderers began to think of themselves seriously as Americans" (1971:106).

While Paredes never explicitly says so, there is the clear implication
that the *fuereños*, with their lesser investment in the local culture of resistance, contribute to the social change coming to the area. The collapse of
the older south Texas society between 1870 and 1930 is to some considerable degree also attributed to the *fuereños*, not only to the *gringos*. But
left relatively unexplored for the moment are those north-bank
borderers—not *fuereños*—who now think of themselves as Americans. I
shall return to these "borderers" in a moment, for they constitute yet
another aspect of the tragic flaw.

This collapse and transformation are signified by the severe attenuation of the *corrido* tradition in Paredes' narrative. In an article with the
telling title "The Mexican Corrido: Its Rise and Fall" (1958), Mr. Paredes
argues that by the 1930s, the great *corrido* tradition of ballads like "Gregorio Cortez" was at an end, the casualty of a society no longer in open
resistance and one also willing to permit the commercialization of the
corrido into less than heroic versions and themes. To write about *corridos*
in the 1950s is to write of popular *memory*, of a world when there *was* a
chaparral, when Catarino Garza (or Mr. Paredes' father) rode and faced
John Bourke with his pistol in his hand.

In the early sixties Paredes continued to offer a cultural poetics about the folklore of *mexicano* south Texas but with a significant shift in his choice of genres, a choice conditioned by a growing class contradiction. Three papers are key here, all based on fieldwork in south Texas. The first paper, "The Anglo-American in Mexican Folklore" (1966), to some extent repeats the argument already noted concerning the *corrido*. The *corrido* represents the dominant Anglo as a less than mythic type and celebrates the heroic, resistive qualities of the old border *mexicano*. With the waning of the *corrido* in the 1930s, however, it is as if another folklore appears to take its place among the *mexicanos*. This is what Mr. Paredes calls "The Stupid American" joke narrative.

> The pattern is a simple one with two main characters, a stupid American and a smart Mexican. Through the Mexican's guile or the American's stupidity, the Mexican gets the best of the Anglo-American and makes the Anglo look ridiculous, beats him, relieves him of his money, seduces his wife, or uses the American himself as the passive partner in sexual intercourse. (1966:118)

While Paredes does not specifically say so, it is quite clear that this kind of narrative emerges in a particular period of this ongoing cultural contact, from the post 1920s until the sixties. "This stage in the Mexican's attitudes," Mr. Paredes tells us, following the *corrido* period, is bound up with a social situation "in which open conflict is no longer possible, with the Mexican finding himself in a disadvantageous economic or social position." Open hostility is no longer possible, so this kind of jest serves "as compensation for a strong sense of frustration and inferiority which was not so keen when open conflict presupposed a possible victory for the Mexican." The war is shifting inward, although still with the Anglo as an indirect offensive target. But another clue for periodizing this genre, one which itself reveals its own kind of internal warfare, is the statement "Stupid American tales are bilingual and bicultural . . ." (1966:118–19), although Mr. Paredes does not note that such bilingualism and biculturalism are already signs not ot all *mexicanos* but of an emerging Mexican-American middle class, those north-bank borderers who now think of themselves as American.

Equally bilingual and bicultural but revealing more of "the direct influence of United States culture" is another distinct joke narrative that Mr. Paredes calls the "self-directed" jest, in which *mexicanos* draw on Anglo-American stereotypes of Mexicans to make fun of themselves. For Mr. Paredes, there is in this second kind of jest a "suggestion of masochism." Even though he still finds some degree of "passive protest" in these jokes, it is a protest that "has not only gone beyond the possibility of violence but has even abandoned an imaginary aggressiveness as satisfactory compensation."

Such masochism—such self-directed warfare—is also the subject of a second paper which examines Mexican-American jokes largely ridiculing the *curandero* (folk healing) tradition of south Texas (1968). Such jokes, collected in Brownsville, Texas, Mr. Paredes' hometown, are parodies of belief tales of miraculous cures performed by *curanderos,* tales called *casos* and narrated by the common, which is to say in post-1910 south Texas, the new laboring *fuereño* class, unacculturated and often illiterate (Paredes 1968:107). On the other hand, those who tell such jokes are

> socially conscious male members of the middle class, impatient about the slow acculturation of the average Mexican American and his low economic and social status. At the same time, they reveal a strong feeling of identification with the unacculturated Mexican . . . the curandero jests release a complicated set of conflicting emotions ranging from exasperation to affection in respect to the unacculturated Mexican American, coupled with a half-conscious resentment toward the Anglo American culture.

But Mr. Paredes tells us more about this middle class which continues a war of "half-conscious" resentment against the "Anglo" even as it conducts another kind of internal warfare. It appears that these are the borderers descended from the old families such as Jovita Gonzalez's who now think of themselves as Americans. He is quite explicit on this point: "These are for the most part descendants of the old Mexican settlers of the region, people with their roots in a past when Brownsville was a 'Mexican' town rather than immigrants or children of immigrants from Mexico . . . they would seem to be completely acculturated, having adapted to American culture and functioning in it in a very successful way" (1968:111).

Mr. Paredes might have said more, drawing out what is implicit in his commentary. For it is the case that Brownsville, this historical social center for the landed families, continues to be a "Mexican" town. These middle- and upper-class informants who tell such jokes "play important roles in community life, not in the life of a 'Mexican colony' but in that of the city and the county as a whole" (1968:111). Paredes is referring to Cameron County, of which Brownsville is the county seat, and therefore one is puzzled by his seeming reluctance to explain why the events narrated in such jokes are said to have occurred in neighboring Hidalgo

County: "Why the events . . . are placed in Hidalgo rather than in Cameron County I am not prepared to say," although "it may be that Mexican Americans in Cameron County feel that their people in Hidalgo live under worse conditions than they do" (1968:114). Yes, indeed, they do. What Paredes surely knew but inexplicably did not say (or is this irony?) is that Hidalgo County, a prime area of Anglo settlement and new towns such as Edinburg and McAllen, is the center of the new capitalist agribusiness of south Texas, and as such also a county of laboring *fuereños*. Further, in his slippage from the "middle class" of Brownsville who actually told him the jokes to the general "Mexican-Americans" of Brownsville who are concerned about "their people in Hidalgo living under worse conditions than they do," the internal class division of Brownsville itself, with *its* large mass of poverty-stricken *fuereños,* is rhetorically erased.

For Paredes, all of these jokes help the class-divided *mexicano* to accept his new world, and, indeed, in this acceptance and self-criticism lies an integrated maturity. For "whatever its limitations . . . it is clear that the self-directed jest expresses much more mature and realistic attitudes than does the jest of the Stupid American type." But it is clear that Paredes sees the middle-class *mexicano* as adjusting and conforming, but not to any simple state of cultural affairs in the new social order. By the 1950s and 1960s when bilingualism and biculturalism were already evident among the middle-class *mexicano* population, the adjustment for this group seems to be to an advanced capitalist urban American culture. Thus, to conclude: "we have seen how the Mexican folk hero goes from confidence and violence to an ineffectual state in which he realizes his insignificance in a complicated and incomprehensible world." In a modernist manner, "the Mexican works through a series of attitudes in regard to the inescapable actuality which the Anglo represents [critically[for him," but, for Paredes, in doing so the middle-class Mexican moves "toward greater wit and wisdom" and attains "a kind of universality as well," as his "humor becomes part of a general *Weltansicht* rather than a cry expressing nothing more than his own particular pain" (1966:126–27).

Paredes ends his drama on a high heroic note, but this is existentialist heroism at some considerable distance from the heroes of that earlier time when there was a chaparral. If we cast the total *mexicano* community of south Texas as the encompassing hero of this drama, then, in this scholar's political unconscious, it is as if the "hero" is historically flawed by a segment of that community which seemingly lent themselves to domination, a change that also ultimately produces the antiheroic, the middle-class, Mexican. It is difficult to believe that this native scholar, born into the

fresh popular memory of the war of maneuver, himself wholly engaged in
the war of position with his work on *corridos,* can find this new posture
wholly admirable, notwithstanding his seeming scholarly distance on the
subject and his acceptance of it. The high antiheroic rhetoric is his attempt, I believe, to put the best face on his not too unconscious perception that, with the hero's tragic flaw as a contributing element, the war has
ended, leaving the middle-class *mexicano* only the politically dubious victory of an abstract humanistic universality, while the *fуereños* go almost
unnoticed save as the referent for the bilingual-bicultural masochistic
joke. But, like the repressed that they are, the *fуereños* return and re-
emerge in Mr. Paredes' narrative.

First published in Spanish in 1966 and reprinted later in English in an
important volume on Chicano literary criticism (Sommers and Ybarra-
Frausto 1977), a third paper, "The Folklore of Mexican-Origin Groups in
the United States," surveys its subject, its plural subject, as Mr. Paredes
argues for the existence of three such groups, each with its own distinctive
folklore. First in his narrative order are again the "regional" groups who
settled the now Southwestern United States during the Spanish colonization and whose descendant communities are to be found over time principally in New Mexico and southern Texas, including Mr. Paredes' own
people. At the generic heart of this group's folklore are the *corrido* and
the historical legend, a corpus marked by early and continuing warfare
with Anglo-Americans as we have already seen (1977:9).

A second group—already noted—appears later on the historical
scene, the at first largely agriculturally based *fуereños* whose folklore Mr.
Paredes does not specifically delineate although it "has much in common
with that of the regional groups, but it is enriched by material recently
brought from the interior of Mexico" (1977:8). Although Mr. Paredes
does not explicitly say so, it is clear from other sources that since its post-
1910 appearance, this is a relatively unstable rural population demo-
graphically giving way as a group to an intensifying process of urbanization. In effect both of these groups, but especially the second, contribute
and give way to a third, the urban population which soon comprises the
great majority of Mexicans in the United States, augmented by direct
arrivals from Mexico into the cities such as San Antonio. We return to Mr.
Paredes for a final assessment of this large urban group's predominant
folklore, which

> comes, for the most part, from the regional groups and from the
> immigrant farm workers, although it has been adapted to the needs

of life in the city. A marked emphasis is given to such forms as the
caló (dialect), the _albur_ (word play), the _blazon popularie_ and to the
chascarillo (joke) . . . (1977:8)

To which Mr. Paredes adds this insight: "bilingual in varying degrees . . .
the member of the urban groups is more subject to external influences,
and is thus also the object of greater hostility, caused by the pressures and
complexities of urban life. As a result, he feels less at ease in his environment than the member of the regional group" (1977:8–9).

In another distinctive line of analysis, the now urban _fuereño_ again
appears clearly if ambivalently, in Paredes' discourse. This final analysis
again contrasts the _corrido_ and its heroic culture to another expressive
genre, this time the bodily self as expressive being. We return to "The
Folklore of Mexican-Origin Groups in the United States" to gain insight
into this analysis, where the _fuereño_ now becomes the _"pachuco"_ and
"pocho."

> An entire generation of Mexicans has since been born and grown up
> in the big cities of the United States . . . These young people have in
> self-defense adopted many ways of behaving different from those of
> their parents, exaggerating these traits as much as those they have
> inherited in the desire to create a new personality of their own. This
> is the origin of the "pocho," the "pachuco"—the child born in the
> ghetto—although his "mores" have been extended in many cases to
> the regional groups and the rural immigrants. (Paredes 1977:12)

We are reminded of and obligated to note the proximity of this vision to an
earlier and more elaborated, now infamous, rendering by Octavio Paz,
who visited Los Angeles in the 1940s and saw these children of the ghetto,
these urban street gang adolescents.

> Since the _pachuco_ cannot adapt himself to a civilization which, for
> its part, rejects him, he finds no answer to the hostility surrounding
> him except this angry affirmation of his personality . . . the _pachuco_
> has lost his whole inheritance: language, religion, custom, beliefs.
> He is left with only a body and a soul with which to confront the
> elements, defenseless against the stares of everyone. His disguise is a
> protection, but it also differentiates him and isolates him: it both
> hides him and points him out. (1961:14–15)

But Paz is not content with noting mere difference and ambivalence; he
must demonize the _pachuco_ with hyperbole that leads us right up to the
Gates of Hell. The _pachuco_'s

dangerousness lies in his singularity. Everyone agrees in finding
something hybrid about him, something disturbing and fascinating.
He is surrounded by an aura of ambivalent notions: his singularity
seems to be nourished by powers that are alternatively evil and be-
neficent. Some people credit him with unusual erotic prowess; others
consider him perverted but still aggressive. He is a symbol of love
and joy or of horror and loathing, an embodiment of liberty or disorder, of the forbidden. He is someone who ought to be destroyed. He
is also someone with whom any contact must be made in secret, in
the darkness. (1961:16–17)

The devil Texas Rangers waged a war of maneuver on a heroic south
Texas *mexicano* culture narratively conceived in Christlike terms. But as
with any Christian vision of God or culture, there is a war within, threatening any such unitary poetics of culture. In a discourse that differs from that
of Paz only in rhetorical degree and not in kind, Paredes reveals this war
within and another kind of bedevilment—the *fuereño* now recast as
pocho and *pachuco*.[2]

But the *pocho/pachuco* also take us to yet another expressive culture
that once again is placed in rhetorical contrast to the heroic *corrido*. In the
old border culture,

the dance played but little part in Border folkways, though in the
twentieth century the Mexicanized polka has become something very
close to a native folk form . . . Many Border families had prejudices
against dancing. It brought the sexes too close together and gave rise
to quarrels and bloody fights among the men. There were community dances at public spots and some private dances in the homes,
usually to celebrate weddings, but the dance on the Border was a
modern importation, reflecting European vogues. (Paredes 1971:14)

Paredes is speaking of the pre-1848 period when little dancing occurred, although obviously some did—community dances at public spots
and some ritually bound private dancing. But, again, with the coming of
the *fuereños,* popular dancing and its accompanying music expands, and
we have a new expressive scene of the twentieth century in which Paredes
sees "the Mexicanized polka . . . become something very close to native
folk form," though that "very close" is instructive. In what I have called
the imbedded, tragic poetics of cultures in América Paredes' entire corpus of work, this "modern" popular music and dancing, like the joke
form, also seems to express the decline of *mexicano* culture in south Texas
from its heroic *corrido* state to a modern one of seeming degradation
associated with *fuereños, pochos, pachucos.*

It is in this bedeviled context that we can best appreciate the following utterance of tragic sentiment by an elderly fictive persona in Paredes' *With His Pistol in His Hand:*

> They will sing of him—in the *cantinas* and the country stores, in the ranches when men gather at night to talk in the cool dark, sitting in a circle, smoking and listening to the old songs and the tales of other days. . . .
>   that was good singing, and a good song; give the man a drink. Not like these pachucos nowadays, mumbling damn-foolishness into a microphone; it is not done that way. Men should sing with their heads thrown back, with their mouths wide open and their eyes shut. Fill your lungs, so they can hear you at the pasture's farther end. And when you sing, sing songs like *El Corrido de Gregorio Cortez.* There's a song that makes the hackles rise. You can almost see him there—Gregorio Cortez, with his pistol in his hand. (1971:33–34)

Américo Paredes' fictive persona tells us of past and present, probably from a post–World War II vantage point. As the elders comment favorably on the *corrido* singing of earlier days, they cannot avoid a disparaging commentary on the present. That heroic *corrido* singing and, by implication, men like Gregorio Cortez were "not like these *pachucos* nowadays," nor, we can assume, were they like those who dance to this "mumbling damn-foolishness." Paredes' persona is critically commenting upon a post–World War II popular music and dancing scene, a scene that becomes a major expressive signification of a lower-working-class immigrant sector that our *persona* negatively signifies through the figure of the *pachuco,* the *mexicano* urban street-gang adolescent.

Writing in the late fifties and early sixties, Paredes offers a modernist existentialist trope to universalize and transcend the socially and culturally defeated *mexicano* that his narrative yields at its conclusion. Yet, for all of his humanistic universality, the *mexicano* is rendered as a figure that has fallen from a primordial pastoral state, a trope that Rosaldo also finds in Paredes' work (1987, 1988). My particular suggestion is that, in Paredes' not too unconscious ethnographic figuration, the *mexicano* himself contributes to this fall and that this decline is registered and measured in the respective folklore genres of the ballad, the joke, and popular music and dancing. But embedded in this fall from grace is the *peon/pocho/pachuco/fuereño,* he and she—for in the dance, unlike the *corrido,* we find a clearly defined *she*—she and he who came to south Texas late and now mumble "damn-foolishness" into microphones and dance to it. In

Paredes analysis, it would seem, the war is almost over and the hegemonic victory of the dominants is nearly complete.

But this is precisely where I shall begin, because this is precisely where I began: with those who joke; who mumble "damn-foolishness" into microphones as I once did; and particularly with those who dance to it as I have done. For, if the heroic ballad was at the center of América Paredes' youth and enabled his scholarly poetics of culture, then the expressive culture I grew up with might do the same for me as I now write about this culture in the 1980s and 1990s.

As a *mexicano* working-class native of south Texas born of *fuereño* parents, growing up in the late forties and fifties, I never knew a time of small ranches and country stores; I knew only the asphalt-concrete *pachuco* mean streets of cities. I knew no pastures, only federal housing projects of *pochos* where, if you walked to the project's father end, you could still hear the radio music—the polka music—from a hundred open windows on hot summer nights. There was no cool dark in the city, and everyone sat outside in the common yards, polkas in the background; women talked quietly, men barbecued, drank, and joked while the children played. But then sirens might cut through the night and an elderly woman might say, "Por hay anda el diablo" (the devil is about), and, as the police cruisers came up the narrow alleys hunting *pachucos,* hunting *pochos,* we *fuereños* would imagine the devil and wage the continuing war.

Interchapter

Chapter Five

Emergent Postmodern Mexicano

War and domination have weighed upon the *mexicanos* of south Texas and so have scholarly students of their culture. In this case and, I suspect, others, anthropological writing is not the simple handmaiden to social domination and power. The same principle of contradiction that I will soon identify in the folklore of my own ethnographic field subjects of the seventies and eighties is also to be found in the scholarly discourses of those who have studied them. In Bourke, evolutionary ethnocentrism and nineteenth-century American racism are manifest. Yet I have also suggested that in an unconscious struggle with his own stigmatized Irish identity, itself a product of Anglo-American domination, Bourke offers a kind of rhetorical redemption which paradoxically issues from evolutionary ethnographic practice itself. It is this unconscious quest for redemption in the face of adversity that lends his anthropological writing the character of Romance. As hard positional warfare became the social order of the day between 1930 and the fifties, Dobie appeared to weave a Comedic binding covering over the ethnic tears and rips in the social fabric of south Texas. Even as this illusory, pastoral covering masked these continuing divisions, his protegé, Jovita Gonzalez, though deeply influenced by Dobie's pastoralism, nonetheless began the revelation of the war lurking below the comedy.

Finally, for me there is the more complex, chronologically and personally more relevant case of Américo Paredes. In Paredes' tragic poetics of culture, with the coming of the *fuereños,* the joke form as well as popular music and dance become signifiers of the decline of culture from its heroic state represented by the *corrido* and Gregorio Cortez to its present-day antiheroic angst. We are left with the complicated figure of a native intellectual who is in political fact organic to his dominated cultural group but who is rhetorically fully organic only to a historical memory of, a specific sense of, that culture now past. In Part II we move from this precursory past into the present to my own assessment of expressive everyday culture.

What follows ethnographically in this book in the next five chapters in some sense departs from a partial and experiential agreement with Paredes' textual conclusion. That is, it partially accepts his rhetorically rendered proposition that by the mid-sixties, the war of maneuver, certainly, but also probably the war of position was at least severely attenuated, if not over. However, it rejects any implication of a total victory for those who dominate. But my therefore implied continuation of warfare is of a distinctive character, not wholly captured by "maneuver" or "position"; rather, I am interested in the ways that the *fuereños* have responded to this pain through art and ritual as political form, as the mode of domination and war began to change to a late capitalist everyday culture of postmodernity. I begin in this interchapter with a general account of this political cultural economy as a prelude to Part II.

THE MARGINAL URBAN MASS

In grand folkloristic fashion, my bedeviled precursors represented their warring subjects but represented them within certain social configurations such as rurality. Even the devil figures that each narratively constructed were markedly rural: Bourke's in the shepherd's miracle play, Dobie's devil goat herder, Gonzalez's outsider devil confounded by the *vaqueros,* and Paredes' devil-like Texas Rangers pursuing Gregorio Cortez, the Christlike erstwhile sharecropper. Sociologically, this ruralized cultural poetics of representation is probably as it should be. Mario Barrera, for example, notes agriculture as a principal source of employment in pre–World War II Mexican-American society, particularly in Texas, as does Montejano (Barrera 1979:76–84; Montejano 1987:1–256).

Yet my precursors tell little about the urbanizing experience of this population, a process already evident by the 1930s (Romo 1977; Montejano 1987:257–308). But perhaps this is to expect too much, given, as I say, the grand tradition of folklore scholarship, which, as exemplified by Richard Dorson, could *in 1971* finally ask the question "Is There a Folk in the City?" (Dorson 1971). Even when Paredes takes us to the city to study joking in Brownsville, it is the joking of a middle-class sector. And, as I have shown, these precursory folkloric worlds are largely male-centered, with the interesting exception of Bourke.

My themes are urbanization, poverty, and postmodernity in relationship to gendered folkloric symbolic action, and I trust my particular effort

for our time adds to the contributions of those who came before me. Before moving to this primary symbolic matter and the construction of my
poetics of culture in the next four chapters, I would like to offer in this
interchapter my own experiential and scholarly representation of this
poor, urban social existence and to do so under the sign of an incipient
postmodernity of the 1970s now well established in our time.

Barrera's study of the Mexican-American political economy (1979) is
of the greatest assistance as an entry point into this social existence.
Within the ca. World War II, decisive transformation of Mexican-
Americans from a rural to an urban-industrial locus, he notes a new, per-
sisting phenomenon, namely,

> the appearance of a transitory marginal group of Chicanos who had
> been displaced from their traditional agricultural roles but for whom
> the new forces of production had not developed to the point of be-
> ing able to reabsorb them. As the new economy developed, those
> Chicanos were incorporated into the productive process in the colo-
> nized sector . . . (1979:150)

On a seeming note of optimism, Barrera continues: "In more recent years
[we are now into our time] there has developed an integrated or at least
substantially integrated sector, "but optimism is quickly and severely tem-
pered, for ". . . along with this development there has occurred a re-
emergence or a marginal sector, this time possibly *permanent*" (1979:150)
(emphasis mine).

While carefully offering this last insight only as a hypothesis (the very
condition or marginality makes it difficult to substantiate), Barrera, nonetheless, fashions a persuasive argument for the marginalization—the
non- or haphazard labor integration of a population sector to the productive economy. Minimally, in 1977, Barrera nationally estimates this more
or less permanently unemployed sector at 10 percent of the Mexican-
descent population, but the figure is probably much higher given the phenomena of discouraged workers and hidden unemployment (1979:155–
56).

Drawing on the theoretical work of José Nun (1969), Barrera explains
that this sector is not synonymous with a classical Marxian industrial re-
serve army of labor, employed periodically when needed, "providing elas-
tically to labor supply and maintaining a downward pressure on wages
(1979:152). Rather, when further aggravated by rapid population growth
as in the case of Mexican-Americans, this marginal sector is yet "another
portion of the surplus population" that, under new labor needs (and re-

dundancy) of a postindustrial economy, "is superfluous to the real labor needs of the economy . . . ," creating a large sector that Barrera after Nun calls "a marginal mass" (1979:152).

Barrera is cautious about unequivocally asserting this condition for Mexican-Americans to the degree that is so evident for African-Americans, but the contemporary statistical economic evidence he marshals is sufficiently persuasive. If, to these persuasive national insights and findings, we add more recent and locally focused data and analysis for southern Texas, there can be little doubt of the continued permanent existence of such a marginalized mass in this area, where seasonal unemployment can run as high as 40 percent, a marginal mass that Maril calls the "poorest of Americans" (Maril 1989).

Alongside these marginalized men and women there are others who manage to maintain some degree of regular employment and are, as Barrera puts it, "substantially integrated" into the productive economy. But Barrera's knowing qualification "substantially" is critical, for even here, within this integrated sector, there is more often social and personal pain than promise.

First, Barrera tells us, in the years 1971–76 (and little changed later) this "integrated" working-class sector, constituting approximately 70 percent of Mexican-Americans, was substantially concentrated in lower-paying unskilled and semiskilled occupations and paid less within these occupations than "Anglos" (1979:151). Overall, Mexican-Americans "improved their income position from 1950 to 1970, but in the process moved into jobs that were, on balance, declining in importance in the economy" (1979:156). We also note the loss of real purchasing power in an increasingly inflated economy. This seemingly integrated sector is also beset by a phenomenon not easily captured in structural and statistical analysis: sudden, unpredictable, disruptive, and terrifying unemployment, usually without mitigating economic resources (savings accounts, health insurance, fuctional automobiles).

Such are the socio-economic prospects of a great many Mexican-Americans in south Texas.[1] We need only add that this structural inequality is clearly conditioned by racial and gender factors beyond that of ethnicity. In Part I we noted the racial, ethnic, and class factors that historically produced a still continuing inequality between "Anglos" and Mexicans in Texas. But we are obligated to emphasize the influence of race, class, and gender within the Mexican-American community. Today in south Texas, a circle of "Anglo" elites exercise considerable dominating power, but they do so often with the active participation of an upper- and upper-middle-class Mexican-American sector that *also* benefits directly from the wide-spread unemployment and depressed wages of the area (Maril 1989:53). Here, one cannot help but also notice the intertwined influence of race as distinct from ethnicity. Borne out by data other than my observations over a lifetime in Texas, the proposition is painfully simple: those Mexican-Americans at the bottom are noticeably *darker* than those at the top (Re-lethford et al. 1983; Arce, Murguia, and Frisbie 1987; Telles and Murguia 1990). Jovita Gonzalez's upper-class "Spanish" Mexicans return to haunt us. The devil comes in many forms.

When Barrera tells us that the marginal sector of the 1970s may be "this time possibly permanent" (1979:150), he is, in one short phrase, tapping into a fundamental shift in the political economy. Why is it *this* time that the marginal sector may be possibly permanent as opposed to some other past time? To invoke such a chronological shift is to invoke the difference between modernity and postmodernity, at least as envisioned by David Harvey and Frederic Jameson, and it is to sense the particular emerging cultural existence of a sector of south Texas *mexicano* society. We are speaking of the consequences of what Harvey calls the transition—for many, the wrenching transition—from "Fordism" to an economy of "flexible accumulation," a transition well under way in the early 1970s (Harvey 1989:140–72). As Harvey interprets it, Fordism re-fers to a social contract extant roughly between 1914 and 1972 in the industrial world, reaching its high point in the post–World War II pe-riod. What are (*were,* for it is now history and a repository for nostalgia) its key features? Using, now as an extended metaphor, the famous orga-nization of the Ford auto assembly plants and marketing techniques be-gun in 1914, Harvey sees their full flowering in the post–World War II period when we saw

> the rise of a series of industries based on technologies that had ma-tured in the inter-war years and been pushed to new extremes of rationalization in World War II. Cars, shipbuilding, and transport equipment, steel, petrochemicals, rubber, consumer electrical goods, and construction became the propulsive engines of the economic growth, focused on a series of grand production regions in the world economy—the Midwest of the United States, the Ruhr-Rhinelands, the West Midlands of Britain, the Tokyo-Yokohama production re-gion. The privileged workforces in these regions formed one pillar of a rapidly expanding effective demand. The other pillar rested rested on state-sponsored reconstruction of war-torn economies, suburban-ization particularly in the United States, urban renewal, geographical

expansion of transport and communications systems, and
infrastructural development both within and outside the advanced
capitalist world. Co-ordinated by way of interlinked financial
centres—with the United States and New York at the apex of the
hierarchy—these core regions of the world economy drew in massive
supplies of raw materials from the rest of the non-communist world,
and reached out to dominate an increasingly homogeneous mass
world market with their products. (1989:132)

But Fordism, as Harvey tells it, was less of a social contract and more of a
truce after a long period of bitter class warfare. "The tense of but neverthe-
less firm balance of power that prevailed between organized labour, large
corporate capital, and the nation state," was not accidental but rather
"the outcome of years of struggle" (1989:132–33). This truce, really a
measured victory for capital, was premised on "the defeat of the resurgent
radical working-class movements of the immediate postwar period," a
defeat produced largely through a manipulated antilabor/communist hys-
teria of the period. Thus, "with their principal adversary under control,
capitalist class interests could resolve what Gramsci earlier called the
problem of 'hegemony' and establish a seemingly new basis for those class
relations conducive to Fordism." In smart fashion, however, Harvey is
clearly aware that "how deeply these new class relations penetrated is a
matter of some dispute and in any case evidently varied a great deal from
one country or even region to another" (1989:133).

If the Midwest was the high regional point of Fordism in the period ca.
1945 to 1972, as Harvey clearly suggests, then Texas was a pale (brown)
version of that capitalist compromise with a disciplined labor force. Here
Montejano provides guidance up to a point (1987).

Throughout his fine book, Montejano is concerned with interpreting
the origins, development, and eventual breakdown of institutionalized
anti-Mexican segregation in Texas as conditioned by economic development (1987:xi). In his final chapters on the post–World War II period,
Montejano argues that, as elsewhere, a "sweeping transformation" of industrialization and urbanization came to Texas in this period consistent
with Barrera's and Harvey's observations. But, equally consistent with
both, Texas and its Mexican population experienced an "uneven development," a less than ideal version of the Fordist contract. Mexicans were
concentrated in the lower end of the socio-economic spectrum and, even in
an urbanized situation, subjected to racial segregation of varying intensity.
For Montejano, this situation began to change for the better by the 1960s,
due principally, he argues, to (1) the secondary effects of the Second World

War, i.e., gradual capital accumulation by Mexicans employed in war industries and by returning veterans educated under the G.I. Bill, producing a
stable "middle class" especially in an urban/military area like San Antoñio,
and (2) civil rights activity from this class. By the 1980s this middle class
expands and racial segregation virtually ends with a "demise of Jim Crow."
Indeed, much earlier in this book I noted Montejano's parallel employment of a war metaphor to write and interpret his historical narrative. But
now, as his narrative comes to a close with this optimistic interpretation, the
war seemingly ends with a Texas version of the Fordist truce, and we live, in
his phrase, in a "time of inclusion." In summary:

> By 1980 the occupational distribution of 1930 had been reversed.
> The unskilled category of farm workers and service workers-laborers
> comprised slightly less than a third (30.8 percent) of the work force,
> while the skilled and professional workers made up slightly more
> than two-thirds (69.2 percent). This occupational division of thirds is
> evident in the 1980 data, but with a further weakening of the un-
> skilled categories and a strengthening of the white-collar categories.
> In 1980, 35.8 percent of Texas Mexicans had white-collar occupa-
> tions; 35.5 percent had skilled occupations; and the number with
> unskilled jobs dropped to 29 percent.
> The importance of these occupational changes for Mexican-Anglo
> relations cannot be overstated. The general effect of an expanding
> white-collar and skilled strata within the Mexican American commu-
> nity was the attainment of a measure of economic stability—
> sufficient stability to enable greater attention to the questions of edu-
> cation, housing conditions, sanitation, and matters of public service.
> This stability also made possible the support of community-based or-
> ganizations. The conversion of the Texas Mexican from farm worker
> into war veteran, urban consumer, and civic actor expressed itself
> ultimately in the civil rights movements of the 1950s and late 1960s.
> Despite the conflict of those years, the rise of stable urban classes
> was ultimately a factor pushing for the moderation and inclusion of
> the present day. (1987:299)

I find myself able to agree with all of this and yet too disagree with the
interpretive tenor of Montejano's narrative. Indeed, where I agree most
is with his passing observation that almost fully one-third (29 percent to
be exact) of Texas-Mexicans still hold unskilled employment. This brief
observation, especially when presented with the optimistic verb
"dropped," is then overwhelmed rhetorically by the uplifting tenor of
the next paragraph with its overall effect of representing Mexican-

Americans as a vibrant, "included" middle and upper class. I do not disagree with the empirical facts, only with the erasure of the rhetorical movement. What happened, I ask, to the remaining one-third? Where are the unemployed in this assessment? In all fairness, Montejano is not entirely without an answer: "In the 1980s, with the weakening of racial divisions as an issue, broadly defined class interests determine the arena of political discussion and debate" (1987:299). And he correctly acknowledges what I've noted previously: "Class divisions and tensions have always existed within the Mexican settlements of the ranch, farm, and city" (1987:300). But one senses that the emphasis placed on such divisions in the earlier parts of the book and the explicit acknowledgment of the unskilled laboring sector lessen at the book's closing, giving way to an almost privileging account of an Anglo-Mexican middle-class politics of "moderation" in which "the politics of negotiation and compromise have replaced the politics of conflict and control" (1987:306).

But unless we are to assume that this middle-class politics of accommodation is consistently in the service of the lower classes, what of *them,* that disproportionately larger lower economic class of *mexicanos* in south Texas, a class now constituted largely of the *fuereños* who flooded the area in the post-1910 immigration from Mexico? Not a heroic class from Paredes' point of view or, seemingly, Montejano's, it nonetheless constitutes a massive pervasive social reality in this region today. It is, further, a reality of poverty that in places rivals the "third world"; of racism articulated on a color/class basis including that of the small but influential middle and upper classes of *mexicano* society; of political class disempowerment that continually vitiates any real possibility of change. What two sociologists have said of Brownsville at the mouth of the Rio Grande is also true of south Texas as a whole.

> No real Mexican-American middle class developed in the small agricultural towns until after World War Two, and even then it possessed few class interests in its struggle over limited resources. A large Mexican-American and Mexican underclass came to populate the *barrios* of Brownsville . . . (Miller and Maril 1979:29)

"Today," another prominent economic analyst recently informed us, "Mexican Americans account for approximately 80 percent" of the Lower Rio Grande Valley's population,

> over half the population lives below the poverty level, and 90 percent of all families in this category are Mexican American. Many of the latter cannot afford the costs of meeting city health and safety

ordinances, so they band together in rural "colonias." These squatter settlements often have inadequate water and sewer facilities, unsafe drinking water, poor health conditions and poor housing. (Hansen 1981:51)

And when Senator Lloyd Bentsen was nominated as the vice-presidential candidate for the Democratic party in 1988, a political reporter had this to say:

> the 67-year-old Senator has deep roots in Texas. He comes from one of the richest and most prominent families in the Rio Grande Valley of south Texas, where the great wealth of a few families contrasts with the poverty of the overwhelmingly Mexican-American citizenry. (Rosenbaum 1988:1)

But we need to emphasize that this is a distinctive kind of poverty in the 1970s and 1980s.

Montejano places great emphasis on World War II and civil rights and less on "economic development" in the production of his middle class. But clearly economic development did assist this transformation, and it is economic development of a particular kind that Montejano does not fully theorize. For this we may now return to Harvey, who explains that by the 1970s the Fordist contract had broken down and a political-economic, cultural shift had occurred, a shift into something else he calls "flexible accumulation."

What does Harvey mean by "flexible accumulation," the central economic/cultural process defining postmodernity, and what does it have to do with the 29 percent, not to mention the unemployed who do not figure at all into Montejano's middle-class Fordist compromise and who ultimately call that compromise into question in our time?

> *Flexible accumulation,* as I shall tentatively call it, is marked by a direct confrontation with the rigidities of Fordism. It rests on flexibility with respect to labour processes, labour markets, products, and patterns of consumption. It is characterized by the emergence of entirely new sectors of production, new ways of providing financial services, new markets, and, above all, greatly intensified rates of commercial, technological, and organizational innovation. It has entailed rapid shifts in the patterning of uneven development, both between sectors and between geographical regions, giving rise, for example, to a vast surge in the so-called "service-sector" employment as well as to entirely new industrial ensembles in hitherto underdeveloped regions . . .

And the Fordist truce gives way to war as

> these enhanced powers of flexibility and mobility have allowed employ-
> ers to exert stronger pressures of labour control on a work-force in any
> case weakened by two savage bouts of deflation, that saw unemploy-
> ment rise to unprecedented postwar levels in advanced capitalist coun-
> tries (save, perhaps, Japan). Organized labour was undercut by the
> reconstruction of foci of flexible accumulation in regions lacking previ-
> ous industrial traditions, and by the importation back into the older
> centres of the regressive norms and practices established in these new
> areas. Flexible accumulation appears to imply relatively high levels of
> "structural" (as opposed to "frictional") unemployment, rapid destruc-
> tion and reconstruction of skills, modest (if any) gains in the real
> wage . . . and the rollback of trade union power—one of the political
> pillars of the Fordist regime. (1989:147–50)

This is a new form of capitalism—late capitalism that now wages war
on lower-class Mexican-Americans and that may also be threatening the
politics of moderation, compromise, and negotiation with the Anglo
Other. We can now envision a war on a different front. It is this condition
of postmodernity that already by the 1970s was becoming the central lived
experience of poor Mexican-Americans as they became either part of the
"relatively high levels of 'structural' (as opposed to 'frictional') unemployment," or, at best, members of a fluid, malleable secondary labor market
by virtue of their skin color and their relative lack of appropriate skills.

THE MEXICANO CULTURAL LOGIC OF LATE CAPITALISM

The production and organization of an economy are, of course, already a
cultural matter, but if I can make a momentary and analytical distinction,
this "economic" existence can be said to be homologous to other realms of
lived cultural experience. If what Harvey describes as "flexible accumulation" is synonymous with both "late capitalism" and "postmodernity,"
then it is possible to shift and blur cultural realms and speak as Jameson
does of "postmodernism" as the "cultural logic of late capitalism" (1984).
What is this cultural logic that he so well describes and conceptualizes and
of what relevance is it to a "traditional," "folkloristic" place and people
like south Texas?

Let us first note that by the very cultural logic of postmodernism, its
very description and conceptualization are immediately "problematic,"
to use a quite postmodern term. Such an effort—and at the outset Jameson is no exception—typically begins (and often ends) in an "enumera-

tion" which "at once becomes empirical, chaotic, and heterogeneous," and typically offers a listing of contemporary artistic, pop cultural, and sometimes intellectual phenomena, among them, to take Jameson's own partial listing, John Cage's music, experimental cinema, the *nouveau roman*, and, in literary criticism, a "new aesthetic or textuality or *écriture*" (1992:2). But Jameson will not rest content with an understanding-by-catalogue; he wishes to have a unitary and fundamental meaning of the postmodern. This he gains by bringing together his general, impressive erudition with, more important, an ethnographer's sense of socially situated meaning derived from field observation and the grand Marxist theory of Ernest Mandel on the stages of capitalism.

Yet immediately we note a critical, though understandable, limitation in the earlier enumeration, now including also Jameson's field data—the new commercial architecture in our cities exemplified by the Crocker Bank Center and the Bonaventura Hotel in downtown Los Angeles. For notwithstanding its defining proclivity to incorporate "popular" culture into its text making, postmodernism as usually conceived is largely a class-confined cultural movement of the elite arts, intellect, and, now, upper-class architecture. To make our point, or better still to have Jameson make it for us, if perhaps inadvertently, we need to reflect on his ethnographic sense of the Crocker Bank Center and its suggestion of the first of Jameson's defining characteristics of the postmodern—the quality of "depth-lessness." This "new kind of superficiality in the most literal sense—perhaps the supreme formal feature" of postmodernism (1984:60), is a formal but presumably moral and political superficiality that

> can be experienced physically and literally by anyone who, mounting what used to be Raymond Chandler's Beacon Hill from the great Chicano market on Broadway and 4th St. in downtown Los Angeles, suddenly confronts the great free-standing wall of the Crocker Bank Center . . . a surface which seems to be unsupported by any volume, or whose putative volume (rectangular, trapezoidal?) is ocularly quite undecidable. (1984:62)

My earlier tentative "perhaps" surely overstates Jameson's presumed inadvertence in admitting a class and racial dimension from "below" into his developing definition of the postmodern. He is too learned and sensitive a critic not to be fully exploiting the evident rhetorical contrast between this postmodern example of "depthlessness" and the low heroics of Raymond Chandler from a quite different and Fordist epoch in Los Angeles history. And he must be equally conscious of his other rhetorical contrast—his figurative positioning of "the great market" below and, one believes, in *difference* to the Crocker Bank Center and its depthless wall. There also, as with Chandler, one suspects that Jameson suspects that in the *great* Chicano market is to be found *depth* as well as other countervalues to the other defining attributes of Jameson's postmodern.

For in interrelated addition to depthlessness, the postmodern is also the definitional site of a world conceived as textualized surface images and in which there is a certain waning of human affect (Jameson 1984:60); a world in which the human subject is no longer just alienated, thus presuming some lost agency and purpose, but rather *decentered* and *fragmented,* incapable of conceiving mission, agency, purpose (1984:63). It is a world "liberated" from *feeling* and from history (1984:63–64) conceived as an informing past, a world whose primary self-representational style is the no-style of what Jameson calls *pastiche*—the random piecing together of any and every thing into representations without motivation or motive in the world. For in contrast to, let us say, parody, which is "the imitation of a peculiar mask, speech in a dead language," pastiche is "a neutral practice of such mimicry, without any of parody's ulterior motives, amputated of the satiric impulse, devoid of laughter and of any conviction that alongside the abnormal tongue you have momentarily borrowed some healthy linguistic normality still exists" (1984:65).

But in the great Chicano market, down *there* below the Crocker Bank Center and the Bonaventura Hotel—Jameson's other great architectural example—our critic in his well-chosen Chicano rhetorical figuration seems to locate depth *and* affect, feeling, laughter, true parody, authentic style, history, and ultimately for a Marxist cultural critic, expressive agency and *resistance.* Or so he must want to believe, and I even more desperately so, and we are probably mostly right, he and I, if one confines this reading to the market scene in a Bakhtinian poetics of culture (Bakhtin 1984). But is the market therefore a metonym for the larger Mexican-American community of, let us say, East L.A. or southwest San Antoñio? Or is it rather an exceptional though very important expressive instance for a "community" that in the 1970s began to experience its own negating class- and race-mediated postmodernism?

What is missing in Jameson's otherwise compelling, persuasive, and largely critical account of the postmodern is a sense of postmodernism not in the interior of the Hotel Bonaventura but on San Buenaventura Street in Westwide San Antoñio. If it is the case that postmodernism is our contemporary "cultural dominant," as Jameson argues, and that its domination began in the 1960s (1984:59), then it is also likely the case that by the

1970s this cultural dominant also begins to appear among *los de abajo* (those below), to borrow Mariano Azuela's title. But this appearance is not a postmodernism of the elite arts and intellect but rather one of what Raymond Williams calls "lived" experience (1977:109–10). Whatever the ideologically flattening, decentering effects of the postmodern on those who check in at the Bonaventura, for those who *live* on San Buenaventura, these effects were experienced in severely negating racial and class terms and consequences in the 1970s and more so today.

We can return to Harvey for more help in elucidating this postmodern experience at "lower levels," although even he doesn't quite get down to mine. Harvey tells us that the primary effect of such a daily lived postmodern culture "has been to emphasize the values and virtues of instantaneity . . . and of disposability . . ." It means "more than just throwing away produced goods . . . but also being able to throw away values, life-styles, stable relationships, and attachments to things, buildings, places, people, and received ways of doing and being" (1989:286). Extending Jameson's art-centered insights to the larger everyday society *including* his idealized great Chicano market, Harvey continues and links economy and daily culture:

> Through such mechanisms (which proved highly effective from the standpoint of accelerating the turnover of goods in consumption) individuals were forced to cope with disposability, novelty, and the prospects for instant obsolescence . . . This transience . . . creates a temporariness in the structure of both public and personal value systems which in turn provides a context for the crack-up of consensus and the diversification of values within a fragmenting society. (1989:286)

Following a review of Mexican-American historiography, Alex Saragoza has this to say about the post-1960s, or what I am calling the period of *mexicano* working-class postmodernity:

> The cumulative cost, particularly it seems since the 1960s, has been a deepening alienation among the poorer segments of the Chicano population, especially youth. Without the resources to acquire the trappings of status defined by a consumer culture they can neither ignore nor escape, poor Chicanos have often turned to alternative, and at times socially unacceptable, forms of expression: increasingly, it appears, self-validation and self-esteem among poor Chicanos reflect a sharp sense of frustration and/or disillusion. The numbers of Chicanos in gangs, youth detention facilities, prisons, and rehabilitation centers of various sorts appear to be growing. (1990:31)

He extends this insight:

> In sum, the social common ground among Chicanos has, it seems,
> lessened substantially. Class differences have been compounded by
> generational change, cultural variations, attitudinal diversity, and dif-
> fering notions of ethnic ideology. In part, this social differentiation
> suggests change endogenous to the Chicano community (e.g, immi-
> gration from Mexico). but this further fracturing of the Chicano
> community also reflects the pressures of American culture and ideol-
> ogy, such as the social imperatives of consumerism, the strong
> ageism of United States popular culture, and the persistence of
> Cold War conservatism.
>
> The key issue remains, nonetheless, the long-term effects of low
> socioeconomic status and its consequences. The combination of per-
> sistent poverty and the impact of American culture and ideology has,
> it appears, *distanced* a growing proportion of Chicanos, especially
> youth, from other Chicanos. As a result, the meaning of these differ-
> ences reflected (and continue to do so) a deepening fragmentation of
> notions of identification among Chicanos. (1990:33)

To speak of an emergent postmodernist culture in relationship to a
marginalized working-class Mexican-American society in Texas, it may
be necessary to posit and now only imagine a historical pre-1970s
Mexican-American culture in Texas with all of the attendant risks of ideal-
ization and verification. Notwithstanding these risks, and keeping before
us a processual sense of culture, we can find warrant for such a construction in Douglas Foley's identification of such a culture ca. 1930 (1977).
This culture probably carried over past the Second World War and, I
would argue, into my own teenage years in the late fifties and early sixties.
It was a culture centered on close family ties, the Catholic parish (for
most), a predominant Spanish language use, a variety of cyclical and daily
rituals including a sense of the worth of the self and others expressed in
the ritualized language of *falta de respeto* (lack of respect), *sin vergüénza*
(she or he without shame), *desgraciado* (born without grace), and
malacriado (badly educated, culturally and morally)—all negative markers for despised violations of the responsible sense of self and others. To
be sure, it was also a deeply patriarchal culture where men controlled,
denigrated, idealized, and protected women.

In the literature, we can clearly detect what most analysts describe as
an "acculturation" process among my folks (Whiteford 1977; Grenier
1985; Peña 1985:165–66; Markides and Cole 1985; Williams 1990). But to
see this process as a uniform, unidirectional acculturation or assimilation

on the basis of a linear model is highly misleading. Leaving aside for the moment the variability in such a general process, I am more concerned with the ahistorical assumption of a culturally constant receiving host usually labeled "mainstream culture" at the other end of the line. The question must be asked: what is the particular cultural character of the "mainstream" at any particular time?

In her sociological study of Mexican-Americans in south Texas also in the 1970s, Williams provides insight into this question in a manner consistent with Harvey's formulation of the postmodern. "In the past," before the 1970s, says Williams, "there was a close connection among life-cycle rituals, religion, and familial integration, a linkage that has been dissolving in recent days" (1990:137). In explaining this dissolution, Williams suggests "that both Mexican American and Anglo families are responding to major changes on the societal and global levels," thereby edging closer to Harvey. But then she momentarily falters as she names these forces: "industrialization," "urbanization," and the "bureaucratization of modern life" (1990:148). This too-simple, anachronistic, Weberian identification of the social determinants of culture change locates these forces in the present rather than in the past ca. World War II when they had already decisively occurred among Mexican-Americans. Something else is going on in the sixties and seventies that, regaining more perspective, she seems to recognize. "Along with these on-going structural changes there have been revisions in the cultural, and notably the belief system." Now quite close to Harvey, Jameson, and Saragoza, she continues: "These cultural changes are interwoven in *complex* ways with *fundamental* structural changes on the societal and *global* scenes" (1990:148) (emphasis mine).

We are at some distance from a postmodernism conceived as an arts movement resident in the upper-class sectors of New York, Paris, London, Los Angeles, and any English department of note in this century. The Mexican-American working-class postmodernism that concerns me—that increasingly pervasive, vivid sociocultural condition I now struggle to describe (I too am tempted to enumerate)—seems to be keyed on a spectrum of class-determined negations of a historically and seemingly relatively stable cultural past. In this south Texas context, postmodernism may be seen as the gradual decentering, fragmenting transformation of this identity into something else—a difficult version of global culture palpable but difficult to verbalize. Although "below," it is, nonetheless, in the same political semiotic universe as Andy Warhol paintings and the Bonaventura Hotel. It is the same fundamental cultural process, although what is lucrative and exciting among the upper and middle classes and the intelligentsia is deadly and enervating among those below, those in the great Chicano market. In the urbanizing areas of south Texas in the late 1970s, one could already sense the clear beginnings—today more evident—of a world characterized by a kind of daily intercultural making-do, a social pastiche of everyday life, a growing depthlessness or, in Harvey's terms, instantaneity and disposability.

In conversations with young workers in south Texas, history, for example, almost disappears as a measure of chronological and cultural depth. They usually—and not always—have enough familial anecdotal historical information to know that their great-grandparents came to south Texas around the time of the Revolution. None of the young people that I met knew their places of historical familial origin in Mexico, although the much older people invariably did. Nor did the young have any clear narrative sense of their subsequent familial history including occupational history save for a loose sense of a parental transition from agriculture to urban day laborers, probably ca. World War II, an identity that continues for them today. For these particular younger workers, there is no longer even the sustaining narrative of adventurous treks northward to pick crops all over the United States.

Almost needless to say, their exclusively mainstream formal schooling did little to fill out this depthlessness as *mexicanos,* nor paradoxically did it have much success in its assigned ideological mission—to firmly weave *mexicanos, etc.,* into the fabric of U.S. mainstream culture and history. Even the great defining ritual of this recognition and integration—service in the armed forces—was, for my male friends much more of an absolute and bloody *necessity* given the inevitability of the draft. In short, while their hold on and sense of anything that could be called *mexican* is tenuous and flat, they do not conversely think of themselves as *Americans* in any ideological sense, although they are active participants in the less expensive aspects of American mass culture.

What schooling they had through high school before they dropped out also contributes to this double negation of identity in another critical way. On the one hand, the schools did not teach them the middle-class English skills necessary for social achievement in the 1970s and beyond, yet it taught them enough to contribute to the gradual displacement of the Spanish they knew as children, although many still do speak it, especially in ethnically marked scenes such as those I will explore. Together with the pervasive influence of U.S. mass media beyond anything experienced by previous generations, this schooling seems to result in a growing general inability to sustain an everyday conversation in Spanish, even a *norteño* (northern Mexican, traditional south Texan) folk colloquial Spanish. They tend to speak in a code-switching style where English is predominant, made up of African-American-inflected, hip pop-cultural speech-style elements interspersed with a few Spanish colloquialisms from street talk—"ese bato" (that dude), "que loco" (how crazy). Only when speaking of marked ethnic forms such as food—or dancing—do they maintain a Spanish code and not for long. This speech style likely affects their occupational mobility, but it also seems to contribute to an ethnic decentering of these subjects in other ways, such as limiting sustained conversations with their elders.

Finally, we come to the fundamental question of what Williams called the "belief system" (1990), expressed for her in terms of familial ties and obligations interlocked with religion and life-cycle rituals. Here again, amongst my companions, we find a certain depthlessness, a surface existence. All of their lives are marked by divorce and shifting relationships. And, if ties to the nuclear family are often tenuous, they spend even less time with members of their extended family, save seeing relatives at a dance by accident rather than design.[2] Only weddings and funerals bring them together and sometimes not even then. While all of them have been co-parents in baptismal rites (*compadrazgo*), there is no consistent follow-through on these obligations. They rarely see either their co-parents (*compadres*) or their godchildren, and there is little, if any, of the traditional gifting for the latter on their birthday. Most telling, when they do see their co-parents—the child's parents—they do not address each other with the honorific *compadre* and *comadre* that traditionally take the place of first names. But above all, notions of self-worth and social responsibility to others are also now in tenuous state. There is precious little socialization of their children with ideas of *respeto, verguénza, etc.,* and the elders among them constantly noted and lamented the absence of this aspect of culture.

But the devil comes in many forms. I participated, I "observed," I read my notes, recollect, and write, but is this not yet another emerging "stereotype," this time in the hands of a "native" anthropologist? Here one is called upon to utter quickly the politically formulaic and readily acknowledge the class-conditioned cultural "diversity" among Mexican-Americans. Yes, of course, as Montejano has noted, there is a south Texas Mexican-American middle class and even a small though highly influential upper class economically defined by a variety of professional and semiprofessional services they provide to the general community. Indeed, one can even readily acknowledge a somewhat more economically stable working class; in Limonada and the Lower Rio Grande Valley centered on the export/import trade with nearby Mexico, and in San Antoñio on the city's military base complex. In their cultural comportment, each of these is different from the others and all are different to a large degree from the "underclass" society where I spent time. But each class sector, it might be argued, is also dealing with its own devil, struggling with its own version of a consumerist decentering postmodernism.

In 1980, the elite-popular magazine *Texas Monthly* published an article called "An American Family," subtitled "Roots: The Mexican Version" (West 1980). There, amidst advertisements for expensive jewelry, Crown Royal liquor, and the Lakeway Tennis Resort, we find a long story about a San Antoñio Mexican-American family. The subtitle says it all as the story traces the social ups and downs but mostly the gradual ups of this family as it moves from the chaos and poverty of the exodus from 1910 Mexico to middle-class success in San Antoñio in the late 1970s. The latter is represented mostly by the scion of the family, a "careful," "responsible," and "cautious" young man who finds gainful employment working politically on behalf of the Mexican Westside and models himself after Henry Cisneros, the charismatic nationally known former mayor of San Antoñio and now member of the Clinton Cabinet (West 1980:180). We have here as good a representation as can be found of Montejano's optimistic but abstract rendering of the south Texas *mexicano* middle class in its ascendancy. But will this young man, in his laudable political engagement with the Westside, really want to model himself after Henry Cisneros, middle-class postmodernist exemplar, as mayor obsessed "with retrofitting San Antoñio as a high tech capital" with low wages (Harrigan 1987:136), described also by Harrigan as "a man of many facets but not necessarily many layers" (1987:91), described even more acutely by the most respected organic intellectual of the Mexican-American working class, Ernie Cortez, as a man who "obviously has the ability to look good on a thirty-second TV spot" but "what we need now are statesmen who have a capacity for reflection and sadness that indicates a real understanding of the human condition" (Harrigan 1987:91). But I digress, for upper-middle-class postmodernism is not my concern, although it may shed reflected light on what I am trying to do here.

As West acknowledges, notwithstanding such stories and such efforts, the marks and the threat of poverty continued in the 1970s for San Antoñio, south Texas, and the national Mexican-descent community as measured by income, education, health, and other key variables. While he can take note, in a kind of urban pastoralism, of the Westside's "shady streets," its "narrow lawns enclosed by rickety fences," and the "street life of children playing," he must acknowledge

> stark landscapes: weedy, dangerous vacant lots choked with garbage and roamed by half-starved, unleashed dogs; water-filled ditches and sumps; burned-out buildings hiding tramps and junkies; and perilous bars like El Molino near Lanier High School. (West 1980:179)

And, as this book goes to press in the 1990s, we learn that today San Antoñio has "the highest rate—39 percent—of all the metropolitan areas in percentage of low-income housing that was physically deficient" and "Hispanics made up the largest percentage of the poor" in such housing (Shannon 1993). And, the war has also gone within as rarely does a night pass without the sound of "drive-by" gunfire.

The *Texas Monthly* story of success amidst such poverty also offers a few tidbits of information that signal something relatively new on the Mexican-American cultural scene in the 1970s—the incipient elements of an emerging ethnic and class postmodern condition. Like Jameson, West also notes a "huge [Chicano] produce market" that in San Antoñio has moved from the downtown area to make room for touristic development, development keyed on a Mexican "image" of San Antoñio. And, although one can still find a few traditional street vendors on the Westside, "anglo fast-food businesses now dot the area" (1980:180). Finally, while the young scion of the family has achieved success, we learn that his cousin's "marriage with a Chicago steelworker broke up and she and her three year old son . . . live with her mother" (West 1980:181).

I have spent time with a working-class sector whose cultural lives in the 1970s and 1980s were beginning to mirror the "stark landscapes," the "weedy, dangerous vacant lots" of their geographical existence, an existence increasingly fed by the thin postmodernist gruel signified by the "anglo fast-food businesses" that now "dot" their lives (West 1980:180). Although it is not nearly as "advanced" as the African-American underclass cultural condition, there is sufficiently a crisis among Mexican-Americans that I find support though little comfort in Cornel West's observations on the "postmodern culture" of African-Americans.

> The collapse of meaning in life—the eclipse of hope and absence of love of self and others, the breakdown of family and neighborhood-bonds leads to the social deracination and cultural denudement of urban dwellers, especially children. We have created rootless, dangling people with little link to the supportive networks—family, friends, school—that sustain some sense of purpose in life . . . This

culture engulfs all of us—yet its impact on the disadvantaged is dev-
astating resulting in extreme violence in everyday life. (1993:25)

Anticipating Cornel West, Gramsci describes what he calls a "state of
siege" that can occur in class struggle, where

> a resistance too long prolonged in a besieged camp is demoralising in
> itself. It implies suffering, fatigue, loss of rest, illness and the contin-
> ual presence not of the acute danger which tempers but of the
> chronic danger which destroys. (Gramsci 1971:239)

Often, in my experience that follows, I felt I was looking upon just such a
state of siege, until, through the interventions that follow, I somewhat
changed my mind.

In what follows, I am not offering a totalistic narrative of siege, decline, and defeat as the postmodern enemy flows through the gates of
traditional culture. Yet I do not wish to minimize the presence and power
of this enemy who first made his decisive appearance among all of us in
the 1970s. To this complicated end, I find more appropriate Victor Turner's observation that, in moments of conflict between strong and weak
social powers, we might look for "endemic, pervasive, smoldering faction-
alism without sharp, overt confrontations between consistently distinct
parties" (1974:41). The war continues by other means.

For my purposes these means involve certain contemporary folklore
practices, an urbanized working-class expressive culture. While the
Mexican-Americans of south Texas continue to have a varied folklore
repertoire, a great deal of it seems to be largely in abeyance, the dormant
disappearing property of passive rather than active bearers of tradition,
and largely the property of the elderly. The very condition of emergent
postmodernity I have described is, of course, not unrelated to this abeyance; indeed, it may be taken as a key symptom of this condition. Yet
though generally reduced relative to the historical worlds of my precursors, an expressive culture does continue with vital force in certain performance areas. These processes could be identified elsewhere in Mexican
America, although perhaps not with this particular density and intensity,
for, I will remind you, the continuing war started in south Texas.

In the chapters that follow I wish to suggest that these contemporary
folkloric practices—indebted to tradition—among marginalized working-
class Mexican-Americans in south Texas and possibly elsewhere are forms
of a continuing, if repressed, war with a late-capitalist urbanized "Anglo"
culture of postmodernity. Through these forms, this sector articulates what

I shall call a critical difference of consciousness in antagonistic contradistinction to this now dominant culture.[3] Through them, this sector seems to maintain a centered historical subjectivity, a creative sense of critical depth against these new, flattening, fragmentary pressures. Although much in the present, these practices are the most distant cousins of Gregorio Cortez, for though not "heroic," they are edges of critical difference. Yet, like Gregorio Cortez and his heroic world, they are not without contradiction, most significantly a gender contradiction and one which, in contradistinction to my precursors, I wish to make salient. Here we must recall that young *mexicana* in San Antoñio as reported by West whose "marriage with a Chicago steelworker broke up and she and her three year old son . . . live with her mother" (1980:181). The experiences that follow are in great part about women who may be much like her. For if, as I have argued, to be lower-working-class Mexican-American amidst the postmodern condition is to live a difficult experience, then to be such a Mexican-American woman is perhaps even more trying as they war with all facets of this experience including the world of men, even as the men themselves are also at war with the Other (Waldman 1980). I begin with a focused explanation of this latter world—this world of men—and progress in subsequent chapters through other, more gender-complicated manifestations of the continuing war and its continuing articulation in conjunction with the devil.

Part II

Politics, Poetics, Present

In this type of work, it is good for the Ethnographer sometimes to put aside camera, book and pencil, and to join in himself in what is going on. He can take part in the natives' games, he can follow them on their visits and walks, sit down and listen and share in their conversations. I am not certain if this is equally easy for everyone—perhaps the Slavonic nature is more plastic and more naturally savage than that of Western Europeans—but though the degree of success varies, the attempt is possible for everyone. Out of such plunges into the life of the natives—and I made them frequently not only for study's sake but because everyone needs human company—I have carried away a distinct feeling that their behavior, their manner of being, in all sorts of tribal transactions, became even more transparent and easily understandable than it had before.

  —*Bronislaw Malinowski,* Argonauts of the Western Pacific

What, then, is the right way of living? Life must be lived as play, playing certain games, making sacrifices, singing, dancing, and then a man will be able to propitiate the gods, and defend himself against his enemies, and win in the contest.

  —*Plato,* The Laws

I am accustomed to consider literature a search for knowledge. In order to move onto existential ground, I have to think of literature as extended to anthropology and ethnology and mythology. Faced with the precarious existence of tribal life—drought, sickness, evil influences—the shaman responded by ridding his body of weight and flying to another world, another level of perception, where he could find the strength to change the face of reality. In centuries and civilizations closer to us, in villages where the women bore most of the weight of a constricted life, witches flew by night on broomsticks or even on lighter vehicles such as ears of wheat or pieces of straw. Before being codified by the Inquisition, these visions were part of the folk imagination, or we might even say of lived experience. I find it a steady feature in anthropology, this link between the levitation desired and the privation actually suffered. It is this anthropological device that literature perpetuates.

  —*Italo Calvino, Chapter VI,* Six Memos for the Next Millennium

Chapter Six

Carne, Carnales, and the Carnivalesque

At two in the afternoon a periodically unemployed working-class man in Mexican-American south Texas puts hot chunks of juicy barbecued meat with his fingers on an equally hot tortilla. The meat or *carne* has marinated overnight in beer and lemon juice. Antoñio or Toñio passes the meat-laden tortilla to one of the other eight mostly working-class men surrounding a rusty barbecue grill, but as he does so, the hand holding the food brushes against his own genital area, and he loudly tells the other, "¡Apaña este taco carnal, 'ta a toda madre mi carne!" (Grab this taco, brother, my meat is a mother!). With raucous laughter all around, I accept the full, dripping taco, add some hot sauce and reach for an iced down beer from an also rusty washtub.[1]

Some sixty years ago the Mexican thinker Samuel Ramos published his well-known and still culturally authoritative *Profile of Man and Culture in Mexico* (1934, 1962), an interpretive general narrative history of its subject since its indigenous beginnings. A kind of secondary precursor to my work, Ramos was trying to explain what he saw as the reduced sense of Mexican cultural life and its contradictions in his time. As part of his contemporary account, a kind of climax to his narrative, Ramos turns into an anthropological, if distanced, observer of everyday Mexican life, particularly male life. For example, the Mexican *pelado* or lower-class man

> belongs to a most vile category of social fauna; . . . a form of human rubbish . . . Life from every quarter has been hostile to him and his reaction has been black resentment. He is an explosive being with whom relationship is dangerous, for the slightest friction causes him to blow up.

According to Ramos, the Mexican lower-class man's

explosions are verbal and reiterate his theme of self affirmation in crude and suggestive language. He has created a dialect of his own, a diction which abounds in ordinary words, but he gives these words a new meaning. He is an animal whose ferocious pantomimes are designed to terrify others, making them believe that he is stronger than they and more determined. Such reactions are illusory retaliations against his real position in life which is a nullity.

For Ramos, these verbal pantomimes, these explosive linguistic reactions are of a particular kind. This lower-class man's "terminology abounds in sexual allusions which reveal his phallic obsession; the sexual organ becomes symbolic of masculine force." The reproductive organs are a symbolic source of "not only one kind of potency, the sexual, but every kind of human power," as this man, "tries to fill his void with the only suggestive force accessible to him: that of the male animal," and, continues Ramos, "so it is that his perception becomes abnormal; he imagines that the next man he encounters will be his enemy; he mistrusts all who approach him" (1962:59–61).

In this chapter—this first instance of my own ethnographic work in contemporary south Texas—I want to discuss what Foucault calls discourses of power as these concern Mexican-American south Texas. You have already heard two examples of such discourses: one, the expressive, all male humor of a group of *batos* (guys, dudes) articulated in and through the ritualistic consumption of barbecued meat in southern Texas, an event called a *carne asada;* and, two, Samuel Ramos' narratively imbedded commentary on the language and culture of the Mexican male lower class, a discourse tradition continued by Octavio Paz in the 1950s and applied directly to the Mexican-Americans of south Texas in the 1960s by anthropologist Joseph Spielberg (1974).

Somewhat mindful of Marcus' recent call upon Marxist ethnographers to provide analyses of the culture of the dominant as well as the dominated (1986), I have elsewhere tried to show how this second set of discourses, this interpretive tradition begun by Samuel Ramos, functions as a discourse of power with a larger international scope (Limón 1987). At critical moments in Mexican and Mexican-American history, this interpretive tradition, perhaps unintentionally, helps to ratify dominance through its negative psychologistic interpretation of the Mexican male lower class and their language. As Ramos' commentary clearly illustrates, this discourse casts these classes in the idiom of human rubbish, animality, aggressiveness, and abnormality—in the Christian realm of the devil, if you will.

This is a view, I might add, considerably shared by those—both Anglo and Mexican-Americans—who hold class power in southern Texas. My chief purpose here, however, is to begin to develop an alternative but critical understanding of this lower-class male culture; to develop a third narrative discourse, if you will, one which I would like to think Foucault might have called an archeology of subjugated knowledges and practices, this in an effort to demonstrate *their* power as a discourse of the dominated even as I draw out its gender contradictions. My analysis will draw from recent Marxist perspectives on language, on the anthropology of natural symbols, but centrally on Bakhtin's sense of the carnivalesque, for these men are, I will argue, Bakhtinian *batos.*

Yet, as I contest Ramos in this analysis, I also wish to remain in dialogue with my primary precursors. Renato Rosaldo notes that "culturally distinctive jokes and banter play a significant role in constituting Chicano culture, both as a form of resistance and as a source of positive identity" (1989:150). Did Bourke and Dobie somehow semiconsciously recognize the cutting edge of such humor, and is this why they largely ignored it? Or did the linguistic complexity of such humor mark the limits of inquiry for these barely if at all fluent speakers of Spanish? Or, even more cutting edge, is the in-group character of humor such that they, as outsiders, were excluded? Jovita Gonzalez certainly recognized it in her jocular rendition of the devil in south Texas, although it is highly unlikely that as a bourgeois woman she could have entered the male *cantina* culture of her time, precursor to these scenes. Finally, as I noted in Chapter 4, some substantial portion of Américo Paredes' career has focused on male humor. More on this.

My rendering of this sociocultural process of "resistance" and "positive identity," as Rosaldo says, departs directly from Paredes' work. Though in this chapter I return to the "same" Lower Rio Grande Valley where he studied humor, it is no longer the "same" semirural society of the 1960s but rather, by 1981–82, an emerging postmodern urbanizing political economy. Here we visit not Brownsville but Hidalgo County also noted earlier by Paredes, still a center of a multinational agribusiness-based economy but one now diversified by cheap labor industrial assembly plants (*maquiladoras*) across the river in Mexico and by drugs. Here we treat not the narrated bilingual-bicultural joke of the ascending middle class but rather the speech body play of a lower-class *fuereño* existence. Here humor becomes not existential angst and cultural ambivalence but carnivalesque critical difference, though never without its own internal contradiction, for the fact that here, in the tradition of my precursors save Captain Bourke, I deal with a world of men from which women are excluded qualifies the "positive" and "resistance" character of this humor.

Later that hot August Saturday afternoon in 1982, another man, a part-time auto parts salesman, in a ten-year-old pickup drives up to our barbecue session on the outskirts of McBurg, a designated "All American" city. He brings with him a couple of pounds of tripe intestines which will eventually be added to other offal and to the *fajita,* or skirt steak, now turning dark golden brown and sizzling in its fat on the barbecue grill. His *tripitas*—for all the meat parts are expressed in the diminutive—are turned over to Poncho, house painter, and the latest cook at the grill; Jaime, this new arrival (otherwise known as "el Midnight" because he is quite dark), begins to shake everyone's hand in greeting, saying, "¿Como estas?" (How are you doing?), etc. Expecting my turn, I put down my beer and dry my hand on my jeans, but Jaime never makes it past the second man he greets.

This is Simón, otherwise known as "el Mickey Mouse" because of his large ears. He has been a construction laborer most of his adult life except for three years spent at the state prison after he got caught on the highway to Austin transporting marijuana intended for the students at the university. ("¡Que pendejada!" "¡Tiré un beer can y me paró el jurado!"—what stupidity! I threw out a beer can and the cop stopped me!)

Simón takes Jaime's hand as if to shake it but instead yanks it down and firmly holds it over his own genital area even as he responds to Jaime's "¿Como estas?" with a loud "¡Pos, chinga ahora me siento a toda madre, gracias!" (Well, fuck, now I feel just great, thank you!). There is more laughter, which only intensifies when "Midnight" in turn actually grabs and begins to squeeze "el Mickey's" genitals. With his own free hand, for the other is holding a taco, "el Mickey" tries to pull away from Jaime, unsuccessfully. Finally in an effort to slip out of Jaime's grip, he collapses to the ground cursing and trying to laugh at the same time and loses his taco in the process. Jaime, however, has gone down on his knees and manages to maintain his grip even as he keeps saying over and over, "¡Dime que me quieres, cabrón, dime que me quieres!" (Tell me you love me, goddammit, tell me you love me!). "El Mickey" finally says "¡Te quiero dar en la madre!" (I want to beat the hell out of you), playing on the double meaning of *quiero* as "want" and "love." He takes a few semi-mock punches at Jaime's body and receives a few in return both carefully avoiding the face. Everyone is still laughing as el Mickey and Midnight, still on their knees, hug each other to a stop. As they help each other up,

Jaime tells "Mickey," "Dejando de chingaderas, anda a traer otro taco y traile uno a tu papa" (All screwing around aside, go get another taco and bring one for your father), referring, of course, to himself. Doing or saying *chingaderas* (fuck ups), that is how these men label and gloss this activity, also sometimes *pendejadas* and *vaciladas* (stupidities, play routines) (see Spielberg 1974).

In the 1950s another distinguished Mexican intellectual whom we met in Chapter 4, yet another secondary precursor, had this story to tell about the Mexican lower-class male personality and his language. "It is significant," says Octavio Paz, "that masculine homosexuality is regarded with a certain indulgence insofar as the active agent is concerned." The passive agent is an abject, degraded being. "This ambiguous conception," he continues, "is made very clear in the word games or battles—full of obscene allusions and double meanings—that are so popular in Mexico City."

> Each of the speakers tries to humiliate his adversary with verbal traps and ingenious linguistic combinations, and the loser is the person who cannot think of a comeback, who has to swallow his opponent's jibes. These jibes are full of aggressive sexual allusions; the loser is possessed, is violated, by the winner, and the spectators laugh and sneer at him. (1961:39–40)

Octavio Paz continues this commentary translated into English in 1961. "The Mexican macho," he says

> . . . is a humorist who commits *chingaderas*, that is, unforeseen acts that produce confusion, horror, and destruction. He opens the world; in doing so, he rips and tears it, and this violence provokes a great sinister laugh . . . the humor of the *macho* is an act of revenge. (1961:81)

"Whatever may be the origins of these attitudes," Paz tells us, "the fact is that the essential attribute of the *macho*—power—almost always reveals itself as a capacity for wounding, humiliating, annihilating" (1961:82).

It is almost six o'clock on this evening outside of McBurg, at what our host Chema likes to call his *rancho* which amounts to less than one-quarter acre of dry, wholly undeveloped land with only a few mesquites to provide some shade from the hot south Texas sun. Chema bought the land, called a "ranchette" by local real estate agents, when he came into a little money from a workmen's injury compensation settlement. He fell from a truck while doing farm labor for extra money. Massaging his lower back for the still lingering pain, he says, "El pínche abogado Chicano se quedó con la mitad" ("The damn *Chicano* lawyer kept half"). Chema's only real notion for improving the property is to build an inevitable brick barbecue pit, but until he can afford it, he will have to haul the portable rusty one on the back of his pickup out to the *rancho*.

A few more men have come with more meat and beer, and a few have left playfully taunted by the others, "Tiene que ir a reportar a la vieja" (He has to go report to his old lady), knowing that eventually they'll have to go report to their "old ladies." The eating and drinking and the talk are still thick, and *conjunto* polka music is playing from a portable radio, although later this will be replaced by guitar playing and singing of, on the one hand, *corridos* with accompanying *gritos* (cries) and, on the other, American tunes from the fifties and early sixties such as "In the Still of the Night" by the Five Satins to which everyone will sing a cacophony of appropriate *sho do be do be doos*.

One of the men keeps insisting that he has to go; with equal insistence he is told to have another beer and to make a taco out of the very last of the cherished delicacy, *mollejitas* (glandular organs), but he is particularly insistent because his kinds need to be picked up at the movies where, we discover, they have been watching Steven Spielberg's *E.T.—The Extra-Terrestrial*. Octavio is almost ready to leave when Chema, our host and ranch owner asks him: "Aye, 'Tavo. Sabes como de dice *E.T.* en espanol?" (Hey 'Tavo, do you know how to say *E.T.* in Spanish?). Before Octavio can even try to reply, a grinning Chema answers his own question correctly by saying *Eh Te,* but he is also holding his hand over his genitals and gesturing twice with it as he pronounces the two syllables. *Eh Te* does of course mean E.T. in Spanish, but is also the way a toddler might pronounce *este* or "this one," dropping a consonant *s,* as in *este papel*—this paper. In saying Eh Te and with his double gesture, Chema is calling attention, particularly Octavio's attention, to his penis—this one. But things get better . . . or worse . . . as the case may be. Chema continues his interrogation of Octavio. "¿Y, como se llaman los dos hermanitos de E.T.?" (And what are the names of E.T.'s two little brothers?). Chema demonstrates the answer with another genital double gesture, this time answering his own question with the Spanish *Eh Tos,* again exploiting the baby play language pronunciation of *estos* meaning *these,* referring, of course, to *these two* meaning his own testicles. Everyone, including Octavio, is laughing and all of us cannot help but look as Chema does his gestures and baby talk, and he isn't through yet. "And what," he asks, "is the name of E.T.'s mother?" This time, however, Octavio, who has obviously been conducting his own ethnography of this speech act, beats

Chema to the answer with his hand at his crotch, loudly and triumphantly proclaims the answer, "¡Mama Eh Te!"; this time, Octavio has exploited the original *Este* (this one) and also the charged ambiguity of *mama* in Spanish, which depending on accent and syntax can mean "mother" or "suck." Laughing with the others, Octavio finally makes his way to the movie *E. T.* or *Eh Te* to pick up the kids; Chema is shaking his head and laughing and complaining about all of the meat juice he has managed to rub all over his crotch.

By seven or eight, more people start dispersing, a few latecomers arrive, a fire has been started, and one of the guitarists sings the *corrido* of Jacinto Trevino about a brave south Texas Mexican who shot it out with the Texas Rangers in 1906 in the town of Brownsville just down the river from McBurg (Paredes 1976). Finally, thinks your ethnographer, I get some real folklore of resistance and not all of the these *chingaderas*.

For at that moment, I am troubled, at least intellectually, by what I have reexperienced, having gone through such events several times in my life in south Texas but also in a few cantinas in Monterrey, in Los Angeles, in Mexico City. Are Ramos and Paz right when they speak of sexual anxiety, of wounding and humiliation? Are the *chingaderas* "unforeseen acts that produce confusion, horror, and destruction" amidst a "great sinister laugh"? And it does not help to have reread a recent anthropological study of such south Texas male humor specifically in this area near McBurg, in which Joseph Spielberg, also a native south Texan concludes that this humor "can be characterized as verbal aggression aimed at another when he is most vulnerable" by his "own lack of discretion in bodily functions, social circumstances or by revealing his sentiments." In the tradition of Ramos and Paz, Spielberg also believes that "the principal theme of this humor" is "humiliation" (1974:46).

These discourses, as I say, troubled me then for they did not speak well of these, my people, and perhaps they do not speak well of me, for frankly, although with some ambivalent distance, I had a good time that Saturday afternoon and have had a good time since.

I had indeed gone to dominated southern Texas in 1982 looking for a folklore of resistance, carrying in my head the examples furnished by Genovese, by Gutman, by E. P. Thompson and George Rude, by Gramsci, and, of course, by Paredes, and I found instead a powerful yet contradictory sexual and scatological discourse—part of a greater Mexican working-class folk tradition left largely unexamined by my primary precursors. Yet, it is a tradition, as I say, delegitimized by the powerful authoritative intellectual discourses of Ramos and Paz and, in a more circumscribed but still effective way, by Spielberg. And I found difficult, and perhaps still do, its relegitimization, because this is at least the implicit burden carried by those who approach such materials from a Marxist cultural perspective. Certainly one alternative is simply to deny the burden and accept Ramos and Paz or perhaps some species of functionalist argument where these behaviors are seen as adaptive steam valves or as "communitas," so that as everyone leaves Chema's ranch they feel prepared to confront the labors they will face on Monday.

How can one rethink these materials as a Marxist narrative of "resistance," especially when they do not nicely lend themselves to such a reading as do peasant rituals of inversion, black spirituals, and English artisans? And when one has to contend with an extant authoritative interpretive discourse, especially one developed by members of the same general cultural group, for these—Ramos, Paz, and Spielberg—are *Mexican* observers; and, finally and most importantly, when one is faced with its manifest gender contradictions?

WRITING WITH A DIFFERENCE

We may begin this alternative reformulation by examining the central sexual symbolization that lies at the heart of the speech play and gesture that I have noted. Tonio's, Jaime's, Samuel's, Octavio's, and Chema's obvious and clear expressive manipulations of body and speech would certainly seem consistent with Samuel Ramos' observation that the Mexican lower-class man's

> terminology abounds in sexual allusions which reveal his phallic obsession; the sexual organ becomes symbolic of masculine force. In verbal combat he attributes to his adversary an imaginary femininity, reserving for himself the masculine role. By this stratagem he pretends to assert his superiority over his opponents. (1962:59–60)

For these commentators, aggression and its generative conditions, inadequacy and inferiority, are directly expressed through anal references and the theme of male sexual violation in this humor. I would not deny the existence of these values and meanings, given my earlier argument for the historical production of aggression. I would, however, argue that such references might be multivocal symbols possessing *several* meanings and not reducible to a single one that fits a preconceived psychoanalytical scheme.

It is too easy to rely on a simple and wild psychoanalysis when dealing with such physical references. Mary Douglas has warned us of the dangers and shortcomings of such simple psychologistic readings when they concern rituals dealing with the human body (1978). Some psychologists are fond of treating such rituals not as social acts but as the expression of private and personal infantile concerns. "There is," she believes, "no possible justification for this shift of interpretation just because the rituals work upon human flesh . . ." Those who make this interpretive reduction

> proceed from unchallenged assumptions which arise from the strong similarity between certain ritual forms and the behavior of psychopathic individuals. The assumption is that in some sense primitive cultures correspond to infantile stages in the development of the human psyche. Consequently such rites are interpreted as if they express the same preoccupations which fill the mind of psychopaths or infants. (1978:115)

She argues for an alternative analytical model for the understanding of the human body in relation to society—one that is "prepared to see in the body a symbol of society, and to see the powers and dangers credited to social structure reproduced in small on the human body" (1978:115). A society's definition and treatment of the body and bodily pollution is, in her estimation, a critical symbolic key for grasping its perceptions of its own structure and of its external relationships. Such pollution—all forms of matter issuing from the body's orifices as well as entering through them—may acquire symbolic proportions, as do necessarily the orifices themselves. The Coorgs of India, for example, are an isolated mountain community sharing with other castes a fear of what is "outside and below" their group. In their ritual behavior they "treat the body as if it were a beleaguered town, every ingress and exit guarded for spies and traitors" (1978:123).

I would submit that the *mexicano* on both sides of the border also has something to fear. This fear may not be simply an infantile concern with one's male group and their simple sexual dominance. Rather, the themes of anality, pollution, and bodily penetration may also be symbolic expressions of an essentially political and economic concern with social domination, not from below, as with the Coorg, but from above—from the upper levels of the structure of power in both countries. The marginalized working and unemployed classes where these expressions abound constitute a body politic symbolically conscious of its socially penetrable status. What Douglas claims for the Coorgs may be at least partially applicable for Octavio, Samuel, Chema, and my other companions of those years:

For them the model of the exits and entrances of the human body is a doubly apt symbolic focus of fears for their minority standing in the larger society. Here I am suggesting that when rituals express anxiety about the body's orifices the sociological counterpart of this anxiety is a care to protect the political and cultural unity of a minority group. (1978:124)

There is certainly some evidence for this view in the often noted tendency of the Mexican male but particularly the lower-class male to turn to the expression *chingar*—meaning sexual violation—to also express social violation, as my companions often did when speaking particularly of their political/economic relationships. "Me chigaron en el jale" (I got screwed at work), or during one of the regular political discussions at the *carne asada,* "Pos gano Reagan, y ahora si nos van a chingar" (Well, Reagan won, now we're all really going to get screwed), and, finally "la vida es una chinga" (life is being constantly screwed), which represents a quite reasonable perception of social conditions for these men in this part of the world.

Others, the dominant Mexican-American and Anglo upper classes— *los chingones* (the big screwers), as these men commonly refer to them— always have the ability to *chingar,* and it is entirely to the point that these are also men. It is here, I suspect, that we can find a possible reason for the conversion of this potential male social violation into the symbolic idiom of homosexuality. The routines, I will remind you, are called "*chingaderas.*" When Antonio seemingly threatens me with the meat that has passed by his genitals; when Octavio triumphantly says "¡Mama Eh Te!" they may indeed, as all Western men do, be expressing their latent anxiety about homosexuality. However, I am suggesting, partially following Mary Douglas' lead, that we need not just stop here. This homosexuality-in-play may also be reversing the sociosexual idiom of *chingar* as practiced by *los chingones* that continually violates the well-being and dignity of these working-class men.

But as I speak of play and games, I want to introduce yet another critical alternative perspective that speaks to a central flaw in Ramos, Paz, and Spielberg's understanding—or lack of it—of this speech play. It is important to recognize that even as my friends introduce the seeming aggressive idiom of sexual and social violation, they do so in a way that reframes that aggressive speech and gesture as play. Ramos, Paz, and Spielberg extract the sexual symbols in this play and give them their shallow reductive interpretations. They are not appreciative of these scenes as dynamic forums that interactionally produce meaning, mastering anxiety by inverting passive destiny through active play.

To begin with, *mexicanos* frame such scenes as ludic moments through native markers such as *relajando* and *llevandosale* (carrying on, bantering, playing), as in "nomas estabamos relajando" (we were just playing). We have a clear recognition of a play world in which open aggression can appear *only by mistake.* Such a mistake can occur when a novice or an unacculturated person fails to "recognize" the scene, or when he is less than competent in the requisite artistic skills. This latter consideration is crucial, for whatever latent aggression exists is not only rendered socially harmless to themselves but is turned into a basis for solidarity. The participants do this by interactionally creating an artistically textured discourse through skillful manipulations of allusion, metaphor, narration, and prosody.

Through interactionally produced play, through artistic creativity which does not deny the existence of aggression but inverts its negativity, the aggression of the world is transformed into mock aggression, mock fighting. What Bateson notes for nonhuman animals is also fundamentally true for these human artistic performers. These men mean something other than what is denoted by their aggressive language. Such language becomes like the "playful nips" which "denote the bite but [do] not denote what would be denoted by the bite" (1972:180). Art and play ultimately create paradox and fiction.

> Paradox is doubly present in the signals which are exchanged within the context of the play, fantasy, threat, etc. Not only does the playful nip not denote what would be denoted by the bite for which it stands but the bite itself is fictional. Not only do the playing animals not quite mean what they are saying but, also, they are communicating about something which does not exist. (1972:182)

Aggression is what would be denoted by an actual bite—it is that something which is the hidden textual model for the playful nip, but is itself not denoted and therefore is negated at the moment of interaction. The playful nips of skillful artistic language produce a paradoxical effect, namely, the interactional production of solidarity, or as Latin Americans everywhere would say, *confianza.* Anthony Lauria notes that in Puerto Rico, "to indulge in *relajos* of any sort in the presence of anyone is to engage in a relation of *confianza*—or trust and familiarity with that person" (1964:62). As Lauria also notes, the ultimate paradoxical social result of the expressive scene is not aggression, humiliation, and alienation, but rather *respeto.* This—*respeto*—is the significance of ending a verbal exchange in mock

punches, a hug, and a laugh. In one of Bateson's metalogues, his persona
and that of his daughter engage in conversation:

Daughter: Why do animals fight?
Father: Oh, for many reasons, territory, sex, food . . .
Daughter: Daddy, you're talking like instinct theory. I thought we
            agreed not to do that.
Father: All right. But what sort of an answer do you want to the
            question, why animals fight?
Daughter: Well, do they deal in opposites?
Father: Oh. Yes. A lot of fighting ends up in some sort of peace
            making. And certainly playful fighting is partly a way of
            affirming friendship. Or discovering or re-discovering
            friendship.
Daughter: I thought so . . . (1972:18)

The artistic disclosure of friendship and respect in the *palomilla*'s interaction is not, in and of itself, ideological. That is, in a social vacuum, one
could only construe it as play, friendship, and solidarity pure and simple.
But, of course, these expressive scenes do not emerge in such a vacuum;
they appear and are embedded in a postmodern political economy and a
hegemonic culture that produce the marginalization and alienation that
prevail among this class of *batos* in south Texas.

In these particular socioeconomic circumstances, play and its concomitant friendship become eminently ideological. As an emergent cultural performance, they represent an oppositional break—or critical difference—
in the alienating hegemony of the dominant culture and society.

In a provocative article, Hearn notes that both mainstream and orthodox Marxist social science construe play as an activity ontologically secondary to the instrumental "real" world of politics and economics (1976–
77). There is in such a construal a reproduction of capitalist categories of
experience, a particularly unfortunate situation for Marxists. Hearn offers a corrective formulation of play which draws upon two nonorthodox
Marxist theoreticians, Habermas and Marcuse. He notes the former's
idea of language as symbolic interaction that "has a transcendental self-
reflexive capacity which permits it to give expression to contradictions
between appearance and reality, potentiality and actuality." Because it is
not totally and automatically bound to reproduce the social order, "language has the potential for emancipating people from a dependence on
reified cultural controls . . ." Thus, people have in their language "the
capacity for reflexivity and transcendence which enables the creation of

evaluative standards, allows the expression of contradictions, and supplies a conception of potentiality, of 'what can be' " (1976–77:147). These
critical possibilities are greater for the least commodified and instrumen-
talized language—the emergent verbal art of marginalized peoples.

Hearn finds similar properties in Marcuse's concept of play. For Marcuse human play is the autonomous production of a dramatized, albeit
temporal, vision of an alternative social order. In authentic, that is, non-
commodified play, there is an emergent promise of "freedom from com-
pulsion, hierarchy, inequality, and injustice" (1976–77:150). In its very
ontology, play is neither secondary to instrumentalism nor its total denial.
Rather it emerges as a critique, a constraint, and a transcendence of all
instrumental activity. Ultimately, play—the free-flowing artistic ex-
changes of the men at Chema's *rancho*—has a subversive quality.

> In play while the limitations of the existing reality are exposed, a
> more satisfying—more equitable and just—order is celebrated . . .
> To the extent that play affirms the possibility of a "better world" it
> retains the potential for highlighting the negativity of and con-
> tributing to the subversion of the prevailing arrangements. (1976–77:
> 150–51)

Mexicans and their verbal art draw upon the domains of language
and play explored by Habermas and Marcuse, to produce a single
phenomenon—human speech play. Through such speech play the participants continually produce a world of human value—of *confianza*
and *respeto*. Such momentary productions, created in collective equal-
ity, negate the alienating constraints of the historically given social order that exists for *mexicanos* and affirms the possibilities, at least, of a
different social order. The participants momentarily overturn the alienating effects even while reminding themselves of the real aggressivism
in the world, that of *los chingones,* such as the upper middle classes of
Brownsville who tell parody jokes about *curanderos* and *fuereños.*

Because the dominant discourse of power—that of Ramos, Paz, and
Spielberg—has focused exclusively on the language of such scenes, I too
have felt obligated to pay special attention to language even while recognizing that language is only part of a cultural contextual scene. Indeed, as
I have suggested, it is the failure to recognize this total context of play that
flaws this dominant discourse. In the world of Chema's *rancho,* it is necessary to recognize other symbolic elements that also constitute this play
world as a temporary forum of nonalienation.

For example, this play scene is itself framed in another form of play—a kind of visible joke—namely, the very existence of Chema's *rancho,* that undeveloped little piece of land surrounded on all sides by huge ranches with oil drills or agribusiness factory farms; just a few miles away, for example, lie the beginnings of the King Ranch, parts of which, according to Mexican legend, were bought and paid for in blood. Chema's *rancho* is itself a source of constant humor, especially when, after a few beers, Chema begins to tell the other guys of his big plans for this little place. Inevitably someone will ask him, where are you going to put the cow? And, how is the bull going to screw her when you can't get them both on the place at the same time? The ultimate joke, of course, is the existence of this ranch dedicated not to capitalist mass agriculture but to friendship and play. While not a necessary condition, the very existence of this visible joke—this humorous incongruity—is productive of more jokes and play. As Mary Douglas says, "if there is no joke in the social structure, no other joke can appear" (1968:366).

Finally, there is my title—*carne, carnales,* and the carnivalesque. As the name of this event—*carne asada*—clearly indicates, and as I have suggested throughout, *carne,* meat, and its preparation and consumption are of central concern here. If, as Mary Douglas says, food is a code, then where in society lies the precoded message, and how does this message speak of hierarchy, inclusions, and exclusion (1971:61)? Or, as Appadurai reminds us, more specifically,

> When human beings convert some part of their environment into
> food, they create a peculiarly powerful semiotic device. In its tangi-
> ble and material forms, food presupposes and reifies technological
> arrangements, relations of production and exchange, conditions of
> field and market, and realities of plenty and want. (1981:494)

What kind of meat is this socially, and what, if anything, is its message, its gastropolitics? These men are preparing and consuming those parts of a steer—the internal organs and the *faja,* or skirt steak—that are (were in 1982) clearly undervalued, low-prestige meats in the larger social economy, and, given their economic resources, that is not unexpected. (As an old Anglo rancher in the area told me, "We used to call that stuff 'Mexican leavings.' ") What interests me is the way in which such meat parts—the discards of capitalist cattle ranching—are culturally mediated to convert them from low-prestige, rather tough and stringy protein into tasty, valued, social food. The use of the affectionate diminutive to name and linguistically "soften" this food—*fajita, mollejita, tripita*—is a case in point here and parallels the physical softening of the protein in much-valued, secretive marinades. (Indeed, it is rumored with awe and disgust that the marinade for Chema's meat, which is considered the best, has a touch of urine in it, some say from his wife.) When I hesitantly asked Chema about this, he said it was absolutely not true; he would never ask his wife to do such a thing. After a few seconds, he added, with a grin, "only a man's piss will do!" In this cultural mediation we get food that is an ever-present reminder of class status but which in its preparation negates that status.

The preparation and consumption of this meat also speaks to class difference in another way. The food is simply prepared, with the only utensils present being a sharp knife to cut the meat, the chiles, tomatoes, and onions for the sauce, and a fork to turn the meat. The sauce is prepared in the bottom parts of beer cans cut in half, and spoons are fashioned from the metal of the upper half. All of this preparation becomes a way for these guys to distinguish themselves from the dominant others—*los chingones*—who use plates, knives, forks, cups, and napkins. They also eat awful things like potato salad and lettuce with their meat which is bought and barbecued for them by their Mexican servants from across the border who cross the bridge to work in their large fashionable homes.

Finally, I am most interested in the way the consumption of food is a kind of interactional parallel to the charged language which paradoxically generated friendship. Everyone brings his low-prestige meat—a symbol of societal aggression—and contributes it to a central collective pile; everyone at some point or another takes a turn at shooing flies away, broiling and cutting the meat, and making the sauce. The tacos are made by everyone in random fashion, and since there are no plates they are passed along by hand, indeed, sometimes going through two or three sets of hands. These men at Chema's *rancho* and many others throughout south Texas, and, I might add, in the Texan outposts of central California, prepare and consume their own once low-prestige food collectively and nonhierarchically, even as they playfully assault each other with the charged language of friendship. The felt result is another discourse of power, but a power that does not dominate; rather and if only for brief moments, it liberates them from the contexts of alienation beyond Chema's *ranchos* where race and class still prevail.[2]

In this world at Chema's *carne* is closely linked to *carnales,* a kinship term used among brothers or close male friends. In the 1960s Chicano college students spoke in too self-conscious and slightly forced ways of *carnalismo.* These men never use this term, although when they hear it they can sense what it means. Rather, they freely use the term *carnal*—this folk term for brother or buddy which seems to me to be an appropri-

ate native gloss for their cultural practice. In one too conscious and too
keenly ideological moment, Chinito ("little Chinese man"), a young man
with Asian features and the most educated among them (one year of college), holds up a piece of raw *fajita* and says, "esta carne es pa' mis carnales, esto es el carnalismo" (this meat is for my brothers, this is brother-
hood). Another man, pained slightly by this apparent intrusion of linear
ideology, immediately replies, "Mira cabron," and going for his genitals,
says, "esta es la carne que te voy a dar" (Look, goddammit, this is the
meat I'm going to give you). And it is only at this moment, when the
others laugh hesitantly, that we see the possibility and the tones of real
aggression. The world of too conscious ideology has intruded and must be
rejected. One does not speak ideologically of friendship and community,
one practices it in the symbolic action of meat, body, and language.

To unify these various revisionary perspectives, I want to think of these
scenes as a present-day example of what Bakhtin calls the unofficial culture of the Middle Ages, the folk culture of Grotesque Realism, of the
carnivalesque, the near realm of the Christian devil. The playful, sexual,
and scatological language, the concern with minimalist consumption of
meat taken from the internal stomach-centered parts of the animal, the
concern with the body—all of these involve what Bakhtin called degradation, a principal aspect of the carnivalesque. But this is not degradation as
the imprisoning bourgeois discourse of Ramos and Paz would have it.

> Degradation here means coming down to earth, the contact with
> earth as an element that swallows up and gives birth at the same
> time. To degrade is to bury, to sow, and to kill simultaneously, in
> order to bring forth something more and better. To degrade also
> means to concern oneself with the lower stratum of the body, the life
> of the belly and the reproductive organs; it therefore relates to acts
> of defecation and copulation, conception, pregnancy, and birth; it
> has not only a destructive, negative aspect, but also a regenerating
> one. To degrade an object does not imply merely hurling it into abso-
> lute destruction, but to hurl it down to the reproductive lower stratum,
> the zone in which conception and a new birth takes place. Grotesque
> realism knows no other lower level; it is the fruitful earth and the
> womb. It is always conceiving. (Bakhtin 1984:21)

However, in adopting this Bakhtinian perspective on unofficial culture, heteroglossia, and the carnivalesque, one also has to note its political limitations and its uneasy relationship to Marxism. In a recent critical
review of this tissue, Young seriously and persuasively questions the Marxist status of Bakhtin's thought on the carnivalesque in culture (Young

1985–86). Taken without critical revision, Young argues, Bakhtinian "carnival offers a liberal rather than a Marxist politics" (1985–86:92). That is, Bakhtin has offered a semi-idealist version of an essentialist humanistic oppositional Other. His carnivalesque is a transcendence of an unspecified general Foucauldian-like domination. Only by specifying the historical moment and social location of some of the carnivalesque; only by accounting for its class (and race) antagonistic character in a specific context can the carnivalesque be read as an expression of class contestative discourse. This I have tried to do. For it is specifically against the ruling bourgeois official culture of contemporary south Texas, including both Anglos *and* Mexican-Americans, that one must understand my companions. Their discourses of sexuality, the body, low food exactly counterpoint the repression and affectation of these ruling sectors throughout the region, a dominating culture whose most visible expression is the high societal celebration of George Washington's Birthday in Laredo, not that far from Chema's *rancho.*

But even as it sets limits to a dominant Anglo and Mexican class, perhaps the most encompassing significance for us of the carnivalesque as a total set of expressive practices is its critical relationship to the urbanized metroplex of cities and shopping malls linked by busy highways that now constitutes the reality of the Lower Rio Grande Valley. This emergent urbanizing postmodern political economy is based increasingly on low-wage service industries, high tech farming, and on the same rapidly shifting patterns of consumption as everywhere else. Low-wage employment and protracted unemployment, as cheaper Mexican labor across the border is manipulated, lead to the long-term marginalization of men such as these on Chema's *rancho,* and, in turn, to the further marginalization of their spouses and to marital strain and divorce.

Finally and perhaps most critically in our own time there is the question of drugs. In the Lower Rio Grande Valley political economy, drugs are a commodity for personal use and, more attractively, for smuggling and dealing. These men, like poor young African-American men in the urban postmodern North, must constantly dance with this devil as a way of getting money and bringing stability and order into their pressured and fragmented lives. But, of course, this temptation to tap into the large amounts of money generated by the postmodern drug industry, wracked as it is by local violence, can only bring further stress. It is a situation captured vividly by the fine south Texas writer Rolando Hinojosa in his novel *Partners in Crime* (1985) as he traces the efforts of his modernist city detective protagonist, Rafe Buenrostro, to find meaning and order in the postmodern drug-fed culture that has descended upon his beloved Lower Rio Grande Valley in the 1970s.

It is not only in critical relationship to Ramos and Paz or the Anglo/ Mexican dominant classes of South Texas that we must view the carni- valesque. The planned use and valuation of a "rural" setting, the insis- tence on simple meats recalling Dobie's *vaquero* cattle culture, the prac- tice of bodily play and speech play to bring men together, all of these processes may also be understood as a critique of the totality of this new postmodern culture that has come to the Valley and the rest of south Texas, a bedevilment most insidious than the earlier coming of *los diablos tejanos,* the Texas Rangers—a late capitalism with no human face.

Yet, as Laura Cummings (1991) notes in a reply to an earlier version of this chapter, the ritual reproduction of this expressive male culture of critical difference comes with a contradiction and at a cost. As I noted earlier, women are pointedly excluded from these scenes. What is cen- trally problematic in the male carnivalesque is the concomitant reproduc- tion of a ritually enhanced sense of dominant masculinity which, its resis- tive edge notwithstanding, may be carried over into other spheres of lived experience with repressive consequences for women.

For this is a scene that has some clear capacity for lurching beyond the carnivalesque into a resemblance of Juan Pedro and his beer-drinking friends in Sandra Císneros' Texas short story, "Woman Hollering Creek." As his oppressed wife and the central protagonist, Cleofilas, watches from the margins, the effort of these men to communicate "bubbles and rises . . . gurgles in the throat . . . rolls across the surface of the tongue and erupts from their lips—a belch. . . ." as they try "to find the truth lying at the bottom of the bottle like a gold doubloon on the sea floor" (Císneros 1991:48).

Where are they, the women, in this male-dominated, too close approxi- mation of the world of Gregorio Cortez? The place of women in the expres- sive world of south Texas—what my precursors rarely noted, including Jovita Gonzalez—and their particular warfare now appear as a revisionary task before us as we move beyond the paradoxical freedom and repression of *carne* and *carnales* to a different sense of the carnivalesque in another part of southern Texas well known to the residents of the Lower Rio Grande Valley—San Antoñio, Texas.

Chapter Seven

The Native Dances

Been doing it since junior high in Corpus Christi, Texas, in the late fifties. But I'm really not very good at it. Never really have been.

She knows it too.

I awkwardly push my body toward hers: she holds me, tightly, and I think she thinks, Well, he'll be better next time.

I know I won't.

I'll never really be good at it. Not like the other guys—Lencho, Tony, *la rata*. All of us drift back to our table after it's over. They with their women; me, with "mine."[1]

Pretty good polka, huh? says Tony. Yeah, well, I think to myself, if you're good at it. I'm not.

Consolation: I'm not here to dance, really. I'm an anthropologist. Forget consolation: maybe I won't be any good at that either. But that is why I am here. Reenter consolation: maybe I can get to be a better dancer, here at El Cielo Azul (The Blue Heaven) Dance Hall in the summer of 1977.

As she expects me to, I help Beatice to her chair as the rest of our friends sit down, except for *la rata,* who stands by the table. Beatrice, or *la Beatrice*, as she is called in Ruperto's Lounge, where I met her, smiles a thank you. She'll help me, I think, in dancing and anthropology, although I've been having a devil of a time explaining the latter to her. Once I do, however, I think she'll help me. I think she likes me. Took her to dinner at Las Brisas. That ought to count for something. Yeah, maybe she'll help me. What textbooks call a key informant.

La rata is asking who wants another round. It's his turn to go to the beer concession. (I have to remember: *la rata,* then me, then Lencho, then Tony. The women never go.) *Cinco* Lone Stars? *Dos* Schlitz? (I have to remember: I had one at Las Brisas, one a while ago, maybe one more and that's it. Fieldwork, *compa.* More observation, less participation.) [See glossary of native terms.]

What about you? *la rata* asks Lencho's date, *la* Rosemary with the big almond-shaped eyes. She uses mostly an accented English and doesn't say much in Spanish.

I want a white wine.

¿Como que un white wine? (What do you mean, a white wine?) In a heavy voice *la rata* reverts to Spanish, and then her own Spanish suddenly emerges, such as it is.

Chingao, you asked me what I wanted! I want a *chingao* white wine!

Lencho rolls his eyes and pretends to be talking seriously to Tony. Rosemary, you see, lived a number of years in southern California before moving back to San Antoñio after her divorce. Worked in a clothing factory in L.A., but now she's a waitress at Las Brisas. Temporarily, she says. Until they call her from the blue-jean place in San Antoñio. She and Lencho met during his morning coffee stop as a truck driver for Zarsky's Lumber. The almond eyes—and the rest—proved irresistible, but Lencho's wife would probably want a second opinion. Not to blame L.A. or anything, but Rosemary's not quite like the others, not like Delia, Amalia, *la* Beatrice—or Lencho's wife. *Más classy,* according to Lencho. The other women don't like her much. *Muy agabachada* (very Anglicized). *Se cree mucho* (thinks she's better). Perhaps it's the well-dyed blond hair, the extra baubles hanging all over her neck and arms. It's not education. They're all dropouts. *La rata* doesn't like her either, perhaps for the same reasons. She also calls him "rat" in English, which really pisses him off. Lencho's wife agrees with all this—and more. La voy a matar a la puta (I'm going to kill the whore). Lencho likes to repeat the line. Tony likes Rosemary, mostly because she's *bien buenota* (has a really good body), but Lencho's got her, and for tonight anyway, *la* Delia, a laundry worker, is with Tony. For tonight anyway.

Rosemary wants white wine and will not be budged. Tony, Lencho, and I are snickering, and *la rata* is up on the fence looking at shit on one side and piss on the other, as Tony likes to say. He leans hard across the table, stares at Rosemary, and tells her, Aqui no hay white wine (There's no white wine here).

She stares back: Go see, she says, drawing only a bit on what are obviously giant reserves of "cool."

Rata looks hard at Lencho, turns abruptly, and goes off to get our stuff. They're tight, these two guys. Dropped out of high school together—*de la brack* (Brackenridge High School). Been drinking buddies at Ruperto's for seven, eight years when Beatrice introduced them to me. Tight. Even if Lencho did go airborne and not into the marines. The story at Ruperto's is that the night before *rata* shipped out to Pendleton, he got drunk, stood on top of the bar, stripped off his shirt, and yelled, ¿Watchan este cuerpo? ¡Se lo voy a dar a los marines! (See this body? I'm going to give it to the marines!).

As the band kicks off another polka, we are left to imagine *la rata* at the bar at the opposite end of El Cielo Azul, this large, Quonset-hut dance hall on the outer, *mexicano* west side of San Antoñio. *Rata* will carefully insert his dark, wiry frame into the seams of a huge mass of Mexican man-flesh clumped around the bar. Big guys, many of them. These days, it seems, *mexicanos* are neither really short nor really tall; they grow simultaneously in all directions. *Rata* will be careful to avoid pushing hard on anybody. The *bato* might shove back and then *rata,* as he says, "would have to call in an airstrike," but right now he doesn't want trouble. He'll squeeze and squirm his way up to the bar, trying to keep his new J. C. Penney guayabera from getting wrinkled. Didn't buy it at J. C. Penney exactly. First, a friend got it from a friend who lifted it at *el centavo.* Then *la rata* got it. J. C. Penney sticker still on it. Marked down. Special. Stuff from Jaske's costs more. Tighter security. *Más classy. Rata,* currently unemployed, can't afford to shop there.

At the bar, surrounded by part-time construction workers, part-time truck drivers, part-time busboys, an occasional full-time drug dealer, all of them still pretty much in native dress, *la rata,* himself a little of each of these, will say—will have to yell—to the fat bartender: Quiero cinco Lone Stars, dos Schlitz, y un white wine. Only to be told: No hay white wine. Everyone will look at him. White wine? Though nobody will say anything. Just smiles. Tight smiles.

Threading his way through the folding tables, chairs, and people—all *mexicanos*—gathered around the large central dance floor, *la rata* then cuts across a corner of the floor to reach our table as couples glide by in the rhythm of the polka. He puts down the beer and spits the bartender's message into Rosemary's once high-school-beautiful, now thickly made-up face: ¡No hay white wine! The rest of us snicker quietly again. Very quietly. *Rata,* I have been told, killed a North Vietnamese soldier with his bare hands and two others with his knife at Khe Sanh in 1968. I'm certainly not going to fuck with him or with Rosemary, who is now deciding whether the world will end in fire or ice. Everybody else, including Lencho, is also staying out of this one.

But a truce is declared for now. One of the bartenders has followed *la rata* back to the table to inform us that the management is sending out for white wine. Aqui nomas al 7-11 ahorita vienen (Just right next door at the

7-11, they'll be right back). Thank heaven for 7-11. The manager thinks
he's onto a new trend, as he will verify later: warm summer nights in the
barely air-conditioned Cielo Azul, hot polka music, and cold white wine.
A gallon at $8.95, twenty cups at $2.50 a cup. Keeps the *rucas* happy. *A
toda madre.* And if they don't drink it, se lo llevo a mi vieja (I'll take it to
my old lady). A real cultural innovator, this one.

Except for Beatrice and me, everyone goes out to dance again, as the
band puts down another throbbing, wailing polka. Neither the traditional
accordion *conjunto* nor the traditional *orquesta* with wind and brass instruments, this six-man group combines a few elements of both—trumpet,
alto sax, rhythm, and guitar with an electric keyboard carrying the stac-
cato lead part of the traditional accordion. Since the 1970s, more and
more of these hybrid small groups are popping up, as young kids, high
school dropouts with band training, try to make it big. They carry names
like this group's—Magia Negra (Black Magic). And they start here in
places like El Cielo Azul—cheaply constructed halls at the margins of
town catering to the *mexicanos* at the margins of society. And though they
play rock 'n' roll, country-western, and Latin American *cumbias,* the
polka is the music of choice, the battle hymn of this republic.

I want to sit this one out because I want to think and mentally record all
that has happened thus far. I actually write a note or two while Bea
watches me with amusement until, her tolerance exhausted, she gives me
the look: I want to dance. So, I'm off to try again.

Better, this time, I think. Beatrice seems to be getting into what I laugh-
ingly call my rhythm. She has me somewhat outweighed and she's about
half a head shorter, but again, she hangs on tight and, with me feeling in
pretty good control, we're off, moving fast and slow, fast and slow, counterclockwise around the large floor, as we ourselves slowly rotate counter-
clockwise as a couple, like the other forty or so all around us. Hey, pretty
good! I think to myself.

At one time I wasn't that bad. Really. Did a lot of dancing growing up
in Corpus. Started at age twelve, as I remember, at the summer night
dances on the basketball court in the Wiggins Federal Housing Project
where I was raised, protected always by our very own gang, los Wolves de
la Wiggins, who lurked in the shadows, holding their women. Later in my
life, Domingo Peña, the famous (or infamous) south Texas dance promoter, had dances every weekend at Memorial Coliseum. Come on, Mrs.
Gutierrez, hurry up! all of us sackboys would say to ourselves at eight
p.m., as the last customer in Biel's Grocery Store on Leopard Street
slowly made her way to the checkout stand. Then she was gone. A fast

mop and we were off as a group walking down Leopard to the dance. Still wearing our jeans, black ties, and sweaty white shirts (we'd steal a bottle of Mennen After-Shave at the store and pass it around), we'd get to the Coliseum and hit the floor for a good time. Getting home was tougher. Gang territories all the way. But the cops were more dangerous. Always the cops. Always. All Anglo then. Stopping. Searching. How come you Meskin kids cause so much trouble? Spread-eagled on the hood of a police car at age fifteen, I once declared war, I now do anthropology, and I've almost forgotten how to dance.

I'm remembering all this as Beatrice and I come out of a fast turn and I'm trying to also "observe." Then it happens. I have my left hand up a little too high holding Beatrice's right, and as we turn I hit him in the face. I turn to say *perdón,* excuse me, but he has already abandoned his partner, who is screaming something like, Don't kill him, Chente! while she grabs him with both arms around a very ample torso. He looks to be on the verge of doing just that when Tony and Delia whirl by. Turns out he knows Tony; they work at the cement plant. Tony mediates; I mumble an apology and endure a very hard stare, a monstrous callused forefinger two inches from my nose, and a ¡La siguiente vez, watchate, pendejo! (Next time, watch it stupid!). At 150 pounds, with ten years of college education and no Marine Corps training, I can only agree. Beatrice takes me in her arms and dances me away. This time, her wiry-stiff, sprayed hair in my face, her thick perfume, the faint popping of her chewing gum are all oddly comforting.

That was close, bro! says Tony, when we're all sitting down again. *Rata* wants to go talk to the *puto.* The marines never leave their dead behind, *ese,* and always retaliate, he says. *Rata* is so comforting. We talk him out of it. Lencho and Rosemary have not joined us, and we see them by the wall. Lencho is working his hands all over her. At a distance she does look beautiful. A few moments later they're gone, probably out to Lencho's car. They'll be back to dance again. After the dance, they'll go to her place. He'll go home at three or four, have a fight with his wife. Get up late the next day. Watch the NFL game, make *fajitas* for the family and have a few. So will Tony. *La rata* is not married; divorced. Maybe he and I will drop by Lencho's tomorrow for *fajitas.* Then maybe Ruperto's. Maybe tomorrow I should write, though.

We dance a few more without sitting down. This time I watch my swings and look out for him. I think he's gone, says Beatrice with a giggle. Am I getting any better, Beatrice? I ask her. Yeah, a little bit, she says. You need to practice. I'll teach you.

When we return, *rata* and Lencho are on their feet on opposite sides of the table. It looks as if at any moment the 1st Marine Division is about to go head-to-head with the 82d Airborne. Rosemary is sitting smugly, half smile on her face, sipping white wine. Smart money says this is about her again, this time with more beer for fuel. Tony talks to *la rata;* I talk to Lencho. Over the last year I've become somehow oddly closer to him. Don't know why exactly. Maybe because, like me, he grew up in a housing project. Casiano Projects. Maybe it's his lumberyard work. I used to do that when I was working my way through Del Mar Junior College. I know about one-by-eight, two-by-four, Douglas fir, yellow pine, sheetrock, and tossing 96-pound bags of cement from the back of a truck under a south Texas summer sun. While the always Anglo foremen watch. War. Maybe it's just our age. We're both thirty-three. The other guys are younger.

Things calm down, for the moment anyway. As I said, these guys are tight, so I think it'll be all right. Everybody goes off to dance again, except for Bea and me. I need a bathrooom break.

The bathroom reeks of everything in this world that reeks. As I am finishing up at the urinals, I become aware of three or four guys watching me intently as they pass a joint among themselves. Tough. Sullen. Long scraggly black hair. Dark glasses. One really big guy, the others lean and gaunt but tough. They all look like they've vacationed in Huntsville, the state prison. The Wiggins Wolves twenty years later. I feel cold all over, and I know it's not the air conditioner at the Cielo Azul. I zip up, turn slowly, and, with a distant approximation of nonchalance, walk by them to the door. As I go by, their eyes follow—even with dark glasses, I can tell—and one of them lifts his head up ever so slightly and softly says, ¿Qu' uvo? (What's goin' on?). I look him carefully in the dark glasses and say just as softly, Aquí nomás (Everything's cool). Then, I am out into the welcome public scene of the dance floor area. Peace. To celebrate the occasion, I decide to get another round for the group even though it's not my turn. I'll have one also. Is this the third or fourth?

When I return, Beatrice informs me that two or three guys asked her to dance and she said no. More dancing; getting better all the time. I even try some of the fancy stuff. Holding only your partner's hand with one of your own, and using the other to give her a slight spin at the waist, you turn her round and round, pass her behind you, swing her in front, take her in your arms again, and pick up the forward motion of the polka on the beat (a move borrowed and adapted from American swing in the thirties). Without hitting anybody. Forty or so moving, swinging couples on the dance floor of El Cielo Azul constitute an expressive, well-armed truce, but perhaps this is a definition of art. Or so it occurs to me as over Beatrice's head I watch *la rata* and Amalia, a single body in two not always discernible parts, smoothly gliding with rhythmic dipping—like the good Mexican cotton pickers that I watched as a boy working part-time on Saturdays in the cotton fields outside Corpus Christi before the machine pickers came—all the while slowly turning on a firm axis. *La rata* even seems to have his eyes closed, no doubt imagining Amalia later, after the dance, but the dancing flows effortlessly. They slip in and out of traffic, sleek and quick, like a lovely black Jaguar that I remember seeing once on the San Diego freeway, a moving form always at the point of violent contact but deftly avoiding it at the last second. Meanwhile, I putt along in my little Honda, watching, with Beatrice along for a rather uneventful ride.

We are gliding by the bandstand when a fight breaks out in a second row of tables near the wall. The truce has broken down. I start spinning Beatrice round and round because I want to see. She soon gets dizzy and has the good sense to say, let's just stop. There's a lot to hear but not much to see since a crowd has quickly built up. Lots of screaming and cursing, and what it visible gives you a pretty good sense of what is going on. With a regular rhythm, a hand holding a beer bottle by the neck appears and disappears, appears and disappears, above the heads of the crowd. Two overweight, older *mexicano* security cops, probably long retired from the San Antonio police department, are making their way into the crowd, but not at a great speed. Even though everyone was frisked at the door, you never know what might be waiting in there. No sense in spoiling a nice retirement, what with the grandchildren and all and your youngest boy slowly getting his pharmacy degree in Austin. I feel a little tug from Beatrice. I turn, she smiles, and we dance away, for the band has not missed a beat.

It's getting late, one a.m.—Amalia wants *menudo* and Beatrice wants to hear the mariachi at Mario's Restaurant. The guys look at each other. Mario's is "classy," so they're thinking money, since they'll have to pay, and *wives,* since it is a key public scene in San Antonio mexicano life. I'm not worried about money. Tony and Delia have only a couple of hours, so they're not coming. We make it a foursome, but *la rata,* after seven or eight beers and a joint, is fading fast even after the hot, spicy *menudo.* The marines always retrieve their dead and wounded, so Amalia drives him home. As they teeter-totter out, she keeps taking his hand off her rump. She won't stay with him tonight. It's too late; she lives at home and it's not worth the fight with her father the next day. She'll take him as far as her house, and then que Dios lo bendiga (may God bless him). She also wants to sleep. She'll serve the lunch and dinner shift to middle-class Anglo San Antoñio at Loopy's Cafeteria tomorrow, on her feet all day.

Through soft slurps of *menudo,* I ask Beatrice more about herself. This will be the first time I've really talked to her at length, although I've known her now two years since I started going to Ruperto's, where she tends bar part-time. Usually she's too busy to talk much, or, in time-honored fashion, I spend more time talking to the men. A mother at sixteen, now twenty-six, divorced. Her boy is living in Arizona with his father. She doesn't explain. I don't ask. Worked at a paper factory running some sort of machine that makes paper cups. Laid off. A cousin has a part interest in Ruperto's, so he got her a part-time job. Would like to get married again. Why work? But, she says, not many good guys around.

We attempt more conversation. You must read a lot of books, she says. She doesn't. Popular fashion magazines, mostly to look at the pictures. Watches TV. *Telenovelas* and also the American kind. The Price Is Right. Come on down! she cries gleefully, causing the other restaurant patrons to look at us, and embarrassing me. (Why am I embarrassed?) I ask her about the dances. Does she go often? That reminds her of the dance floor incident, and she laughs, repeating Tony's line—That was close!—and adds, what if you had been killed! What would your professor friends at the university think? And your wife? I tell her, I don't know what they would think, and I'm not married. Not exactly single, though I don't tell her that. There is supposed to be a someone. So what am I doing here? I ponder myself dead on the dance floor and envision a headline in one of the yellow journalist San Antoñio newspapers: Professor Zapped. Said to be Doing "Fieldwork." Had It Coming. ¿Quien le Manda? (Who said he should be there?).

So what about the dance, Beatrice? She doesn't say much. It's something to do. Guys ask her out now and then and this is where they usually take her. To dances. Like me. We were at Ruperto's on a Saturday afternoon. Lencho and Tony wanted to go. Said they knew some *rucas.* Beatrice was off for the night, they said. Why don't you ask her? Why not? We seemed friendly enough. So here we are. Getting to know her.

Does she enjoy dances? A seemingly stupid question until she says, no, not really. Like I said, it's something to do, she says. It's about the only place to meet guys. But usually those that ask her out or that she meets there when she goes with girlfriends, pues nomás no (well, thank you, but no thank you). Maybe it's different in the "better" dance halls, but she doesn't get asked there and she can't afford it. Nonetheless, she thanks me for taking her out and for dinner. Usually she doesn't even get dinner, and they all want something. I don't mean you, you understand. You're not even my type anyway. She laughs: you can't even dance good! That was close, José!

Anyway, she continues, I like to dance but I don't always like the dances, ¿me entiendes? (you know what I mean?). There's too much *borlote* (trouble) all the time. Y los guys, pues nomás no. They really are bad places sometimes. You shouldn't be going, really, José. My mother says that's why the devil has been coming. El diablo chulo (the cute devil).

Yeah, I think to myself, I've heard about the devil, but I think nothing more of it then.

Time to go home. We leave Mario's, turn on Commerce, and drive into the deep west side, past run-down or boarded-up stores and shops, lots of cantinas, and, on the side streets, small houses with the predictable profusion of flowers and bric-a-brac in front. I drop her off at one of these houses, which she shares with two other women. She invites me in. I thank her, say no, and lie, It's getting late. But I am thinking, this is enough. No more. Can't do it. Besides, I'm not her type anyway. Can't even dance good . . . I mean, well . . . but I am learning, again, with women like Beatrice. My people. My people? As I now reflect on these women, I think of the Chicana character Arlene in Viramontes' short story "Miss Clairol"; she who, accompanied by her ten-year-old daughter, Champ, in preparation for a date shops at the K-Mart "wearing bell bottom jeans two sizes too small" and "a pink strapless tube top. Her stomach spills over the hip hugger jeans." In indecision, she tells Champ, "Shit, mija, I dunno," as she

> smacks her gum, contemplating the decision.—Maybe I need a change, tú sabes. What do you think?—She holds up a few blond strands with black roots. Arlene has burned the softness of her hair with peroxide; her hair is stiff, breaks at the ends and she needs plenty of Aqua Net hairspray to tease and tame her ratted hair, then folds it back into a high lump behind her head. For the last few months she has been a platinum "Light Ash" blond, before that a Miss Clairol "Flame" redhead. . . . The only way Champ knows her mother's true hair is by her roots which, like death, inevitably rise to the truth. (Viramontes 1988:101)

Later, with a can of Campbell soup for dinner, Champ (real name Ofelia) is left alone with the TV as her mother leaves with her date "in the blue and white shark-finned Dodge" to

dance until her hair becomes undone, her hips jiggering and quaking
beneath a new pair of hosiery, her mascara shadowing under her
eyes from the perspiration of the ritual, dance spinning herself into
Miss Clairol, and stopping only when it is time to return to the sew-
ing factory, time to wait out the next date, time to change hair color.
Time to remember or forget. (1988:104–5)

Sunday Morning. Actually wrote a bit, then went out for *barbacoa*
tacos and coffee. Declined invitation for breakfast at friend's home in
exclusive Alamo Heights. Wealthy Mexican-American attorney with Anglo society spouse. Coffee and oranges in sunny chairs, green cockatoos
and all that. Didn't seem quite the thing after last night and later this
afternoon. After the tacos, I'll come back to the apartment, write a bit
more, then to Lencho's for the promised fajitas. Pick up Tony and a
couple of six-packs. Maybe *fajitas* too; Lencho is probably broke. Before
I get a chance to leave, my mother calls. How are you and why aren't you
at Mass? (Because nobody else is in Mass, *mamá*. Not me. Not Lencho.
Not Tony. Not Rosemary (especially not Rosemary). Not the wealthy lawyer and his wife. Only old ladies and middle-class *mexicano* lawyers running for office with their manicured wives and kids.) She tells me it is very
hot in Corpus (already) this late Sunday morning. Is it hot there in San
Antoñio? (yes, *mamá*), and then updates her weekly narrative about the
family and the neighborhood: unemployed relatives, trial separations,
divorces, pregnant teenagers, a couple of killings on Agnes Street, the
mexicano bar strip a few blocks from the house. (And so it goes.)

    She does offer a new motif: Mr. Sánchez, that nice man down the street
(you know, the one married to that girl you dated in high school) was
arrested for drugs at the U.S. Customs checkpoint. I make the mistake of
asking about the rest of the family in Limonada. Ay, dejame decirte lo
que paso (Oh, let me tell you what happened). Killings over drugs, pregnant teenagers, divorces y desocuparon a tu tio Alfredo (and your uncle
Alfredo was fired). Yes, the lawyers do stay busy and *mamá* records it all.

Sunday Afternoon. The *fajitas* are nicely grilled. Lencho's kids are
playing in the street under his strict orders—quickly disobeyed—to stay
away from the street gang corner near the Apache Bar. His wife is lying on
the old flowered sofa in the combined living/dining area of their two
bedroom/one bath on the southwest side of the city. Long ways from Alamo Heights. In the direct blast of an old floor fan, she watches some old

sentimental movie on an equally old TV. I've tried to engage her in polite conversation with almost no success. A touch testy. Probably holds me complicit in Lencho's doings. La voy a matar a la puta. I wouldn't doubt it. On the Westside, I doubt nothing.

We eat outside standing around the barbecue grill. Lencho chops up *fajitas* until we're full. He also sends in a plate with one of the kids for their mother. As we eat Lencho serves notice that Ruperto's Lounge, before a possibility, is now a necessity if we are to watch the Dallas-Pittsburgh game. She-on-the-flowered-sofa intends to watch the movie for the next two hours fortified by Lencho's *fajitas* and a couple of Big Reds. After last night and this morning, Lencho isn't up to a struggle for household hegemony, especially since Ruperto's isn't a bad idea anyway. Better TV, and Tom, the owner, keeps the place and the beer cold. Money is a small problem. I'll buy extra. Assistant professor largesse.

Third and Very Long. ¡Va a pass! (He's going to pass!). Shit no bro. El Franco Harris is goooood, *compa.* 'Tas pendejo, tiene que pass (You're dumb, he has to pass). Almost all eyes glued to the 21-inch color set above the bar. Dallas calls time out. ¿José, no hay jale en la university? (Is there work at the university?). I need work bad, bro; el "unemployment" [benefits] done gone! Danos un round, Tom (Give us a round . . .). A voice from the back: te toca shootrear, Tony (It's your turn to shoot . . .). Tony waits, cue stick in hand, watching the set. Tied and third and very long on the Dallas thirty, Dallas denies Franco Harris and Pittsburgh lines up for a field goal. It's good! Awwwright! Tony yells; 17-14! He's not rooting for Pittsburgh. Those are my numbers, bro! It's not over *buey, la rata* tells him. Just three more minutes and I score, bro! Pot's mine and I'm buying for all you *cabrones!*

Dallas returns the kickoff to their thirty-five. Staubach takes them forty yards. Fourth and long. Herrera puts it though the uprights. Tony explodes: ¡Pinche mothafucka! That hondo was mine, mothafucka! *Rata* snickers. The voice in the back yells, hey Tony, where's your Dallas spirit, *ese?* Dallas is going to win, bro! ¡Chinga su madre, spirit! ¡Chinga su madre, Herrera! ¡Pinche raza! Hey José, the Greek chorus continues from the back, apáñale jale en UTSA pá que no este chingando (get him a job at UTSA so he's not fucking with us). Everyone laughs; Tony shoots a finger at the Greek chorus. I wonder about the brunch across town. They are probably watching the game also. Same game, different drinks, no pot.

Game Over, No Overtime, Alamo Heights Wins. Nine p.m. Tony, *la rata,* and me. Almost out of money, otherwise we might still be at Ruperto's. Better this way; I teach tomorrow. First week. We were also hungry, Tony, *la rata* and me. Lencho's gone home only a little drunk. He'll get cold *fajitas* and cold wife.

¿'*Ta toda madre, la chicken, que nel?* (Chicken's damn good, no?) says Tony. We're sort of standing, sitting around the hood of Tony's 1965 Ford doing a bucket from the Colonel's. Fries and jalapeños, too. Fucking, finger-licking good, as *la rata* says. Also a final six-pack. That's all "we" could afford. I thought about taking them downtown for *menudo* or something at Mi Tierra. Always open. They take VISA. But I've paid for them maybe too many times. Bad "fieldwork"? Besides the Colonel was just down the street from Ruperto's. Downtown poses another problem. *La rata* would want to stop by El Esquire; nomas una (just one). I've had it. I "chip in" for the chicken and buy the Bud at the 7-11. We think about doing the chicken on the 7-11 lot, but management and the cops aren't cool about that. We drive our cars down to the big K-Mart parking lot down the street. As we spread the food, I tell them my Chicano K-Mart joke: What are the first words in English that a Chicano kid learns? Answer: "Attention K-Mart shoppers, we have a special on Aisle Four." They don't get it. I gnaw on a bone and ponder the complexities of the new bilingual joke. My wealthy lawyer friend likes it a lot. So do I. We're virtually alone on the K-Mart lot. Halfway through the bucket, my car next to Tony's, it occurs to me that we might look like a dope deal in progress to some passing police cruiser. Oh Lord. I wonder if *la rata* and/ or Tony are carrying stuff as they sometimes do? Cold fear. *San Antonio Light* headlines: UTSA Prof. Deals Dope. Dissertation not Done. Prof. Done Gone. Will my university benefits cover a good lawyer? Small fat chance. Chicken. Gnawing fear. I stand on the car bumper to get a better look around. Whatcha doing, bro? asks *la rata.* I don't answer, but I mentally rehearse my routine: Oh no, officer. You see, here's my faculty I.D. I have a Ph.D. . . . almost. Fat small chance. I wonder if there's a library in Huntsville. Will they let me out for the defense? In the light of the few parking lot neons, *la rata* notices that Tony's car inspection sticker is expired. Shit! Tony says, gotta get a job, or gotta deal, one or the other, don't give a fuck. When I hear "deal," I decide to move things along, forgoing what looks like a pretty good chicken wing. Extra crispy. I decide to "lend" Tony ten bucks for the inspection. I am overwhelmed by the thought that he might be stopped for an inspection sticker with nickel bags under the seat. And he would be searched. Yes he would. From the SAPD's point of view, Tony and *la rata* are walking, talking Probable Cause. Will the car pass inspection? I ask him. Like all of us, it has seen better days in the sixties. Yeah, he knows this garage, but he still needs the ten bucks to pay off. Maybe the guy will take a nickel bag. Nothing's free, you know.

Gotta go, bros; I tell them, watch you later. *La rata:* ¿nos watchamos en El Cielo Azul el Saturday? (We'll see you Saturday at El Cielo Azul?). No, not this Saturday. Dinner with a lady on the Riverwalk. *Más classy.* I don't tell them this and make up some lie about work. They won't be at the Riverwalk. Improbable Cause. ¿A poco te escamó el diablo? (Does the devil scare you?) Tony asks and tells us that the devil appeared at another dancehall Saturday night, at El Camaroncito (The Short Shrimp). At least according to some *rucas* he heard talking about it.

It's a hot south Texas night. With the AC on full blast, I find the street to my place. By now, the hyenas of the Westside—the roaches—are picking over the scattered chicken bones on the K-Mart parking lot. Big, Mexican roaches—sauntering roaches, as my friend Victor Nelson says—munching away. I can hear them: ¿'ta toda madre la chicken, que nel? I'll head home. Maybe stop by to see the classy lady. In Alamo Heights. Have a Drambuie. Won't stay up long. Tomorrow is the first day of classes. 9 a.m. "Mexican American Culture and Society." I'll start with the Aztecs, of course.

Me cae chingos bailar (I like dancing a fuck of a lot), he says through large mouthfuls of Big Mac quickly swallowed into a wiry brown body dressed in a greasy mechanic's uniform. On his shirt, "auto break specialist," right there below his name, "Garza," but his companions, and now you and I, know him as *la rata.*

He's not a full-fledged mechanic, although he had some training in "Auto Shop 123" before he dropped out of high school to eventually give his brown body to the marines, who taught him only one thing and it wasn't auto mechanics. (I remember his kind in high school—the "vocational" kids, mostly Mexicans, a few blacks—practicing on faculty cars in the courtyard in front of the vocational building. I would watch them through the window of my advanced chemistry class as I patiently waited for the results of my experiment, knowing it would be fine; fully deserving of an "A"; yet another to add to my collection. Bound for college, not Khe Sanh.) Now I look at him and wait patiently for the results of this ethnographic chemistry; my certainty of an "A" all gone. At a dance, I mentioned that I had been having brake problems, so he tells me to come by next week and he will personally do them. I'll have to pay, of course, he says, since it's not his shop. That's OK. They take VISA too. On this Wednesday—his third day on the job—he finished my car. It's nearly lunchtime, so he invites me across the street to the McDonalds. It doesn't need to be said. A miniparty celebrating his new job. We debate stopping at the Quickie Pickie next door for a couple of beers to sneak into the McDonalds but decide against it. He has to work this afternoon and I have to teach. With a crisp ten dollar bill, he pays for two Big Macs, a double order of fries, two cokes, and two little apple pies; almost like mother's; fresh made; miles away. I don't want the pie but he insists. Tan a toda madre (They're mother-fucking good). Who am I to get in the way of a man celebrating his vocation? I take the pie.

Simón, Chingos (Yep, a fucking lot), he continues, in answer to a question I pose to him as I chew on my Big Mac: Do you ever miss a weekend dance? I try not too, he says, me cay chingos bailar. Simón, chingos. We talk more about dancing and finish our Big Macs. As it turns out, *la rata* will not buy anyone else lunch for awhile. Two weeks later he is once again unemployed, a seasonal adjustment in the "national" economy, the business pages of the *San Antoñio Express* tell us. Yet, I have no doubt I will see him on the floor at some dance hall in the weeks to come, again and again, for I intend to dance again.

Why do my people dance? In the very asking of such a question another devil appears to torment us, for is this not one of those stereotypes? Mexicans dance, don't they? That is, they indulge but do not discipline their bodies to work and save. That is, they—especially their women—indulge their sexual bodies, ignoring "higher" matters of spirit and intellect. Such is the interpretive sense—the cultural poetics—one gathers from the first, outside, which is to say, largely Anglo observers of my people's ancestors as the latter danced in Texas in the first half of the nineteenth century, the dance and event (not polka then) called fandango:

> Whenever whites discussed the Mexican's moral nature, references
> to sexuality punctuated their remarks. The fandango, for instance,
> was identified with lewd passions and lasciviousness. The erotic na-
> ture of this traditional Mexican dance often led to prudish comments
> from onlookers. Señoritas were described as especially sensuous
> when participating in the dance . . . (de Leon 1983:37)

But as de Leon astutely notes, it was not really *the* Mexicans who were guilty of moral laxity, only *most* Mexicans, and another devil yet reappears among my people.

Anglos generally stated that only certain elements of Hispanic society were attracted to the revelry of the fandango. In San Antoñio, for example, the educated families, the elites of the city, the better society whom whites likened with themselves, were thought to be in control of their morality. The ones who gathered to enjoy the obscene dance were described as the lowest species of humanity—the poor, the uneducated, the mixed-bloods. (de Leon 1983:37)

Why do my people dance? But also, by what right does a working-class/Mexican-descent anthropologist dare approach the sordid edges of such a stereotype? Because, perhaps like General Walker, these Anglo observers were superficially correct: "only certain elements of Hispanic society were attracted to the revelry of the fandango . . . the poor, the uneducated, the mixed-bloods." In the 1970s I danced and drank (yet the other stereotype) with the continuing poor, uneducated, mixed-bloods of south Texas, but, unlike Walker's ancestors, I offer another cultural poetics, one, no doubt, also carrying its own repressions and contradictions, like those of my ethnographic precursors.

But a step forward toward this cultural poetics requires another step back toward history, for between the fandangos of the mid-nineteenth century and polkas of the Cielo Azul of the 1970s, dancing music continued to figure in the lives of Mexican-Americans in Texas. We know that a variety of musical dance forms appeared among this population in the nineteenth and twentieth centuries, always conditioned by the growing presence of the dominant Other. By the 1930s, however, this music/dance variety had largely given way to a predominant polka style played by a predominant ensemble at least for the mass working classes: the *conjunto* with its lead accordion, guitars, rhythm, and vocalizations of new and old lyrics. We can note a major exception to this trend, another kind of ensemble, the modern orquesata (orchestra) tejana (Texan) (or American-style "big band"). The appearance of the American style "big band" also signals the emergence of a musical/class division within Texas-Mexican society as a small middle-class sector identifies with orchestra music. (Limón 1983; cf. Peña 1985)

As part of more general festivities such as weddings, loosely called *funciones* (functions), music and dancing occurred principally in the forum called a *baile de regalo* ("gift" dance):

the baile de regalo acquired its name from the customary practice of requiring young men to offer their female partners gifts of candy, sweet bread, peanuts, or other condiments for the privilege of dancing with them. (1985:37)

Peña also notes that this dancing forum had "ceased to exist by 1930" and had, indeed given way to a competing scene, the *baile de negocio* (business dance), a predominantly working-class, commercial dance scene with the *conjunto* as its ensemble. Here peanuts, candy, and sweet bread did not suffice. Here,

> women in attendance who received an invitation from a man to dance collected from him a chip that he had bought at the door for, say, fifteen cents. Each woman collected all the chips given to her and turned them in before she left the dance, receiving five cents for each chip she had accumulated. The remainder was the empresario's profit, out of which he recovered the salary paid the musicians. (1985:48)

Peña cites one of his older informants as he amplifies on this wage form and surplus value generated from the use of woman's body, echoed again in El Cielo Azul.

> "They came to work, it was work . . . single women who had no man, who had nothing. They came to dance and made their living that way." But often, as Ayala said, in order to keep working they had to resort to prostitution. (1985:49)

At the other end of history, Peña tells us less about the post-1960 period, for it is not his principal concern. Yet, he does speak of the relative decline of the *conjunto* as an autonomous stylistic rendering of working-class consciousness and notes the efforts to merge the *conjunto* and big-band ensembles into smaller groups partaking of both. These later musicians imitated, he tells us, "often in degraded fashion, the accomplishments of the 1950s and 1960s" (1985:160). From Peña's point of view, it would appear that this "degraded" fashion refers to the hybrid sort of highly amplified ensemble drawing on elements from the big band and *conjunto*. And here we find Peña perhaps too influenced by Américo Paredes, his mentor as well, as he speaks without hesitation of the *degradation* of musical culture from the high, resistively "pure" moment of the *conjunto* to groups such as La Magia Negra at El Cielo Azul.[2]
    Peña offers us another entry point into our world of dance, although it too is not without its complications. In another study, he too would take us dancing, although historical time, class, and his interpretive framework make this a very different dance scene. Sometime, in the cusp between the sixties and the seventies (he is not specific on this point), Peña studied the dancing culture of Mexican-Americans in Fresno, California, many of

them probably with Texas roots. He typifies these California folk as "exclusively Chicano and working class," regularly employed as blue- and white-collar workers in an age range of thirty to sixty, "members of an increasingly affluent working class" (1980:56–57). We are then offered a telling, mostly physical, description of the dance scene. For example, the dancers enter the scene by paying admission at "a small table with tickets and money change . . . set up at the door," where "one or two women from the sponsoring organization" collect the money. "By long established custom, the nature of the celebration called for semi-formal attire. Most of the men wore dress clothes . . . the women often dressed rather lavishly" (1980:57–58). Following a description of musicians, music, and the dance's friendly social interaction, Peña offers this interpretive summary of the dance scene's cultural significance, drawing on Victor Turner. The dancers move "from the outer hierarchic structured and Anglo-dominated world" into a "new reality"

> . . . where in the course of the dance, everyone shed his customary
> social status and entered into a shared state of communitas, born of
> a common sociocultural identity and a more or less shared (if not
> actually acknowledged) sense of alienation from the dominant Ameri-
> can culture . . . a spirit of communitas prevailed, in which all the
> people contributed to and partook of a strongly Chicano ambiente.
> (1980:65–66)

And finally, at evening's end, the "revelers" go "out into the night . . . to their respective statuses in structured Anglo society, their sense of identity reaffirmed by their renewed communion with fellow Chicanos" (1980:66).

Is it class or regional differences, a different historical moment, or perhaps an overwrought interpretive nationalist sensibility that produces this vision of communitarian resistance? Yet I confess that I once and momentarily held such a Turnerian view in an unpublished paper on my Texas dancers that I wrote and circulated in 1977 and later published (1983). I now doubt its applicability at least to the world of El Cielo Azul. If there is communitas in Fresno, it is of a middle-class kind and comes at another social cost which Peña almost erases as the rhetoric of communitas gets going. It is a brief telling observation: "To be sure, there were other levels of Chicano society, namely those occupied by farmworkers . . . that were seldom represented at the dances." He explains and doesn't explain why: "The reasons for this are complex, but they are based on such things as ascribed status and the differential identities related to that status." As he lapses thus into the language of mainstream sociology, these distinct statuses and identities are then said to constitute "in short . . . the cultural diversity that existed among Chicanos in Fresno . . ." (1980:57). But really, and even shorter, the explanation is, in a word, *class,* or, *fuereños.*

Whatever its interpretive sense for Fresno, I certainly doubt this Turnerian vision for the dance world of lower-working-class San Antoñio, where a different ambiente prevails, one where tension, faction, and disorder also reign, and where simple Turnerian visions make little sense.

> The influential (if not exactly "official") voices of Anthropology spend an enormous effort in repressing the second term of the pair, order/disorder. By and large it is simply ignored. At other times (as with Carnival when the very point of the ritual is to create disorder) it is held to but further invigorate order, while an important third strategy condemns disorder to the "anti-structure" of that primeval ooze of "communitas" represented by Victor Turner as a sort of womb-like paradise of sheer humanity beyond both social structure and Hobbes' infamous warre. (Taussig 1984:109)

I cannot be certain about Fresno (for that matter I cannot be certain about anything), but in San Antoñio, as one glides across the floor, one clearly senses that there is little here that is beyond social structure and warre. Indeed, it might well be said that the negating postmodernity I have described, like a killing fog, seeps into the dance as a scene and we are at some distance both from *los bailes de regalo* and Fresno. I have danced in a world organized by a multimillion-dollar booking and recording industry of companies, agents, contracts, and dancehall operators. It is a world one enters by paying relatively high admission fees and often being subjected to searches by and the watchfulness of bouncers and security guards, trying to make sure no one dies from "communitas." Once inside, it is also a world of heavily promoted alcoholic consumption with highly visible beer concessions, not at all a small part of the profitability of the dance scene. And if all of this is late capitalism making war on its postmodern working-class subjects, fueled by alcohol, the subjects are quite capable of making sudden, unpredictable, violent war upon each other, notwithstanding the searches at the door. For often the fights merely begin here but end on the parking lot or on the back streets of the Westside where firepower is available.

In a highly specific way, many of these effects of the postmodern ultimately come to be sited on the body. It is the working-class body, already punished by labor and a varying nutrition, that now comes to be visited by substance abuse and physical violence. It is a physical infliction that takes a particular toll on men, yet this seeming gender asymmetry is balanced by another negating infliction upon the female body and self. For it is women who, in yet another internal war, are continuously forced to contest the sexual commodification of their bodies. The men who take them to the dances, the men who frequent the dances, singly and in groups, do so often with the expectation of what they call *movidas* (sexual moves and pickups) with these underclass women. While the female sexual targets may be single, the men sometimes are not, as in Lencho's case; one's impression is that wives are rarely taken.

The single women who attend these dances—the Beatrices and Delias—know all of this full well, but they faithfully attend anyway. Some, sometimes, are there indeed for *movidas* or perhaps just for fun in an otherwise tedious existence. But, in conversation, more often than not, one senses clearly another set of expectations centered on their desire to lend care, coherence, and stability to their difficult lives through marriage. Between Delia's expectation and Tony's (lies) lies a specific ongoing negotiation over her body. For Delia, this negotiation issues forth in her uncertain knowledge that the man now pressing against her breasts or sliding his hand over her buttocks may be "the one." He too more than likely expects her to be "the one" as well . . . for that night. Often, these women tell me, they reject these bodily proposals for one-night sex after the dance, settling for and momentarily accepting their single status, at least until the next dance. If nothing "permanent" happens, as it rarely does, there is, for them, the consolation of "siquiera salimos" (at least we went out). They see people, drink a little, talk, and momentarily get away from low-paid, tedious jobs, small crowded houses and apartments, TV and popular magazines that tell them about lives they will never have, and relatives who are constantly harassing them with ¿Cuando te casas? (When are you going to get married?), yet another negotiation over their bodies insofar as these are made to represent the interests of their families. Ironically, of course, marriage is precisely what they are trying to effect by going to the dances, even as relatives criticize them for the sexual implications of these dances.

These men and women finally come to the dances for a fundamental and defining reason: to dance. For, lest we forget or become too distracted by my rhetoric of the negating postmodern, amidst and, I now claim, against such inflictions on the body, those bodily subjects dance: that is, they spend most of their time on the dance floor, jointly propelling their bodies in coordinated fashion counterclockwise around the well-polished floors. Yet, strangely, in an article on Chicano dance, Peña says almost nothing about the actual motor act of dancing itself, bearing out Foster's recent admonition to anthropologists who say a great deal about dance scenes but little about dance itself (1992:365). Let me try.

"¿Quieres bailar, female reader?" Or at El Cielo Azul, I might just walk across the floor to your table and silently offer you my hand. We begin with a conventional ballroom dancing stance—my right arm firmly around your waist, palm flat on the small of your back; your left arm lightly around my neck and our other hands interlocked and held up next to my left shoulder; our bodies separated to a degree settled upon by silent gender negotiations, though usually things will tighten up to make more continuous body contact and my face may wind up touching your hair as we begin to move to the music's quick tempo. The idea is not to skip, hop, and jump or pump our arms—as "Anglos" often do when they attempt this dance—the bodily idea is to sensuously slide and glide around the floor, "Subtle and smooth, the smoother the better," as another observer of this dance has noted (Broyles-Gonzalez 1985:E5). My left foot moves forward with my right sliding, sometimes slightly dragging behind, and, as I do so, you take sliding complementing backward steps, or at least until I take us through a half turn—for I am leading, of course—and gently now pull you toward me and around the floor. There will be several such half turns as we by now complete one counterclockwise circle and we're back more or less where we started but still going.

But in all of this, we are not holding our bodies rigidly straight up in the manner of a waltz, let us say. Rather, whether moving forward or backward, I am slightly bent over at the waist toward you in a slight right-leaning crouch, my right leg also slightly bent at the knee. By necessity you will be bent slightly backward at the waist, not too uncomfortably we hope. By this time our relative body proximity may have changed. I probably have your right hand and arm pulled toward me close to my left ear, perhaps even over my left shoulder. Solely for purposes of control, of course, I may be holding you more tightly around the waist to facilitate our constant counter-clockwise turning on an axis between our bodies even as we move counter-clockwise around the floor.

To exaggerate any of the above, e.g., lower crouch, more bend to the knee so as to push against your thigh, a tighter hold, might draw a disapproving glance from anyone watching at a more middle-class dance, let us say in Fresno, for it marks the couple as proletarians, perhaps even as a culturally diverse "farmworker." But at El Cielo Azul, it is not an unusual dance stance. I make a half turn—and there will be many—and gently pull you toward me and around the floor.

Finally, if I wish to, I may release you from the waist at irregular times and, holding you only by your right hand, take you through a series of swinging motions around and brushing my centered body even as we continue to move forward around the circle. But this is "fancy" stuff, and most of the time, I'll be holding you or Beatrice and wondering what I'm doing here so focused on bodies after spending so many years on my mind. The dance over, I'll walk you back to your table having said little or nothing during the dance. Talk is minimal and the silence may continue as sometimes the woman simply resumes her place and no "thanks" is necessarily uttered from either direction. I walk away, check out other possibilities . . . perhaps I'll come back to you . . . you were pretty good . . . what's a nice readerly woman like you doing in a place like this?

"Any study of the colonial world," Frantz Fanon once told us, "should take into consideration the phenomena of the dance and of possession." Dancing, he says, is "the native's relaxation," which

> takes precisely the form of a muscular orgy in which the most acute aggressivity and the most compelling violence are canalized, transformed, and conjured away. The circle of the dance is a permissive circle: it protects and permits. (1963:57)

"At certain times on certain days," he continues,

> men and women come together at a given place and there, under the solemn eye of the tribe, fling themselves into a seemingly unorganized pantomime, which is in reality extremely systematic, in which by various means—shakes of the head, bending of the spinal column, throwing of the whole body backward—may be deciphered as in an open book the huge effort of a community to exorcise itself, to liberate itself, to explain itself. There are no limits—inside the circle. (1963:57)

But between the first and second quote we can detect a shift in Fanon from the trained psychologist that he was to the interpretive critical anthropologist that he could be. In the first instance, he offers a rather conventional, which is to say functionalist, interpretation of colonized expressive life in Africa, where imposed violence is "canalized, transformed, and conjured away through muscular orgy." But, in his second and more political role, already evident in this same paragraph, the "circle of the dance," while "a permissive circle," nonetheless "protects" as it "per-

mits." Here we begin to see form and political signification. Form and
critical order continue to be elaborated as he notes for us the regularity of
performance "at a given place" with a sense of collective responsibility—
"under the solemn eye of the tribe." What at first appeared as orgy, as
"seemingly unorganized pantomime," is now seen as "extremely systematic." The result is no longer formless, meaningless, purely muscular orgy
but rather a formed social text to be "deciphered as in an open book," a
decipherment that yields a political unconscious—"the huge effort of a
community to exorcise itself, to liberate itself, to explain itself" in a context of colonial violence.

Yet the language of "book," "explain," "decipherment" suggests a ref-
erentially symbolic, perhaps even allegorical performance. But among
the Mexicans of south Texas, such an understanding of polka dancing
does not obtain; it cannot be readily deciphered in such a fashion, save
perhaps for the counterclockwise circle that perhaps symbolically suggests group cooperation and protection against the "outside" (Hanna
1979:169).

Several of Hanna's acute insights into dancing provide a strong interpretive platform for my own thoughts. When she tells us, for example,
that the "the overemphasis on the verbal and the technological in the
United Stated undervalues dance for the population at large but as a consequence many subcultures exist which overvalue dance precisely on this
account" (1979:147), we immediately think of the south Texas world.
When we learn that "in the city of Junchtitan, Oaxaca, Mexico, privileged
upper class groups cling to their dance as a symbol of cultural identity in a
milieu which has become heterogeneous and threatening" (1979:143), we
sense the paradoxical relationship of this world to my dance world, these
fuereños dancing so far from the upper classes of Oaxaca.

We sense these interpretive relationships, but useful as they are, they
are still at some distance from the dance as form rather than event. But as
an astute student of dance form, Hanna offers two seemingly contradictory observations that bring us closer to our mark. Citing Maurice Bloch
(1974), she suggests that "repetition and ritualization" in dance "de-
creases the range of possible messages and thereby reinforces the status
quo" (1979:141). This, however, is to assume that the status quo, our
postmodern status quo, invests its late capital in orderly repetition rather
than, as it does, in a planned random flux of alienation and consumption,
against which the repetitive ritual of the polka may be the critical message. Or to take her second insight, such dance may be, after Bernard
Siegel (1970), a form of "defensive structuring in which members of a

society attempt to establish themselves in the face of felt, external threats to their identity . . ." (1979:142). These insights bring us closer to the central idea of dance form as politics, but both also seem to work on a social assumption at variance with my world, namely, the image of a discrete "inside" culture, à la Fresno, threatened by a distinct "outside" culture, out there beyond the dance hall doors. What I have sensed and tried to render is the continuing penetration of the postmodern so-called "outside" into the dance scene, creating a continuous movement of disorder/order, a struggle for meaningful identity, a struggle sited upon the body.

Randy Martin (1985:55) offers us a way to see dance form as a "decidedly non-symbolic and non-signifying politics." He analogizes the human bodies in dancing to the body politic, proposing that dance produces in an artful and deeply satisfying way a desire that he says is present but usually not acted upon in society, "the desire to act politically." In the absence of such periodic action there can only result an attenuation of consciousness. Dancing can act as an organized resurgence of such desire, in which art and collective will are marshaled to a transcendent end—transcendent, that is, beyond the "normal," dominated character of society (1985:56).

But how is a dance enactment—a moment seemingly free from politics—an analogy of thwarted desire expressed in collective art, rather that an escape into an art from all these social repressions? In a particularly insightful move, Martin reminds us of the role of the choreographer to show us the politics of the dance:

> The dance company, while poised for the production of desire in performance, could stand for any community or totalized agent bound by some means of authority or regulation. At the onset of the rehearsal process, choreographer and company exist as state and people, capital and labor, patriarch and gender, as a totality which finds its representation and as such identity or consciousness of itself through an external authority. In this sense, authority can be said to symbolize totality without the means to realize it. Initially, the company looks to the choreographer for dancing as people look to the state for government. What is obscured in this signifying gaze is exactly who wields practical power over social action. (1985:57)

We need not qualify Martin's dynamic model much to appropriate it to our purpose. At its "best," when couples at El Cielo Azul glide across the floor in seemingly synchronized fashion, all their turning moves well executed, the dancing approaches the artistically articulated desire that Martin would have us valorize as a physical politics, a pure form that speaks, nondiscursively, of people's desire artfully to assert their presence against choreography. One can detect an emic awareness of this desire expressed in a different pure form in the *gritos,* long cries of celebratory approval, coming from the men sitting or standing at the bar, as they watch a particularly artful execution on the floor.

But, to continue with Martin, this collective desire is not articulated against a repressive domination form beyond the dance hall. Rather, the adversarial culture is present within the dance hall; the site of contestation is at the point of dance production. To understand this local struggle and to see why pure dancing is political, we need critically to identify our own version of Martin's authoritarian, totalizing choreographer—our own representative of the state political economy. In El Cielo Azul, such dominating power emanates, paradoxically, from two unlikely sources both seeking to control and subvert desire.

In his previously cited study of such dances in Fresno, California, Peña (1980) describes the role of the dance band and its leader in stage-managing the dance. Such groups obviously generate the dancing, even as they attempt to impose their externalized sense of order upon it. They do so, for example, by deciding when a too stimulating, energetic polka will not be played, substituting instead a slow, saccharine, romantic song that does not require great dancing art. Further, as a professional group, the band to some degree embodies the profitable political economy of the dance, with its marked tendency to treat the dancers as commodities and consumers. The disjuncture between art and commodity occasions the disputes that sometimes mark the end of the dance: the crowd wants more music, while the band and the dance hall promoter are thinking about their labor and profit (Peña 1980:62–64).

But there is another kind of paradoxical choreographer at the dance, one directly sited on the human body itself. The inseparable triad of hard, working-class labor, substance use, and sexual desire may initially motivate the dancing—a desire to relax tired muscles; a sexual desire consummated in a cheap hotel or a car seat; and alcohol as a desire that drives the other two. This triad choreographs the dance even as it can produce a fourth desire: to take the race and class war within oneself, perniciously transform it into "manhood," and sometimes inflict it upon other men—perhaps on the slight pretext of a bump on the dance floor or a prolonged stare at one's woman. In the sudden violence of a fight, we see the ultimate disarray, the sometimes too final fragmentation, in the continually fragmented lives of these people.

Yet amid incipient violence, to watch a Cielo Azul couple on the floor at its best, to hear the sharp, well-formed class-consciousness of the *grito*, is to realize that, for a moment, some measure of artful control over these forces—some measure of victory—has been achieved in the never-ending struggle against the choreography of race, class, and, one has to say, gender. For transcending sexual intention on both sides, or, better still, sublimating it, the dance, in its best moment, even with the male in ostensible control, makes the couple look *como si fueran uno* (as if they were one). And, for a moment, gender domination appears overcome . . . for a moment. The Chicano poet and historian Juan Gomez-Quiñones knows about dances:

> Solo en la danza
>   hay union
>
> Solo en la danza
>   se une
>   espirita, alma y ser
>   por eso nos gusta
>
> (Only in dance
>   is there union
>
> Only in dance
>   Do spirit, soul, and self
>   Unite
>   That is why we like it)
>   (1974:13)

For these "natives" under their own species of now postcolonialism, a colonialism inflicting domination upon their bodies, it is precisely the formalized yet flexible, artful and complex if momentary control of their bodies that affords them an opportunity to control some aspect of their lives. Always, it is a complex control posited against a formless, unstable "outside" that attempts the saturation of their very bodies. In the 1970s this "outside" could already be identified as a negating postmodernity for urban working-class *mexicano* south Texas.

If the *corrido* was the major signifier of the critical politics of Américo Paredes' heroic world, then I take the polka as that of my own world—the polka not so much as a musical form, but as a dance. I opt for the dancing rather than the music because, as Peña has clearly suggested (1985:157–61), the music is increasingly more open to late-capitalist and postmodern commodification, while, in my view, the dancing stands at some critical distance from the postmodern effect. Amid a world of alienating postmodernity, the polka is something else. At the same time, I do not think of it as the "rebellious, syncretic and creative" side of postmodernism (Clifford 1988b:15). It is creative, but not the made-anew-in-the-historical-instant manner that Clifford seems to imply in this formulation, and it is not particularly rebellious, at least in any manifest sense. On the other hand neither is it a pure local narrative of "cultural continuity and recovery" (1988b:15). The polka is something else.

For Randy Martin (1985), dancing is the artful management of the human body in the sentient and ultimately political articulation of form, critically transcending the domination that initially creates it and tries to control it. I suggest that this artful control over the effects of a negating, postmodernist climate is what *mexicanos* achieve in their dancing. There are, of course, great differences between these dancers and the ones Martin writes about; the *mexicanos* are working-class ethnics, not innovative "art" dancers on the New York stage. They draw on what Raymond Williams might have identified as a "residual tradition," formed in the past but made politically serviceable in the present (1977:121–27) Williams' identification of the creative, critical unifications of past and present seems wholly consistent with Ellman and Feidelson's sense of a critical modernism. The modern

> finds its character by confronting the past and including this confrontation within itself as part of a single total experience. It is more than a cultivation of immediacy, of free or fragmented awareness; it is the embodiment in current imagery of a situation always larger than the present, and as such it is also a containment of the resources and perils of the present by rediscovery of a relevant past. In this sense, modernism is synthetic in its very indeterminacy. Modern writers, working often without established models and bent on originality, have at the same time been classicists, custodians of language, communicators, traditionalists in their fashion. (Ellman and Feidelson 1965: vii)

Written in the early sixties, this passage conceives of a modernism of arts and letters that is a paradoxical synthesis of tradition and innovation, and socially critical in its character and intent. While a number of influential critics have lost confidence in high modernisms and their critical capacity—always, of course, for the elite audiences of such modernist texts—they also seem to maintain some skepticism toward that which has presumably supplanted it, namely, postmodernism (Foster 1983). I be-

lieve Ellman and Feidelson were already implicitly and negatively identifying postmodernism when they spoke approvingly of modernism as
"more than a cultivation of immediacy, of free or fragmented awareness."
Sharing this skeptical stance toward the postmodern in thought, literature, the arts, and social practice, Marshall Berman, above all others,
seems intent on restoring modernism's muted critical voice (1982).

This is not the place to enter fully into this large debate, but let me
attempt a contribution by proposing that whatever the fate of modernism
in other circles, the nineteenth-century-derived, pure formal dancing at
El Cielo Azul is very akin to a modernist critical performance, by its very
"embodiment in current imagery of a situation always larger than the
present, and as such . . . also a containment of the resources and perils of
the present by rediscovery of a relevant past."

But as this modernism gets articulated round and round out there on
the floor, a new dancer enters—he doesn't pay admission, no bouncer
dares to stop him, all the women notice, a real "looker," and by his walk
you know he's a good dancer, probably the best there is. The women
know this. They know it well. And they tell his story.

Chapter Eight

The Devil Dances

"¡Es puro pedo do viejas!" (It's all women's crap!), Mendieta told me as we sat at the bar in the mostly empty dance hall on a Monday morning in the summer of 1979.[1] We were effectively alone as we each sipped a late morning beer save for an elderly janitor cleaning up after the Sunday *tardeada* (Sunday afternoon dance). Mendieta, part owner of this slightly decrepit dance hall, continued to talk: "Mira, Limón; el pedo pasó allá" (Look, Limón, the shit happened over there), motioning toward the far corner of the dance floor; "pero, pa' mi . . . que un bato le metio mano a la ruca" (but, if you ask me, some dude grabbed the broad's ass), telling me this with a yellowed toothy grin while grabbing a hammy handful of air. He paused and leaned toward me. "¡Pero eso que dicen del dia-blo . . . es puro pedo! ¡pedo de viejas!" (But all that stuff they're saying about the devil is just a lot of crap! Women's crap!). "Ye si quieres saber la verdad, anda ver a la ruca; se llama Sulema y es mesera en el restaurante San Miguel" (And, if you want to know the truth, go see the broad; her name is Sulema and she's a waitress at San Miguel's restaurant). "¿Quieres otra vironga, carnal?" (Would you like another beer, bro?), he asked, and without waiting for my answer, he half waddled to the other side of the bar and pulled another two out of the ice, dismissing my effort to pay with a wave and a flash of ring-laden hand. However, he was only part owner of El Cielito Lindo (The Beautiful Little Heaven) dance hall, so, from a well-loaded money clip extracted with some difficulty from a deep pocket of his yellow matching leisure-suit pants, he peeled off a couple of dollars and put them in the cash register, taking his change as well. One beer and a few pleasantries later, I was off to San Miguel's restaurant in search of Sulema and the devil, but not without Mendieta's parting shot, "No se te olvide, Limón, es puro pedo" (And don't forget . . . it's just a lot of crap).

Now, as I finished a delicious *fritada* (goat stew) at the restaurant,

168

Sulema, to whom I had briefly introduced myself already, was done with the lunch rush hour and had a little time to come over and talk to me during her own thirty-minute lunch break. While Señor San Miguel checked his Rolex and eyed us both suspiciously, she munched her tacos, sipped her *tamarindo* water and began to tell me about the devil.

As it turned out, according to her, Mendieta was mistaken. Nothing, she said, had actually happened to *her*. It was some other *muchacha* (some other girl), though she knew her. "Nos salimos de high school at mismo tiempo hace seis años" (We dropped out of high school about the same time, six years ago), she added, with only the slightest trace of embarrassment crossing her face, which looked older than the twenty-four to twenty-seven years of age I now calculated her to be. But how did she know about the incident? Well, while she wasn't involved in it, she had been at the dance at El Cielito Lindo the night it happened. "Tocaron Shorty y los Corvettes y andaba con mis amigas" (Shorty and the Corvettes played that night and I was with my girlfriend.) But did she actually *see* the devil, I asked, in a silly, too hurried, anthropologically adolescent fashion. "Pos, no, pero una de mis amigas lo vio" (Well, no, but one of my girlfriends saw him). "Yo nomas se lo que dice la gente" (I only know what people say).

I was about to ask her just what it was that people say, but our lunchtime had run out and Sr. San Miguel and dirty dishes waited. Could I see her again, and perhaps her girlfriends? I inquired. Long pause . . . and I knew. I had made another mistake. She didn't have to say it; her long hesitation said it all: Familia? (family) ¿Quien eres tu? y que quieres de deveras? (Who are you? and what do you really want?) and, the ultimate deep normative structure of greater Mexico, "¿Que va a decir la gente?" (What will people say?). I pulled back slightly in silence as we stood at the restaurant door. Perhaps sensing my discomfort, she quickly and expertly negotiated this tricky cultural terrain for both of us. Well, she said, she lived with her parents since she was single, so she wasn't so sure about my coming to their house, since they didn't *know* me, nor, we had established earlier, did they know my relatives well, although one of her brothers had known a friend, Tony, in high school before he was killed in Vietnam. There was the restaurant as a place to meet, like today, but there was only the lunch period like today . . . and then there was Sr. San Miguel. As for some other place . . . after hours . . . well, ¿que va a decir la gente? She didn't have to say it.

Then she had a bright thought. Could we meet Wednesday night at the Denny's Restaurant on the highway? She and her friends went there almost every Wednesday night for lemon meringue pie and coffee. Good pie, she assured me. I couldn't, at least not this Wednesday. I was on a preliminary field scouting trip, making initial contacts such as these and establishing a place to live for the summer. And, I had to return to Austin for the rest of the week, but I would be back on Friday, I explained to Sulema, and I would see her at the Denny's the following Wednesday.

She had another bright thought. There was a dance at El Cielito Lindo this Friday night, and if I liked dances maybe I could come and maybe she and her friends would be there and maybe we could talk. A la mejor. ¿Quien sabe? (Maybe. Who knows?) San Miguel glared and waited impatiently. His $2.50 an hour was being used up with no labor in return. Later, I would also discover that he, in his married state, periodically tried to get Sulema to go to bed with him. "I'll see you there," I said. As we parted, she told me with a smile, "¡Y no se preocupe de diablo, nomas se la aparece a las mujeres!" (And don't worry about the devil, he only appears to women).

No sooner was I resettling into south Texas, and there I was again, on my way to a dance. Did I like dances? Sulema had asked. Oh, I like dances alright, and I was pretty good, courtesy of *la* Wiggins, Domingo Peña, and *la* Beatrice. *La* Beatrice. And Beatrice? She had married an *indocumentado* and was living somewhere in southern California. Maybe she too would develop a taste for white wine like Rosemary. I had, at UCLA, after leaving San Antonio in 1978. But now, once again, it was Miller Time. Back to *el baile* (the dance), this time at El Cielito Lindo, this time with a Sulema and with the possibility of finding my devil.

That Friday night, after paying my $5.00 admission, being frisked for concealed weapons, and making my way past a huge bouncer who wholly engulfed the stool he was sitting on, I met Sulema and her friends, Ester, Blanca, and Dolores or Lola. I politely asked if I could join them and there were introductions all around, with Sulema prefacing the whole thing with a "this is the professor I told you about, es anthropologist y quiere saber del diablo" (he's an anthropologist and he wants to know about the devil). Ester, a hairdresser, wanted to know what that had to do with digging up old bones, since the local newspaper had run a story about a team of anthropologists who had a dig going near the town. On the other subdisciplinary hand, Lola, a salesperson at Woolworth's, wanted to know was it really true that anthropologists could teach monkeys to speak English like she had read in the *Time* magazine in the beauty shop. Blanca, who worked at the ticket window of the local theater, made a joke that such anthropologists should come to south Texas if they really wanted a challenge. Everyone laughed. I mumbled something about the different kinds of anthropologists and somehow explained my interest by saying in not too convincing fashion then that cultural anthropology is something like history.

Throughout the evening we talked when Los Cadetes de Linares (The Cadets from Linares) weren't playing a particularly loud polka or between their sets. We drank a little; me, to keep a clear head; they, perhaps as well, and as a matter of social discretion. One would inevitably run into cousins. I had beer while they shared one purse-sized pint bottle of Bacardi rum (bought for them by Blanca's older brother, just recently released from prison). They passed the bottle around either under or flat across the table and carefully poured tiny amounts into mostly Coca-Cola and ice-filled cups. With a small penknife, Ester cut up slices of Mexican lemons since the establishment did not provide any with their setups. (This also led to the usual conventional personal joke about not cutting up Limón.)

Finally, we danced. And, once again, as we swung around the floor, I had the sharp sense of the expressive well-armed truce, a sense that the guys in San Antoñio had substantially verified and which would acquire additional substantiation from the men I would meet in Limonada.

> Simón, compa. Tienes que moverte de aquellas y no pegarle a nadie.
> Sino se vuelve puro pedo. (Sure buddy, you've got to move nicely
> and not hit anybody. Otherwise everything goes to shit.)

Moving *de aquellas* (well, nicely, good) meant the artful execution of movement in and amongst other couples while also turning, and at moments of high artistry, swinging one's partner in "fancy" turns, periodically throughout the dance sequence. *Se avientan* (they go all out, they're great), it would be said of such couples. Yet within this underworld, a certain paradox was evident: such artfulness was produced by people with relatively sullen faces, who avoided eye contact, engaged in minimal conversation, who primarily drank and danced, the latter with great finesse and energy.

Throughout the evening I danced with each of the women in turn. By dancing with each of them and moving myself around the table each time we returned from the floor, I tried to solve a probable cultural problem. I wanted other men to feel quite free to come up to ask any of them to dance, the ostensible reason everyone was here. However, I suspect I produced another possible cultural problem for myself. After all, I was just one guy dancing with four women. I could just hear the men, particuarly the large group of unaccompanied men gathered around the bar, saying, "O es muy chingón, o es joto." (Either he's a big fucker or he's a fag), that dark fate that haunts so many men at the edge of their masculine consciousness. In terms of local principles of homosexuality I'm sure my slight build, buttoned down shirt, and glasses didn't help. (I was reminded of the times when I visit my parents and go out to drink and shoot pool with a two-hundred-pound working-class friend. "Damn it," he says after a few beers, "why don't you get some fucking contact lenses?") At any rate, I negotiated myself past this possible dark fate throughout the night with only occasional slightly amused glances, and, perhaps, paradoxically, with Mendieta's unsolicited help. He was serving behind the crowded bar resplendent in another—this time, light blue— leisure. The bar scene differed little from El Cielo Azul. As I came up to get another beer and a second setup for the women, he gestured "hello," with outstretched hands, rolled his eyes and headed toward the women, and, in front of all the men, made an obscene gesture with his hand suggesting sexual intercourse.

But amidst drink, dance, and talk, I was after the devil, and he indeed appeared, not in any visible dramatic form, but as the principle figure in a collective narrative produced by the women that night when I asked about him, and reproduced in varying versions throughout my summer. Amidst moments of intense concentration, nervous laughter, and occasional glances toward the dance floor, this is how I came to know the devil. I offer it as a general dialogue of voices, including my own.

Dice la gente (the people say) that sometimes at night when a Mexican-American dance is in full swing in southern Texas, as so many are, especially on weekend nights; as couples glide in almost choreographed fashion counterclockwise around the floor to the insistent, infectious rhythm of *conjunto* polka music; as men, women, and music and not small amounts of liquor all blend in heightened erotic consciousness, it is then that the devil may appear.

He comes in the form of a well-dressed, quite handsome man. "Estaba bien cute" (He was real cute), says Blanca, but hastens to add that she didn't really see him, this is what she was told by a female cousin. The devil is tall and strong in appearance. "Con shoulders asi" (with shoulders like this), demonstrates Ester with outstretched fingers. Sulema cannot resist. "¿Estas segura que nomas los shoulders?" Laughter. Embarrassed looks and glances. It's a few moments before we can continue and they can look at me again without laughing. What does he look like? How is he dressed? I ask. "¡Muy elegante, con suit y todo!" (Very elegant with a suit and everything). "Es güero, asi como Robert Redford" (He's blond, like Robert Redford). I think of Robert Redford, as I take note of the young Mexican-American men around me, at best, one or two in inexpensive suits, most with thick dark hair and shirts open to mid-chest or lower revealing on some the Virgin or Guadalupe resting on an Indian bare, brown skin.

The narrative stops, perhaps because I have been looking away. So what else happens? I finally ask. Is that it? A handsome guy appears? Oh no, then comes the good part, Ester continues. They say that after he came in right over there, motioning to the entrance at El Cielito Lindo, a girl sitting with her friends spotted him and she really wanted to dance with him. Blanca interrupts. "Well, everyone does!" "I know," Ester replies, "pero esta la hace ojos" (This one makes eyes at him). I ask them to slow down as I try to jot down at least the main points of the story and their reactions. So, Ester continues, she makes eyes at him and he comes over to ask her to dance. In parody and with a laugh, Lola flicks her own heavily made-up eyelids quickly up and down. So he asks he, y salen a bailar (and they go out to dance). At this point Sulema covers her eyes. Blanca whispers, "this is the good part, this is the good part," and gets a *Shhh!* from Lola.

Up on the bandstand, Los Cadetes de Linares are coming back from their break, and around us men, very occasionally a woman, walk by carrying beers and setups to their tables. As in El Cielo Azul, the few all-female groups like the one I am with will try to get a male friend or relative to bring them beer and setups to avoid going up to the male-crowded bar. And so, Ester continues, as they're dancing, "la girl le mira los feet" (the feet of a chicken). "Goat! goat!" Sulema says loudly trying to correct her. Clearly exasperated, Ester sharply replies, "¡Chingado, lo que sea!" (Goddammit, whatever!) and apologizes for using a bad word. On my small pad, I scribble as fast as I can, missing a lot but concentrating on the narrators. Ester continues: "y cuando le vio los feet, la girl grito" (And when she saw his feet, the girl screamed). "And then she faints right there on the floor," Sulema quickly adds and gets a dirty look from Ester for her unsolicited contribution. "And then she fainted, Mr. Limón," continues Ester (who can't seem to call me José), and he ran to that corner over there and disappeared in a puff of smoke! Lola adds a denouncement. "My brother says that he was in that corner that night but he only heard the scream, he didn't see smoke or nothing. Quien sabe?" A puzzle remains. I say to them: Sulema told me that one of you did see the devil. Which one was it? "¡Que liar, Sulema!" Blanca explains. You told us that

you saw him when you were going to the ladies room. Sulema looks embarrassed. In the final analysis, however, the issue is not really that important, and I decide to leave it alone, as well as the true identity of the
woman who encountered the devil on the dance floor.

    What is important is that a recurrent belief exists in the form of an
emergent collective narrative; that it exists for these women and, to
judge from other, less systematic data, for women like these throughout
south Texas, including San Antonio and the extensions of Texas everywhere, for the devil has also been reported in the agricultural labor
camps of California and Wisconsin. In another fashion it exists for men
as well, as I will show in a moment, but first let me say a bit more about
these women and their interpretive images of the devil as I continued to
engage them in later conversations principally over too many lemon meringue pies at Denny's. What is the devil all about; what does it mean, if
anything, for you? Why do you think such an unusual thing happens?
Why does the devil appear to women like yourselves at dances? Before
answering me directly, they first summarize what *la gente dice* (people
say), which really turns out to be synonymous with what the elders say,
as I will show in a moment. However, in more extended conversation, it
turns out that Sulema, Ester, Blanca, and Lola have their own distinctive consensus perception of this figure and its relation to their lives.
Ester: "I don't know . . . I kind of like him!" Why? (I feign surprise.)
He's a devil isn't he? Si, pero, he's so *different!* ("Different from what?"
I think to myself. Do I need to really ask, or having met Mendieta is the
answer clear?) Esta bien chulo (He's so cute, attractive), Ester continues. Lola adds, "I once met a guy like that in Houston." What do you
think he would be like, I mean, as a person? I ask. "Te apuesto que es
bien suave" (I bet he's real kind, soft, sweet, suave). But he's a devil! I
insist in mock argument. What about the goat's feet? "Ay, who cares?"
says Sulema. And with a gesture of putting shoes on a little child, Blanca
adds, with a nice laugh, "¡Nomas le pones zapatitos!" (You just need to
put little shoes on him!).

    But, as I say, there are other perceptions of the devil in this community.
Let me briefly summarize two others. For example, there are the elderly,
both male and female. The devil, they say, comes because today things are
out of hand. Girls go out to dances by themselves. En nuestro tiempo, no
se via eso (In our time, you didn't see that). There is too much drinking.
Outside the dances and even inside, you see *marijuanos* (marijuana smok-
ers). A seventy-year-old man tells me "La ultima vez qaue fue, tuve que ir

al escusado, y allí estaban los cabrones fumando mugrero" (The last time I went to a dance, I went to a restroom and there were the bastards smoking trash). And the music is so loud, says another, con todos esos aparatos (With all those electronic things.) And, for all this, they charge so much! "¡Se imagina Ud. Señor Limón, *Diez dolares!* ¡Ni que fueranos ricos!" (Can you imagine Mr. Limón, ten dollars! As if we were rich!). Ya no son como las bailes de antes (They are not like dances used to be [in our time]). Por eso viene el diablo (That's why the devil comes).

I carried my same questions to another social scene; the daily afternoon, all male, quiet slow drinking scene at the bar at Mendieta's place. Here is another view more or less shared by the married and the single men who drink there. Like Mendieta, they think of the story as women's noise, chatter, crap, and, they claim, they do not go around telling the story, although they've heard it from women. Nonetheless, what do they think the devil is all about?

"Los viejas quierien *batos* asi, tu sabes, batos gabachos" (Broads want guys like that, you know, like Anglos). It is the married guys at the bar who offer a more extended analysis. "Women," you know, "always want more of everything. They're never satisfied. It's like my wife," one tells me, "Comprame esto, comprame el otro" (Buy me this, buy me that). Se vuelven locas con las credit cards (They go crazy with the credit cards). Chinge, chinge, con que vamos al mall, vamos al mall" (Nag, nag, let's go to the mall, let's go to the mall), says another.

I don't quite see the connection. What does that have to do with the devil? It's like the church says, like Eve, tells another one. ¡Queria la pinche manzana! (She wanted the damn apple!). So this rich *white* guy, real high society, appears and he tempts them but he disappears pa' que aprendar que no pueden tener todo (so they can learn that they can't have everything). But they think they can or they want to, *por eso se imaginan todo este pedo* (So that is why they imagine all that shit).

But why at the dance? I wonder out loud to them. Why does this rich white devil choose the dance? Why do the women see him there and not some other place? After a hearty belch, a city sanitation worker exclaims: "¡Porque aqui nosotros mandamos! ¡Chinga que si!" (Because here, we rule! Goddam right!). Here (at the dance) we (*mexicanos*) rule or predominate, is what this man means at one level. But how is the dance a scene of *mexicano* predomination? I pursue him on this at Mendieta's linoleum-top bar as we all munch deep-fried *tripitas* (chopped intestines) for *botana* (hors d'oeuvres). Others join the conversation.

¡Aquí no entran gringos!
(Gringos don't [can't] come in here!)

¡Vale mas que no!
(They better not!)

Pero los viejas quieren que entren. ¿Me entiendes?
(But the broads want them to come in. Do you know
what I mean?) Por eso hacen ese pedo del diablo.
(That's why they make up that crap about the devil.)

¡Y hasta eso, los gringos no saben bailar!
(What's more, gringos can't dance!)

To the author of this last comment, a postal employee, I point out that the
devil, who looks gringo like Robert Redford, is reputed to be a great
dancer. He comes right back with devil logic.

Si, pero para el diablo todo es posible.
(Yes, but for the devil everything is possible.)

Asi son los gringos; para
ellos todo es posible.
(That's the way gringos
are; for them, everything
is possible.)

Menos el baile. Un gringo
entra aquí nomas en forma
de diablo. (Except for
the dance. A gringo can
come in here only in the
form of a devil.)

¡Ni Willy lo puedo parar!
¿Verdad, Willy? (Not even
Willy [the bouncer] can
stop him? Right Willy?)

Willy, who is leaning his three hundred pounds on the bar drinking beers
in a few swallows, firmly cups his hand over his crotch and bellows: "¡Es
todo lo que necesito pa' un pinche diablo!" (This is all I need for a damn
devil). Another man gives a *grito* and orders another round. Meanwhile,
outside, in the beer-can-littered area behind El Cielito Lindo, Mendieta
has started a *carne asada*. Lured by the fragrance of *fajitas*, the comrade-
ship of *carnales*, and the consequential carnivalesque, we all drift
outside—all of us—for this is part of my fieldwork, is it not? A few beers

later I can almost see him there just outside the circle, observing but not joining us, leering at us, a well-dressed *bato,* "bien cute." The *menudo* tastes particularly good this morning at San Miguel's restaurant. After some pretty heavy drinking last night at Mendieta's (less observation, more participation), I've stopped in for the necessary *menudo* but also to say goodbye to Sulema. San Miguel went across the street to the bank to make a deposit so we have a little more time to sit and talk as I slurp my broth. Sulema nonetheless keeps her eye on the bank through the window.

I tell her about last night at Mendieta's, and she confesses that she and *las girls* have been worried about me. I'm not like the other men, she says. The girls were afraid I'd get hurt or that people at the university might find out that I was hanging around with people like that and I might lose my job. I'm sure professors don't drink, she says . . . . Those aren't places for a man like me, she says. What's a man like me, I ask? You're different, she replies. Like the devil? I ask. She giggles and says nothing, but I strongly suspect what she's thinking: the devil is *handsome* and he can *really* dance. Did I find out what I wanted to know? About the devil? Well, yes, I think so, I tell her. I'll be more certain when I return to Austin and think about it. I really shouldn't write about things like the devil, she tells me, even though she personally likes him. What if he brings bad luck to your writing? I should write about the nice things about the people in this area, she advises, like the George Washington Celebration in Laredo very close to Limonada. You should come to it, she says. There will be lots of beautiful girls there, she tells me, "your type, con college y todo" (with college and everything). It'll be in February and maybe I should come, she repeats. Well, I'll think about it, I tell her. Right now, with my head and notebook full of devils and the reexperienced poverty of the *mexicano* lower class, such an elite celebration with its parade and debutante balls is of very little interest to me, although frankly, fantasizing about the "y todo" part helps my slight headache.

San Miguel has not come back, so she walks me to my car and says goodbye and tells me to "juegate la fria" (play it cool). Funny thing to say, I think, as I drive out and note the 99 degree reading at 10 A.M. on the time-and-temperature sign at the bank. A few minutes later I'm on IH-35 North. Out of Limonada. In the back seat in a cooler, I'm carrying a free six-pack on ice, courtesy of Mendieta. It's a long drive to Austin, where I start teaching and writing this fall. Maybe I'll stop in San Antoñio. Downtown. Check out El Esquire. Not far from the Alamo. Far from Alamo Heights. Later, *tripitas* at Mario's Restaurant. I wonder what Rosemary is doing? Spend the night. I look over to the passenger seat—for a moment I think I see him sitting there. Funny. He doesn't look at all like Robert Redford. More like Gregorio Cortez? "Not too dark and not too fair, not too thin and not too fat, not too short and not too tall, and he looked just a little bit like me." Except for the feet. He grins: "Let's go, bro!"

The devil comes in many forms. He came to my precursors in various guises and now he comes to me chiefly on the lips of women—*mexicana* working-class women—who speak his story in southern Texas in the 1970s. It is not a new tale; it has been uttered before in other times and places,[2] yet it is new in another sense. In the 1970s, it seems to be spoken by women with greater frequency, with keener intensity. It seems to be the devil's special time.[3]

By the late seventies and early eighties, the devil was moving around Mexican America, often crossing borders, ignoring them as does postmodernity, the cultural logic of late capitalism. Another scholar, María Herrera-Sobek, found him in Tijuana, across from southern California where this cultural logic looms largest (1988). The collective narratives she presents vary only somewhat from the general narrative pattern I've suggested, and her secondary informants are all men, although they appear to be repeating stories originally uttered by women. To make interpretive sense of the dancing devil—in Tijuana he prefers discotheques— Herrera-Sobek rises to a level of interpretation that bypasses the situated condition of her informants in this ultimate site of the cultural logic of late capitalism, especially the situated condition of Tijuana's young working-class women. For Herrera-Sobek, the materiality of this cultural practice and its social conditions seems to count for little; the devil's origin lies elsewhere. The devil who dances with these women and is spoken on their lips is to be understood in the realm of pure religious value. His story "articulates ideas about sin, guilt, defilement and punishment into a cohesive structure we are capable of understanding," since "ever since humans conceived the universe in terms of opposed pairs . . . they have been forced to confront the problem of evil, its purpose and origin" (1988:155).

Another colleague also met the devil, also in southern Texas as I did. Here it is not religiosity but "culture" that dominates Glazer's analysis of his collected texts, with little by way of ethnographic context (1984). It is "culture" analytically deployed in a reified static manner, as Joseph Sommers once critically noted of Chicano "cultural" readings which take culture "as the central determinant of the [Chicano] people's experience," subordinating or wholly erasing "the idea that culture might be bound up with the social condition of class, as well as the view that cultural forms evolve as a response to the specifics of the historical process" (1977:58). Glazer posits a singular, wholly dominant patriarchal culture in south Texas, one in which there are no openings, breaks, or contested sites. So deep and pervasive is this dominance, by his reading, that even the dancing devil legend though told by women, is wholly in the service of patriarchy. Finding no possible resistive interest in their own utterances, Glazer makes such women narratively complicit in their own domination. Viewed in conventional and Christian terms as a symbol of singular evil, the handsome, sharp dancing devil appears "to keep rebel spirits in tow . . . to punish behavior which is viewed as being deviant [that is, attending dances] and not conforming with social norms" (1984:125–26). And, to be sure, as I will suggest later, some people in south Texas view the devil in these conventional functionalist terms, but not all, and not the very women who regularly utter these stories.

Herrera-Sobek's religiosity and Glazer's culturalism put us at some unsatisfying interpretive distance from the materiality of late-capitalist postmodernity at the U.S.-Mexico border. Even less satisfying is their interpretive removal of the legend from the expressive repertoire and cultural practice of these women of the border into the service of patriarchy and religion.

If the reasons were not cultural, or religious, why did the devil dance with such intensity in southern Texas in the 1970s? Why does he seem to come more readily to the lips of women, although others note his presence as well? Informed by other colleagues more attentive to the material and gender locus of such devils, I take his intense presence in southern Texas and later in all of Mexican America as a register of the society's initial and shocking encounter with the cultural logic of late capitalism. Like some of my folks, the devil is a migrant over space and time. In a nondancing yet expressive stance, he has been seen in other parts of the greater Latin American world. Among the peasants of Bolivia and Colombia, also in the 1970s, he appears in a more traditional expressive idiom as a critique of advanced capitalism and the imposition of wage labor (Taussig 1980). And, closer in time and gender, Ecuadorian peasants, particularly women, imagine him as their critical response to a broader form of advanced capitalist class domination (Crain 1991). But in southern Texas at the edge of late capitalism, the well-dressed, good-looking, sometimes blond figure dances in multiple signification in the dance halls spawned by the collision of tradition and postmodernity. In this respect he is less a folk figure than in South America and more, yet again, like the dancing, a modernist figure indebted to the past but open and available as flexible and critical tool for reading and critically evaluating a threatening present.

In what follows I want to suggest that this intensified appearance at this historical juncture may have signaled a multiple and critical reaction to an increasing saturation from the "outside" by an intensifying culture of post-modernity. But why then does the devil not appear just anywhere, let us say, in your backyard in the dead of night? I would suggest that this saturation eventually threatened the one major area of critical distance and difference—the dancing body politic as I have described it in the previous chapter. As more drugs, alcohol, opportunistic sexuality, and violence begin to mark the dance scene as a site of cultural contradiction, the devil also enters the dance to mark this contradiction. And it is contradiction, for there is no singular culture here as the devil answers to the varying needs, especially the varying gender needs, of my folks under this new form of warfare.

To make specific interpretive sense of this narrative, I turn to the theo-retical work of Fredric Jameson, even as I attempt a critical revision of that theoretical framework.

For Jameson the largest critical project is to discover how any given symbolic act embedded in capitalism, particularly any given narrative— *Heart of Darkness, Light in August,* or the devil at the dance—becomes a part of what he, and I agree with him, takes to be the master narrative of world history. Such narratives

> can recover their original urgency for us only if they are retold
> within the unity of a single great collective story; only if, in however
> disguised and symbolic a form, they are seen as sharing a single fun-
> damental theme—for Marxism, the collective struggle to wrest a
> realm of Freedom from a realm of Necessity; but only if they are
> grasped as vital episodes in a single vast, unfinished plot. (1981:19)

"It is," he continues, "in detecting the traces of that uninterrupted narra-tive, in restoring to the surface of the text the repressed and buried reality of this fundamental history, that the doctrine of a political unconscious finds its function and necessity" (1981:20).

For Jameson each narrative (and for that matter any symbolic produc-tion) is open to an analysis which will restore its "repressed and buried reality," its "traces," in a way that brings out its relationship of meaning with the master narrative. To this analytical end he proposes a threefold model of analysis which demonstrates a narrative's meaning in increas-ingly wider social contexts (1981:75). However, Jameson's formulation appears to have a certain bias toward the last two levels of interpretation, those which seem to encompass a larger measure of social reality and history.

I choose to begin with Jameson's third and widest, ultimate horizon of reading, where he invokes the Marxist concept of modes of production. A narrative read at this wider horizon may express, though in a deeply disguised and quite indirect way, the conflict between wholly different cultural periods or modes of production; a narrative may evidence "that moment in which the coexistence of various modes of production becomes visibly antagonistic, then contradiction moving the very center of political, social and historic life" (1981:95). The narrative is now to be read as "a field of force in which the dynamics of sign systems of several distinct modes of production can be registered and apprehended" (1981:98). At this level this registering and apprehension of conflict between different modes of production do not occur through a reading of the symbolic "contents" of the narrative to the same degree as is the case at the other two levels. At the third horizon, he argues, *form* becomes the focus of the interpretive move. We want to concern ourselves with the way the ideology associated with a particular mode of production is captured not in context but in form; we are concerned with what Jameson calls the "ideology of form" (1981:99).

Let me suggest that it is the elders who tend to read the devil in this manner. For while they, like others, depart from the contents of the narrative to offer their reading, it is only they who seem to be concerned with form, though not with form in any conventional sense but rather with social form, with the form of society, with their folk sense of the modes of production. The narrative for them signifies something more historically embracing, namely, the perceived long-term changes in their lives as they have undergone conflict and change in what they perceive from a folk perspective as shifts and overlaps in the modes of production. To speak of *los tiempos de antes* is to invent a tradition, for in the historical lives of the elders they, in fact, experienced a more virulent and intense race and class domination both in Mexico and in Texas: strict codes of racial segregation, lynchings, hurrying to step off the sidewalk when an Anglo approached, picking cotton at dirt wages from sunup to sundown, unchecked diseases treated only by *curanderos* because no Anglo doctor would accept Mexican patients. These were the conditions experienced by these elders. Yet as they speak of the past, they invent a tradition, for amidst intense domination they developed a moral economy based on a number of moral principles and an etiquette, both of which were in evident display at the dances they remember. For all its hardship *era bonita la vida* (life was lovely), and the dance is always used as a signifier of this illustration. This tradition of moral economy associated with an orthodox stage of agriculture capitalism is brought to bear on the present moment of advanced capitalism, in which domination continues in covert forms *and* in which the critical moral economy is, in the eyes of the elders, rejected by the young, who have given way to the psychological penetration of late capitalism. "Estos huercos cabrones," says an old man, "toman lo peor de los gringos" (These brats, they take the worst of the gringos).

A second interpretive horizon, which Jameson calls the "social," becomes operative "only at the moment in which the organizing categories of analysis become those of social class," more particularly the antagonistic and active relationships between "a dominant and a laboring class" whose ideologies and symbolic acts are also involved in an active, dialectical, and antagonistic relationship (1981:83).

In this kind of class-based analysis "the individual utterance or text is grasped as a symbolic move in an essentially polemic and strategic ideological confrontation between classes." It is, however, an uneven symbolic confrontation from the perspective of global power. Because of the class nature and authority of writing, Jameson implies (echoing Foucault and Benjamin) that "the cultural monuments and masterworks that have survived tend necessarily to perpetuate only a single voice in this class dialogue, the voice of a hegemonic class." What is required at this level of analysis is the interpretive reconstruction of the voice of the dominated, "a voice for the most part stifled and reduced to silence, marginalized, its own utterances scattered to the winds, or reappropriated in their turn by hegemonic culture" (1981:85). At this interesting juncture in his exposition Jameson subconsciously recognizes the power of what so many of us call *folklore*, although he cannot name it, an interesting historical repression in itself. This is "framework," he tells us,

> in which the reconstruction of so-called popular cultures must properly take place—most notably, from the fragments of essentially peasant cultures: folksongs, fairy tales, popular festivals, occult or oppositional systems of belief such as magic and witchcraft; . . . only an ultimate rewriting of these utterances in these terms of their essentially polemic and subversive strategies restores them to their proper place in the dialogic system of social class. (1981:85–86)

At this level symbolic acts, particularly folkloric symbolic acts, may be understood as expressive diagnostic instruments for making evident the social forces that dominate and for critiquing them, much as the men do in the bar setting. By experiencing only the everyday domination of race and class but not of gender, the men have the privilege, as it were, of interpreting the devil narrative in terms of race and class relations; thus their resentful, angry focus on the well-dressed man and/or "Anglo" who dares enter the dance hall, that most intense, protected scene of *mexicano* life.

In this male construction we are reminded of that other well-known literary figuration of the devil also set in this general part of Texas. I refer to Aristeo Brito's novel *The Devil in Texas* (1990), which spans generations of a Mexican-American community in the Upper Rio Grande valley town of Presidio. A wealthy Anglo landowner, Ben Lynch, oppresses this community. The figure of the devil is omnipresent in the community and in the novel, leading the book's best critic to comment: "The devil is Ben, is Texas, is American capitalism, all creating a real and present hell in this valley" (Alarcón 1980:43) (translation mine). Yet, this antagonist in the race and class war, to the even greater resentment of these men in Limonada, enters the dance, draws the admiration of "their" women and evokes their desire.

It is a form of desire, palpably experienced, that connects Sulema, Blanca, Lola, and Ester to their story. It is a desire conditioned by their class but certainly more by their gender experience, a historical experience that the narrative addresses in a manner that approximates Jameson's first level of interpretive narration, where the narrative symbolic act registers the literal events of lived experience and is understood as such, including most fundamentally and literally for these women their sheer presence at the dance. For, in the most literal of terms, they tell me they are there to meet a special kind of man, although as with Beatrice and her friends in El Cielo Azul in San Antoñio, the dance also affords temporary escape from the tedium of female working-class labor, small cramped houses, and complaining parents who paradoxically nag them with a constant "¿Cuanda te casas?" (When are you going to get married?).

But they live in a world of Mendietas, a world where someone special is rarely to be found. When a marriage does occur, there is risk that it will be, indeed, to a version of Mendieta after such a woman settles for what is available in her class-constrained world. She may, in fact, go *against* the advice of the Mexican women's proverb "Es mejor vestir santos, que desvestir borrachos" (It is better to dress saints than to undress drunks). And while she searches, she dances, and while she dances with the Mendietas of her world who come to her table, her version of the war continues, over her body out there on the floor.

Into this void of hope unfulfilled, walks the devil—good-looking, good dancer, good money (you can tell by his clothes)—and, in this version of Jameson's first horizon of reading, the women produce and read a text not as a moral conflict of modes of production, not as an allegory of race and class forces, but as a text with a very proximate relationship to the Real of their lived historical experience, though now rewritten symbolically. For it is important to stress that, read at this level, the text does not merely reproduce the Real though it stays in an "active relationship" with it, drawing the elements of the Real—the devil *as dancer*—"into its own texture," carrying "the Real within itself as its own intrinsic or immanent subtext," though not a merely reflected, inert reality. While working closely with the plentitude of the Real of gender and reading it in this fashion and not in abstractions, the text, even at this level, is symbolic action, not direct "reflection," and

> symbolic action . . . is a way of doing something to the world, to
> that degree that what we are calling "world" must inhere within it,
> as the content it has to take up into itself in order to submit it to the
> transformations of form. (Jameson 1981:81)

The evident Real of the dance and dancer in their night lives is transformed by the formal accretions of poetic language—physical attractiveness, smoothness in dancing, "suave" personality—as the symbolic act generates and produces "its own context in the same moment of emergence in which it steps back from it, taking its measure with a view towards its own projects of transformation" (1981:81). These active artisans of language, these *fuereña* makers and critics of literature, working with the palpable Real materials of their gender existence, take and transform the Real so "that the literary work or cultural object, as though for the first time, brings into being that very situation to which it is, at one and the same time, a reaction" (1981:82), a creative critical reaction, I would add. Through this "literal" recording of their immediate historical experience, though poetically and formally transformed, these *fuereñas* give critical voice to their aspirations beyond a sexist and labor oppressive world not of their own making, even as that very world constrains the very form and content of those narrative aspirations. But there is more, and it takes us into the extratextual features of this narrative performance and ultimately offers insight into another dimension of their critique. This devil—who is such a moral threat to the elders, such a race and class threat to Brito's fictive community and these men, a source of resentment and jealousy—

appears to be a sexually charged site of admiration, delight, and playfulness for these women.

Like Milton's Satan, this devil, in Alicia Ostriker's words, "is fascinating and complex—passionate, intelligent eloquent, capable of introspection, responsive to experience and situations, sexually attractive . . . and arousable," unlike Milton's God (and many of these men) who is "tyrannical and dull . . . disagreeable, egocentric, legalistic and self-justifying" (1987:209). What others make symbolically fearful in their version of the continuing war is for Blanca, Sulema, Ester, and Lola an ally, a potent imaginative playful ally generated in narrative performance. These women have created their version of a Bakhtinian universe of the carnivalesque, excluded as they are from other versions. In a sense it is also a more democratic universe, for one man is admitted but only on their transforming creative narrative terms, terms that reject the oppressive totality of the Real even as they directly confront it.

In setting out these multiple readings and glossing them in Jameson's Marxist terms—as horizons of reading, all occasioned, in the final analysis, by capitalist race domination—I have tried to suggest how it is that folklore can, in its most disguised and symbolic form, speak critically to such domination.

Folklore, however, and the social nature of the folkloric performance also afford us an opportunity to critically revise Jameson's theory. I have already suggested how his levels and concentric circles tend to delegitimize the immediate and concrete and, therefore, in this case, the intense lived experience of women in favor of the more abstract "social." However, let me point to another problem. Even as Jameson takes note of the power of folklore, he misses the folk and their interpretive power. For Jameson, as with so many literary critics (though not all), there is always the assumption of the ideal *individual* reader/critic, he or she who consciously or unconsciously reads and registers at the three levels of analysis. There is in such a model the hegemonic internalization of individualism as the proper stance for all reading. In contrast, we have the shared, collective model I have proposed here, where a community takes multiple readings of the same text and in doing so produces and enhances their collectivity even while allowing their different perspectives.

I have tried to lend emphasis to the lives and perspective of a group of single, working-class women in Limonada, south Texas. It is they, it seems to me, who experience the ongong war with late-capitalist postmodernity in its most intense form, where race, class, and gender come together in a single sharp point. Their narrative dance with the devil is their elaborated critique, a critique that is symbolic while anchored in the Real, a critique establishing their critical difference. This same emphasis on women's difference continues in the next and final stanza of this book, even as we expand our sense of the critical folklore repertoire at war in southern Texas.

Chapter Nine

Culture and Bedevilment

It seems so long ago, but I clearly recall a time in my childhood—I was nine—when I accompanied a playmate and his family to the pilgrimage site of Don Pedrito Jaramillo just south of Corpus Christi. It was 1954 and my playmate's older brother, age nineteen, had just returned to south Texas from service as an infantryman in General Walker's army in Korea and a subsequent stay in a stateside military recovery hospital. At night, in the semidarkness of the housing project courtyards he had left at seventeen, we boys sat around this teenager turned soft-spoken man, and were awed by his halting accounts of the shelling; of the shrapnel still in his body; of the Chinese soldier who ran him through with a bayonet as he stared up from the ground. He had survived that war to return to another, and, from his mother's point of view, his survival and return to native ground had everything to do with his photograph and her supplication to Don Pedrito. Now, in 1954, in two full cars, his family and I drove down to the site to retrieve the picture and to have her pray her thanks to Don Pedrito, this key resource in the continuing war, past and present.

J. Frank Dobie knew of him. Although he offers no extended commentary, he does note that sometime at the turn of the century, one of his Mexican *vaquero* mentors, Antonio de la Fuente, had "contracted a cough that no home remedy could cure" and "rode three days to consult Don Pedrito de Jaramillo famous among all the Mexicans of Southwest Texas as a medicine man" (1980b:viii).

John Gregory Bourke also thought him famous and left us a more extended ethnographic commentary.

> There is a native quack doctor calling himself "San Pablo" and claiming to be in some way under the guidance and control of the Apostle, who now lives near the village of Los Olmos, Cameron County, Texas and has gained a great ascendency over the minds of his dupes. He will prescribe for all sorts and conditions of men, but

places no value upon his services, trusting to the gratitude of those whom he frees from physical and mental ills. (1894b:608)

Even as he misidentifies Don Pedrito and maligns him, Captain Bourke manages to grasp some truth. Notwithstanding his racism and his ongoing literal war with Mexican-Americans, I find Bourke's figurations— "quack," "dupes"—an odd lapse even for this evolutionary anthropologist. It is as if the "normal" delegitimizing language of evolutionary discourse—"primitive," "superstitious"—will not do in this instance; as if Jaramillo as a cultural figure requires a more popular and potent negating language precisely because the captain unconsciously perhaps recognizes this figure's potency. The rest of the text reveals such grudging recognition of this "quack's" social significance: he has gained "a great ascendency"; he prescribes for "all sorts and conditions of men"; he "places no value upon his services, trusting to the gratitude of those whom he frees from physical and mental ills."

The latter is a set of descriptive characteristics carried over into the work of Ruth Dodson, a Dobie colleague born in 1876 and raised on a ranch in south Texas near Jaramillo's pilgrimage site. In a history of this folk healer's career published in 1951, she provides mostly descriptive matter but also a social assessment consistent with Bourke's and Dobie's. From her we learn that Jaramillo was born near Guadalajara, Mexico, in 1829 and that he came to south Texas in 1881 at the age of fifty-two, having already identified himself as a folk healer in a traditional way.

> Don Pedrito related that when he was a poor laborer in Mexico (some say he was a shepherd), working for half a bushel of corn and the equivalent of five dollars a month, he suffered an affliction of the nose . . . One night he said, he was suffering so much that he went out in the woods to a pool of water. He lay down and buried himself in the mud at the edge. This relieved him. He stayed there treating himself with the mud. At the end of three days he was well; but his nose remained disfigured. (This disfiguration of the nose is always associated with the gift of healing that is credited to Don Pedrito). He returned to his house and lay down and slept. After a while a voice awakened him and told him that he had received from God the gift of healing. (1951:12–13)

After arriving in south Texas in 1881, Jaramillo immediately established his medical practice on a small ranch, then still owned by a Mexican family, called Los Olmos after a small elm-bordered creek that ran through it. From this site in the center of south Texas, his medical influence gradually grew from healing the local ranch Mexicans such as Dobie's Antoñio de la Fuente to a more regional presence as the Mexicans from greater south Texas, including those from Laredo, San Antoñio, Corpus Christi, and the Lower Rio Grande Valley, came to see him. Soon he also began to travel to these sites as well on extended medical visitations, and he began to receive mail asking for medical advice. At times, when he was away on such trips as many as five hundred people would be awaiting his return, camped out along the banks of Los Olmos Creek. Soon his fame took on international proportions as people from Mexico also began to come to him for help, although his major clientele were the poverty-stricken Mexicans masses of south Texas (Dodson 1951:19). Dodson offers this assessment consistent with Bourke's and at the same time a radically different cultural poetics.

> From 1881 until his death in 1907 and even thereafter, . . . there never has been another so honored and appreciated among the Mexican people of South Texas as this *curandero*, this folk healer, Pedro Jaramillo. It can also be said that no one else in this part of the country, of whatever nationality, religion, economic or social standing, had done through a lifetime, as much to try to relieve human suffering as this man did through the twenty-five years that he lived in South Texas. He gave to his work the days of his life and the many thousands of dollars presented him by those who felt that they had been helped through him. (1951:16)

Dodson's work provides a historical descriptive basis for the next major ethnographic assessment of Jaramillo. I refer to the work of Octavio Romano (1964; 1965), a Mexico City native who emigrated to the United States, fought in World War II, became an anthropologist (Ph.D. Berkeley) and a major figure in the Chicano intellectual political movement of the late sixties.

Romano draws extensively on Dodson's descriptive history while adding considerable data of his own. To the sense we already have of the healer, we now add something of his healing practices. While spiritualism and the use of herbal medicine are practitioner traits often attributed to Mexican-American folk healers, Don Pedrito had a distinctive technique and was known

> primarily for his rapid, almost immediate, prescriptions, his common recommendations for water as a cure (both internally and in baths), and for periodic departures in which he would prescribe black coffee without sugar, a nip of whiskey, or canned tomatoes. But the drink-

ing water and the recommended water therapy were his trademark.
(Romano 1964:96)

To this essentially physical treatment, Jaramillo also added therapeutic
counseling—though not spiritualism—as part of his healing repertoire
(Romano 1964:99).

His services to the mostly *mexicano,* mostly poor community of south
Texas and beyond were not confined to healing. Working side by side with
a group of local women volunteers, the healer of Los Olmos also provided
food on a daily basis for those patients who came to see him but also for
anyone who was hungry in that region. Such need was particularly acute
during the great south Texas drought of the mid-1890s which, like all natural calamities, had a more adverse effect on the poor. Yet while he mostly
treated the poor, he also treated some Anglos and members of the Mexican upper classes. Indeed, there is evidence that the latter furnished him,
at times, with material gifts such as the small plot of land at Los Olmos so
as to assist his practice. But it is also quite clear that, as even Captain
Bourke acknowledged, Jaramillo accepted no personal compensation for
his services, lived a simple frugal existence, and used all monetary donations to further assist the afflicted (Romano 1964:87–100). Finally, Don
Pedrito dedicated himself wholly to this service. He never married and he
had no family of his own.

Beyond this descriptive account, Romano has three principal interrelated theoretical objectives in making a case for Jaramillo's cultural significance. The first is to locate the healer within a binary model of south Texas
Mexican-American masculine culture which will then be related to the
other two: locating Don Pedrito within a multiple hierarchy of healing and
identifying him as a charismatic figure.

Romano posits a masculine behavioral culture operating between two
mutually exclusive poles. Most men, especially in their younger years,
tend toward an atomistic social practice, which "emphasizes mistrust and
suspicion as well as general uncooperativeness," a practice of withdrawal-
avoidance of close social relations beyond the kin group. At the other end
of this code of male conduct is a more ideal practice of altruistic, coopera-
tive, communitarian values. But, it would seem, most ordinary men
rarely venture into this ideal terrain except, and only sometimes, older
men who acquire the honorific title of respect, *don,* and who at moments
extend themselves beyond the kin-friendship network to the larger community (1965:1154–55).

The large clear exception to this otherwise normative male behavioral pattern is the male *curandero* or folk healer such as Don Pedrito, especially in the degree he has risen in what Romano argues is a healing hierarchy. This hierarchy begins in the domestic realm, where an elder daughter or a mother can perform healing tasks for their immediate family. The hierarchy then moves up or out through ten levels based on two manifest principles: spatial geographical, as the healer attends to an increasingly larger physical area of responsibility; and increasing full-time specialization as a healer with each ascending rung. There is, however, yet another principle operating in Romano's hierarchy, although not as clearly noted, and that is gender. The lower levels—the scenes of domesticity and neighborhood healer—appear to be a woman's realm, but *men* become more prominent as the levels rise all the way to "international religious folk saint" and "international religious formal saint," the highest levels. Healers can be found at all levels and over time can move up or down the hierarchy (Romano 1965:1156–58). As the male healer ascends, however, he is bound to the communitarian side of the male behavioral culture. He is obligated to serve his community as Don Pedrito did, and "the alternative pattern of withdrawal-avoidance is not open to him" (1965:1155).

Finally, in a critical application of Weber, Romano argues for the potential and sometimes achieved charismatic status of the healer who has ascended to the top rungs of the hierarchy, a charisma drawing on his abilities as a healer but also on a force of personality. Romano concludes that as an international healer between 1881 and 1907 and later, a folk saint healer wholly in the service of his community, a male of a very different cultural kind from the everyday norms of the community, Don Pedrito achieved charismatic status but of a particular kind. Rather than charisma of radical innovation in the classic Weberian formulation, Don Pedrito's becomes a "charisma of conservatism" based not on innovation but on "renovation," on the powerful maintenance of tradition. In conclusion, Romano see this cultural charismatic conservation as a "type of influence" produced between healer and patients, constituting

> that component in folk-healing and folk-healers (charismatic medicine) which is complementary to the expectations (psychosomatic predispositions) among the clientele, for by its very nature it provides a meaningful point of stability during a moment of instability which has been brought about by an illness or incapacitation of some kind. (1965:1170)

We pause here and wonder, perplexed. A powerful healer. Communitarian values at odds with an atomistic masculinity. A culturally conservative charisma. A meaningful point of stability in a moment of instability defined as an illness or incapacitation of some kind. Eighteen eighty-one to 1907, a critical historical phase of south Texas political and economic life. And, it is precisely this last consideration—history and its absence in Romano's analysis—that gives pause, wonder, and perplexity.

Octavio Romano—who in less than three years would emerge as the most radical of critics of social science, who would critically note the lack of a Mexican-American *historical* presence in the social sciences (1967)—here in 1965 brings us so close that we can only wonder what prevented him from taking the next step, to heed the classical left injunction, always historicize.[1] Only then can we fully appreciate Don Pedrito's critical difference.

To complete this larger task, to build upon the findings of Romano, this important secondary precursor of mine, we need to recall the story told in Part I of this book, a story of the war of maneuver and hard positional warfare at the turn of the century. We need not fully restate but only recall the massive, often violent displacement of *mexicanos* from their land; their linguistic, cultural, and racial exclusion from politics and school; the lynching-as-criminal-justice system carried out against *mexicanos;* the depredations of the Texas Rangers; the violent suppression of labor strikes; and, most fundamentally, the redefinition of nature from subsistence to capitalist commodity, that is, the transformation of the meanings and uses of land and water in the service of a new international, agribusiness, advanced capitalism, all of this within Don Pedrito's healing lifetime.

In the most elemental way, at the level of brute physicality, the new world order imposed on south Texas by "Anglos" with the collusion of the upper-class *mexicanos* inflicted injury and pain upon the literal *mexicano* body/politic. The stress of hard labor combined with poor diet, and a continuous exposure to the hellish south Texas sun, by themselves would be sufficient causes of ill health. To this one can add the physical repercussions of sheer terror, such as that visited upon the Mexican population of south Texas in 1915.

It is only the most literal of assessments to say that the hundreds who visited Don Pedrito every week at Los Olmos were bringing to him the physical and psychological consequences of the new world order, including starvation. But Don Pedrito provided something else beyond his medical treatment and his food, and Romano's commentary on cultural charismatic conservatism and meaningful stability against "incapacitation of some kind" now takes on radical social significance.

As the old social order disintegrated and as the south Texas Mexicans experienced social stress and anxiety over this change, Don Pedrito became a symbolic figure of dissent from the new social order and its value. As the community was shattered and scattered by new economic forces, he, and his shrine afterward, located in the center of south Texas, provided a central unifying person and place where *mexicanos* could anchor their identity. In addition to this general function, Don Pedrito may have had more subtle meanings for a people who were seeing their traditional values threatened. Against the new advanced capitalist ideas of competition, acquisition, and profit on the basis of human subordination, Don Pedrito stood as a figure who worked incessantly on behalf of those whom he made his equals in an economic sense. He shunned economic privilege by refusing monetary rewards and by redistributing his goods, even while maintaining a moral hierarchy based on his status as an elder. This symbolic interpretation can also be applied to Don Pedrito's healing methods, which drew upon natural, minimally mediated elements such as water. His use of water, with its meanings of healing and purification, was in direct contrast to the use of water for the new commercial agriculture, which relied upon extensive, environmentally degrading machine irrigation to maximize profit.

Romano offers us another beginning, actually better than a beginning, but yet again, in 1965, not brought to its utmost fulfillment and yield. Here I am less perplexed because in 1965 we should not reasonably expect an awareness of gender issues so much before us today. We must recall the manner in which Don Pedrito Jaramillo's social existence and practice are interestingly gendered. We can note a number of features. The healing hierarchy Romano develops is gendered female at the outset, that is, at the "lower" domestic levels. But it would appear that at the higher levels, such as that of international healer, the hierarchy is not masculinized as such; rather, it is *joined* by men, but men of a particular kind. Romano quite clearly spells out this kind: the male more bound, indeed, wholly bound over to a nurturing, communitarian social existence rather than to the more decisively "masculine," atomistic, uncooperative, withdrawal/avoidance social order.[2] If to this communitarian ethos, we add Jaramillo's nonmarriage, his labor alongside women, and, as Romano reports it, the majority number of women who after his death continue to come to pray and supplicate at his grave site (1965:1163), then we are well on our way toward a distinctive cultural poetics of the healer of Los Olmos. This is a poetics that would lend emphasis to his historical significance as a figure of critical difference to the enveloping capitalist social order between 1881 and 1907, but it is a critical difference with a particular gender inflection. As Macklin astutely notes in her study of female healers,

> the role of highly successful, full-time healer demands that all of one's time and energy be devoted to "humanity"; conflictive obligations of any other role cannot be met. Further, the role demands an androgynous combination of nurturing compassion and openness along with a willingness to exercise the power, authority, and decisiveness necessary to confront and conquer spiritual and existential dangers. In these senses, then, full-time healing constitutes a role that transcends gender. (1980:130)

This powerful figure of androgynous critical difference—this figure who refused to dance with the devil—continued his work after his death in 1907, such was his power. It now became a politics of healing critically relevant to the mass of working-class *mexicanos* in south Texas as they were incorporated as a dominated laboring class in the advancing capitalist social order. As Romano following Dodson tells us, Jaramillo's grave site at Los Olmos Creek soon became a pilgrimage site. Over time, with the aid of benefactors and small donations, a chapel-like structure was erected near the grove. Here the greater Mexican community, but especially those from south Texas, came to pray and leave written supplicatons asking for his help in matters of physical health but also mental, as well as a host of other social problems: unemployment, overextended credit, school difficulties. A photograph of the person in need was sometimes left.[3]

> Don Pedrito I ask of you do me the favor of curing my son and daughter, that they get well and help me in my work and I promise I'll come and watch over you and bring flowers.
>
> Don Pedrito, what I ask of you is to pass in English and graduate.

And, by interesting coincidence, the following:

> On May 9th I leave for Korea and, with faith in Don Pedrito Jaramillo, I wish to return happily home. (Romano 1964:130)

But one particular kind of visitation and supplication stands out as it speaks to the laboring masses of Mexican-Americans in the twentieth century.

> Another form of visitation includes many who are part of the thousands from South Texas who join the annual migratory agricultural cycles each year . . . according to the local residents in the vicinity of Los Olmos Creek, truck after truck momentarily stops at the

shrine of Don Pedrito each year as the agricultural cycles begin. Here they request his protection on the trip and good fortune during the harvest. (Romano 1964:112)

And, as a distinctive practice reinforcing these many visitations, the greater Mexican working-class community also has a store of legends or *casos*, emphasizing Don Pedrito's charisma and his miraculous cures as they do for other Texas *curanderos* (Graham 1981). It is these legends, we recall, that were the butt of the ambivalent *curandero* jokes told by Professor Paredes' middle- and upper-class informants.

He's originally from Weslaco in the Lower Rio Grande Valley, he tells me, although he now lives in Chicago. I have met him and struck up a conversation in the shrine's parking lot. He was sitting there on his car hood, his car somewhat blocking mine, as I was getting ready to leave after visiting the shrine in the summer of 1980. A ready excuse. Could he please move his car, Illinois plates and all? Then before he could gladly do so, I asked him if indeed he lived in Chicago where I had a sister, and soon we were into talk, my leaving momentarily delayed. About thirty years old, a factory worker, an ex-marine, I find out, ¿Y usted? From Austin, anthropologist and the devil knows what else. ¿Que es un *anthropologist?* he asks.

He is waiting for his mother who is inside making a supplication. He's got a six-pack on ice in the car, asks me if I want one; hesitantly in *this* parking lot I say yes. Laughing as he swallows a long pull on this very hot typical south Texas day, he tells me that it concerns the beer. The supplication that is. He came home to Weslaco to see his mother and family, and she promptly motherly coerced him into driving her up to the shrine. She was not coercive enough to talk him *inside* the chapel, so she settled for half a loaf. She's worried about his heavy drinking, I find out, and his being so far away especially now that he is single. Two divorces. The first with a *muchacha mexicana* from *Edinburgo* he says, right after he got back from Vietnam in 1969. The other just a couple of years ago with a *ruca polaca* (Polish broad) in Chicago. Left for Chicago after the first divorce and not being able to find steady work only part-time driving a vegetable truck. ¿Y usted? Well, anthropology, a pretty good job in Austin. Not married . . . yet. Trying to find out something about the people who come to the shrine for a book I'm writing. He's been to Austin, he tells me. He ran some *carga* (a load) there a couple of times. He says it with a slight grin so I'm not sure *what* kind of *carga* he means, for in greater Mexican slang, *carga* can also mean heroin. The grin and lowered voice tells me its the latter. He's going for his third beer since we started talking. ¿Y usted? I politely decline. Now I must go. It's a Sunday afternoon, and I promised some friends in Kingsville, just up the road, that I would join them for a *carne asada* before I return to Austin. No women. Just *batos*. There will be beer a-plenty so I'll probably spend the night. Have breakfast at my parents in Corpus the next day. I leave him waiting for his mother still inside the shrine.

Inside the shrine, around an altar and a large picture of Don Pedrito, earlier I have seen them, today's supplications for help, with the accompanying photographs. Like those Dodson and Romano saw, many of these discourses of the 1980s continue to ask for Don Pedrito's help with medical problems, unemployment, school; but almost too predictably, and in contrast to Romano's sample (1964:130–32), they now compete for space with articulations of drug abuse, wife battering, divorces, pleas for help for men doing time in prison, help in someday reuniting in south Texas families now probably permanently scattered to Toledo, Los Angeles, Utah, Michigan, Oregon, Chicago.

> My most esteemed Don Pedrito please help my daughter looking for work in Houston. She's a good girl.

> Don Pedro, highest of saints, bring my son safe home from the jail in "Honsvil."

> You who protect us all, my husband is in great need of work.

> You who are ours and in the heavens, ask *la virgencita* (the Virgin Mary) to keep Raul and Mary together.

> Don Pedro, our saint, my boy wants to go back to school, help him please.

> Light of our existence, my boys need help with *la droga,* help them please.

> You of all charity, bring my children back to *el valle* (The Valley).

Is Don Pedrito up to the task? Can "he" help the *mexicanos* of south Texas fend off these new devils as he did the devil's older representations for this now urbanizing, postmodern community? Will he continue to be a point of stability and healing in these most incapacitating and unstable of times for these my people? To see the many cars and people still coming to the healer of Los Olmos is to know that the lower-class *mexicanos* of south Texas believe he can, that "he" remains a figure of critical difference in their lives, beset as they are by a new postmodern form of domination.

"He" has been and continues to be for them a powerful charismatic folk saint, but one always critically relative to history. "He" was and continues to be for them a folk hero, not like Gregorio Cortez, with his pistol in his hand, a hero for the war of maneuver, but rather an androgynous hero speaking to women and men and thus, perhaps, better suited for the longer continuing war of position and endemic protracted struggle for the maintenance of community.

Yet, even as Don Pedrito, this androgynous persona, continues his heroic healing power over time, he is still "Don," and it is *his* power. We must still think him male and critically recall those other many levels in Romano's healing hierarchy, those many levels populated largely by women—*curanderas,* female working-class healers—those many levels unintentionally diminished in Romano's gendered hierarchy as he himself (and I as well) are captured by Jaramillo's charisma. What about them? "Folk medicine," Silvia Bovenschen tells us, "before reaching professional status and being subsumed under the control of men, was practiced almost exclusively by women" (1978:102). Today, at these "lower" levels of the hierarchy, it is predominantly such women who continue to deal with the plentiful illness in southern Texas (Trotter and Chavira 1981).

We can gain ethnographic and theoretical entry into this substantially women's practice by turning to an important literary work from southern Texas. This turn will also permit me to acknowledge another important secondary precursor for these efforts and to offer some encompassing concluding remarks.

This study had its earliest beginnings in 1975 while I was serving as a member of the faculty at the new University of Texas at San Antonio as a quite junior assistant professor, still in fact ABD. Originally conceived as a first-class urban campus—the "UCLA of the Texas system," some said—UTSA promised innovative academic excellence. And its location in San Antoñio promised a social relevance for education of great importance for many of us who went there, especially those of us who were of Mexican descent and veterans of the Chicano student movement of the sixties. The powers-that-be actually seemed to affirm this promise by appointing as Vice-President for Administration Tomás Rivera, the fine Mexican-American literary intellectual and former migrant worker from Crystal City in south Texas. Rivera had just published his beautiful and powerful novel, *y no se lo tragó la tierra* (. . . *and the Earth did not part*) (1971).⁴ Serving under his leadership and living in San Antoñio, the cultural capital of south Texas, could do nothing but delight me.

We had first met shortly after Tomás received the Ph.D. in 1969, and we would meet again in 1972 under less pleasant circumstances, in a context of academic warfare. Américo Paredes best reports these circumstances in which he first came to know Rivera.

> I first met the man about the time I became acquainted with the
> book, . . . *y no se lo tragó la tierra.* I was then Director of the
> brand-new Center for Mexican-American Studies at the University of
> Texas at Austin. José Limón . . . suggested that we try to get Rivera
> appointed to a joint position in Mexican-American Studies and Span-
> ish and Portuguese. So Rivera came to our campus and Limón intro-
> duced us. Tomás Rivera was a very pleasant person with a ready
> smile, but there was an air of self-assurance about him as well. The
> iron determination that had carried him so far, and that would carry
> him much farther yet—that was not evident in his demeanor; and
> those who did not know him well may have sometimes been de-
> ceived as to the man they were dealing with. Tomás gave the usual
> lecture expected from candidates for appointment. But our Spanish
> Department was not interested at the time in a Mexican-American
> born in El Cristal, so nothing came from his visit. (Paredes 1986:24)

Rivera went to San Antoñio instead where, with shared great hopes about UTSA, I joined him when he hired me in 1975, willing to risk my ABD status when I had no other job possibilities in Texas.

Rivera shared these thoughts with me over beers at a quiet place in the Westside, far from the campus. I always thought he looked more at home there than he did in his nice UTSA office. We talked about the war there amidst the war, interrupted regularly by working-class folk who knew him. Ultimately and again, the war came home personally to him too. When the presidency of UTSA became available, he thought of applying, but a leading member of the Board of Regents told him that the University of Texas system wasn't ready for a "Mexican" president. Tomás left, eventually to become chancellor of the University of California at Riverside during the brief democratic opening afforded him by the Jerry Brown administration before Reaganism descended upon California and then the country. There, he eventually died, too many stresses on his heart. He liked his beer and tacos, but that probably wasn't what killed him. His unfailing courtesy belied the war raging within.

All of us who are enlisted in the continuing war have reason to remember Tomás Rivera, but as I close this book whose early beginnings I shared with him, let me now express my ultimate debt and gratitude to Tomás by drawing on his novel to address the world of *curanderas* in their critical difference from the Real of history and as figures for the political poetics of ethnography.

The central protagonist in Rivera's novel *And the Earth Did Not Devour Him* is a young male figure coming to terms with his existence in a harsh dominated world of Mexican-American migrant farm workers, like those who stop at Don Pedrito's pilgrimage site. Developed in thirteen interrelated short sketches, this protagonist comes to a critical consciousness and a knowledge of domination even as he also comes to know his own culture. Early in the book we have a foreshadowing of this second line of inquiry. At night, to ward off illness and in keeping with Mexican folk medical tradition, his mother would place a glass of water under his bed.

> What his mother never knew was that every night he would drink the glass of water she left under the bed for the spirits. She always believed that they drank the water and so she continued doing her duty. Once he was going to tell her but then he thought he'd wait and tell her when he was grown up. (Rivera 1987:86)

This opening account is followed by a series of recollective sketches flowing narratively from this young male protagonist's emergent consciousness and amplifying his growing awareness of culture and domination. "A Prayer" signals for us the absurd futility of a mother's prayer for her son in the Korean War. "The Children Couldn't Wait" tells us of the oppressive reality of farmworker labor in the hot hell-like agricultural fields of south Texas. Driven to sneak off for water, a child is shot "accidentally" by an Anglo rancher trying to scare him. Yet another sketch, "It's That It Hurts," teaches us about racism and limited opportunity for this working-class sector, while a more extended piece, "Hand in His Pocket," again notes for us the masking character of traditional Mexican-American cultural practices. So that he may finish the school year, the protagonist is entrusted to the care of an elderly Mexican-American couple who carry the honorific titles of Don and Doña by parents who presumably have left early for the migrant labor circle. Gradually he watches the honorific turning horrific as these culturally "valued" elders cheat people, serve him putrid meat, and finally murder an itinerant Mexican undocumented worker.

Rivera traces for us a protagonist becoming aware of domination but also in a process of deconstructing his own native culture so as to know its limitations. Ultimately he comes to a climactic ultimate test of culture and domination, as Rivera, an intellectual who also knows his folklore, draws

upon and transforms a traditional rite of passage for young south Texas
men: standing in an open field at midnight cursing the devil and daring
him to appear.

In the climactic two sketches—"It Was a Silvery Night" and "And the
Earth Did Not Devour Him"—we learn that this young-man-coming-to-
consciousness is aware of this traditional folklore. Given all that has gone
before, he decides to try it.

> And how do I call him? Maybe he'll appear. No, I don't think so. In
> any case, if he does appear he can't do anything to me. I haven't
> died yet. So he can't do anything to me. I'd just like to know
> whether there is or there isn't . . . If there isn't a devil, maybe there
> also isn't . . . No, I better not say it. I might get punished. But if
> there's no devil maybe there's no punishment. No, there has to be
> punishment. Well, how do I call him? Just, devil? Or, imp? Or, de-
> mon? Lucifer? Satan? . . . Whatever comes first. (1987:108)

The young protagonist does call him. He does not appear. He curses
him. He curses the devil's mother. Still, he does not appear. "There was
no devil . . . No, there's no devil. There isn't" (1987:108).

> Two or three different times he sensed someone calling him but he
> didn't want to turn around. He didn't get scared because he felt sure
> there wasn't anyone nor anything. After he lay down, very careful
> not to make a sound, certain there was no devil, he began to feel
> chills and his stomach became upset. Before falling asleep he
> thought for a good while. *There is no devil, there is nothing.* The
> only thing that had been present in the woods was his own voice. No
> wonder, he thought, people said you shouldn't fool around with the
> Devil. Now he understood everything. Those who summoned the
> devil went insane not because the devil appeared, but, to the con-
> trary, because he didn't appear. He fell asleep gazing at the moon as
> it jumped through the clouds and three trees, as if it were extremely
> content about something. (1987:109)

This scene enables the next sketch, where the protagonist's family becomes quite ill after suffering a heatstroke while working in the field. In
his raging oppression the protagonist tests yet another complementary
folk belief: if you curse God, the earth will devour you.

> He cursed God. Upon doing this he felt that fear instilled in him by
> the years and by his parents. For a second he saw the earth opening
> up to devour him. Then he felt his footsteps against the earth, com-
> pact, more solid than ever. (1987:115–16)

As his family recovers, "he left for work and encountered a very cool morning. There were clouds in the sky and for the first time he felt capable of doing and undoing anything that he pleased" (1987:116). The best commentator on this novel, the south Texan Ramón Saldívar, has persuasively argued that the protagonist's

> almost Nietzschean serenity, a liberating joyful wisdom, is the direct result of his appropriation of the site of God's former existence as the place for his own self-determined presence . . . the religion of Job reconciled or of Christ crucified here has not diminished but rather added to man's burden of suffering to the extent that it has been used as a justification for the historical crimes that people commit against other people. By rejecting that religion and its idealist metaphysics and moving as it were beyond good and evil, the protagonist implies that in this life *understanding,* the source of collective power, is the first step toward historical materialist salvation. (1990:83)

For Saldívar, this "first step," this encounter with devil and God, leads to the protagonist's amplification of his new knowledge beyond himself so as to know and speak collectively in subsequent sketches his community's travail, identity, and mission in the novel's closing moment of "collective power," of "historical naturalist salvation" based now on "understanding" (1990:86–90). In these final scenes, the protagonist recalls a multitude of migrant farm worker voices from his past and reflects:

> I would like to see all of the people together. And then, if I had great big arms, I could embrace them all. I wish I could talk to all of them again, but all of them together. But that, only in a dream. I like it right here because I can think about anything I please. Only by being alone can you bring everybody together. (Rivera 1987:159)

Our young protagonist achieves a collective utopian emancipation based on "understanding," on his desire to think, but it is a paradoxical achievement. For I submit that Tomás also presents us with another dimension to this young protagonist, a dimension relatively unacknowledged by Rivera's critics in their valorization of his protagonist's utopian achievement against an idealist, religious metaphysics (Olivares 1986). Tomás teaches us something else yet, a more difficult lesson, namely, that nothing is gained without a cost, a cost in this case borne by women as *curanderas* and by those who would write ethnographies reproducing dominating power. To grasp this aspect of the protagonist—the more complex figure that Rivera skillfully created—we need to revisit the protagonist's narrative progress. Here we need to recall Rivera's key opening scene and the manner in which he poses this problem, this tension which the prevalent criticism will tend to resolve in favor of the emergent rationality of the male protagonist who lays claim to true knowledge and true politics. The boy's mother places a glass of water under his bed to ward off bad spirits, and he responds with condescension based on his assured emergent rational self. Patricia de la Fuente offers the beginnings of a dissenting reading of this scene. "This incident," she observes, "displays a deliberate focusing on the mental landscape of Rivera's protagonist" who "brands her as ignorant, superstitious and easily gullible." In so doing, he "reveals indirectly, but irrevocably, a blind faith in his own superiority" (1986:84). What this feminist south Texas critic does not but could easily note is that in her desire to ward off evil spirits, this mother is acting as a *curandera* at one of those several female-populated "lower" levels of Romano's hierarchy, and that it is *as curandera* that she is branded as ignorant, superstitious, and a prisoner of an idealist metaphysics. Who is she, this working-class *curandera?*

We noted Captain Bourke's knowledge of such women—powerful women—such as his principal informant, Maria Antoñia Cavazos de Garza who "had been married four times and had borne seventeen children." Her conversations with Bourke "ranged from folk *materia medica* to *brujeria* or witchcraft," even as she cautioned and prescribed against those "who had sold their souls to the devil"; those whose souls "after death . . . roamed about seeking sanctuary" though they would not enter certain houses: "a person who made a cross of mustard on the wall near their bed was protected from the wandering ones" (Porter 1986:293). Today, at these "lower" levels of the hierarchy, such women continue to deal with the plentiful devils of southern Texas. From specialized healers to more ordinary women, such as our protagonist's mother, who labor primarily in their homes, it is such *curanderas* who daily and relatively uncharismatically engage with late capitalism's baleful effects on the *mexicano* body politic as they continue a struggle with the devil.

They carry out this struggle materially sited on the body, but as they do so, like Bourke's informant, they simultaneously struggle with yet other forms of the devil, even as they too, like the women at El Cielito Lindo, also choose to dance with "him." As Macklin notes, in her public roles as healer, such a woman

> epitomizes all of the *good* associated with feminity; she is knowledgeable, self-sacrificing, nurturant, caring, submissive yet protecting,

loyal, chaste, and close to divine power; but the same arcane knowledge and ability to traffic with spirits suggests all that is dark, mysterious and *bad* in the power of being female. (1980:127)

In their dance with the dark and the mysterious such women risk the label
of *witch,* for even as they oppose the bedevilment of illness and dance with
one form of the devil, yet other devils rise in opposition to their practice
and the more fundamental threat that it poses; again, Bovenschen:

> it was the charge of complicity with the secret powers of nature
> (which seemed to the populace identical to those powers which were
> exploding society's framework), which was the basis for suspecting
> witches. The sympathetic relationship of women to nature, its suc-
> cesses (using herbal drinks), its failures (the laying on of hands),
> being as they were secular attempts at controlling life, threatened
> the church; but they simultaneously stood in the way of the triumph
> of instrumental reason. The latter fact explains why the representa-
> tive of the new science of natural law, the protagonists of modern
> rationality, were of so little help to witches. (1978:98)

In his struggle for knowledge and collective emancipation, Rivera's
protagonist does contend with an idealist religious metaphysics, but in his
triumph he also critically and rationalistically attacks his mother's traditional form of knowledge and cultural practice. With supreme rational
objectivist confidence, the young protagonist discovers that there is no
devil, but this seeming discovery is itself a rationalistic ideological covering for *our* discovery of a more profound truth: there *is* a devil in this boy's
universe. Tomás Rivera, good writer, learned scholar and thinker refused
by the University of Texas at Austin Spanish department, knows his Faust
and bedevils critics who privilege his young protagonist as a rational, "political" intellectual (a figuration of the Chicano movement masculinist
intellectual politics of the sixties?) In a telling scene largely ignored by the
novel's critics, we learn of the protagonist's first memory of the devil even
before he calls him out, and we are reminded yet again of Captain John
Gregory Bourke and his shepherd's play:

> The devil had fascinated him as far back as he could remember.
> Even when they had taken him to the shepherds plays at his Aunt
> Pana's, he was already curious about how it might be. He thought
> about Don Rayos, with his black metal mask, with its red horns and
> black cape. Then he remembered how he found the costume and the
> mask under Don Rayos' house. One of his marbles had rolled under
> the house and when he reached for it he found everything all full of

> dust. He pulled everything out and dusted it off, and then he put on
> the mask. (1987:106–7)

Later, we also learn that

> Mother had a painted picture of hell at the head of the bed and
> since the walls of the room were papered with images of the devil
> and since I wanted salvation from all evil, that was all I could think
> of. (1987:118)

Finally, as we have seen, he calls the devil, only to discover there is no
devil, there is no God, but on the eve of his encounter, as he voices his
rational, political skepticism to his mother at their moment of crisis, we
discover that indeed there is a devil, and it is his mother as *curandera* who
knows his identity: "Oh please my son, don't talk that way. Don't speak
against the will of God . . . you scare me. It's as if already the blood of
Satan runs through your veins" (1987:113). And indeed it does; it is the
blood of masculinist universal reason which, while permitting him to question idealist religious metaphysics and dominating power, is nonetheless,
itself, a complicit exercise of power. From here he will ostensibly grow
into a critical figure who speaks for the collective utopian emancipation of
his community. But before his growth into these final collectivist emancipating scenes, we recall his sheer indulgence in his Faustian-
Mephistophelian moment when his desire to *know* is all. We need to recall
his serenity at *his* own victory—*his* triumph. The moon hovered overhead
for *him*, not yet for his people, not yet for a collectivist utopia, and the
price for this is his erasure of another, nonutopian, communal, female-
centered way of knowledge and politics. She who dances with the devil to
heal the body politic of south Texas is disowned and subordinated, first in
the privileging of the male charismatic *curandero*, and now by a youthful
masculinist will to power driven by universal reason, a will to power that
now reminds us of the project of ethnography as a general concern of
these pages.

   While my chief purpose in this my final chapter has been to amplify our
sense, our cultural poetics, of the expressive world of women and their
critical difference in southern Texas, the *curandera* now also becomes
available as a figure for the construction of ethnographic discourse in relation to domination, a fundamental concern of this essay in both of its
parts. For, in her multivocalic reliance on and transformation of a range of
material and nonmaterial resources—including her own persona—to produce a healing discourse, the *curandera* eschews any singular model of

rationalistic, distanced, objectivist discourse. Rather than singular ratio-
nalism and empiricist representation of ills and cures, the *curandera*, it
might be said, works by *evocation,* as, some believe, should ethnography.

> The whole point of "evoking" rather than "representing" is that it
> frees ethnography from mimesis and that inappropriate mode of sci-
> entific rhetoric which entails "objects," "facts," "descriptions," "in-
> ductions," "generalizations," "verifications," "experiment," "truth"
> and like concepts which, except as empty invocations, have no paral-
> lels either in the experience of ethnographic field work or in the
> writing of ethnographies. (Tyler 1987:207)

Like Rivera's *curandera,* Tyler also warns us of the devil who fascinated
the young protagonist and many anthropologists:

> Ethnographic discourse is not part of a project whose aim is the
> creation of universal knowledge. It disowns the Mephistophelian
> urge to power through knowledge for that, too, is a consequence of
> representation. (1987:208)

For Tyler, a better, which is to say, a "postmodern," ethnography is a
text that, like the *curandera*'s practice, exists in tension and paradox, "neither denying ambiguity nor endorsing it, neither subverting subjectivity
nor denying objectivity, expressing instead their interaction in the subjec-
tive creation of ambiguous objectivities that enable unambiguous subjectivity. The ethnographic text will thus achieve its purpose not by revealing
them but by making purposes possible" (1987:213).[5]

This is the general orientation I have tried to bring to the two worlds of
Parts I and II that I have rendered in this extended essay. In Part I, I
explored the world of my precursors and their ethnographic texts founded
upon the continuing war, tension, paradox, and repression, particularly
on the question of gender. As I now look back through the prism of my
own time and Part II, I sense myself in a paradoxical position. Those who
have now read this and any of my other work and know the trajectory of
my career can clearly trace the manifest influence of Américo Parcdes,
my nearest precursor and mentor. Yet, taken together, the key terms of
this essay—war, the postmodern form, the negotiation of personal identity, and most centrally the question of women—now put me in a powerful
and complicated relationship to all of these figures including the most
distant and unlikely Anglo/Irish evolutionary soldier-anthropologist, Captain John Gregory Bourke.

For me, he becomes like Renato Rosaldo's William Jones, who pre-

ceded Rosaldo as an anthropological fieldworker among the Ilongot of
the Philippines at the turn of the century, at about the same time Bourke
was making war and anthropology in south Texas. Something of an adventurer and warrior also—he contemplated organizing a band of Harvard
men as "Rough Riders" under Teddy Roosevelt for the coming war with
Spain—Jones also had deeply ambivalent feelings about his fieldwork
community, the Ilongot. Indeed, like Bourke, he displaces unto his subjects and their land his anxieties about his former identity as an Oklahoma
cowboy and the vanishing open range of the West. For Rosaldo, Jones,
like Captain Bourke, is a distant figure in time and politics. Rosaldo and I
can acknowledge, in Rosaldo's words, our precursors' mutual "zestfully
innocent . . . romantic pursuit of the exotic" and their "rugged frontier
character"; we can, perhaps, even feel toward them what they felt toward
the Ilongots and Mexicans they studied: "awe, respectful, puzzled, an-
noyed and angry," indeed, at various moments and with varying empha-
ses, I have had these feelings toward all of my precursors. Yet for all of
their varying distance in time and politics and our own ambivalences, we
can still learn from *all of* them, recognizing "that science progresses
through a movement, not toward truth, but away from the errors of less
adequate theories" (Rosaldo 1980:1–8).

   With my precursors—but especially with Captain Bourke and his
female informants in mind—I progress, or at least lurch forward, toward
my cultural poetics of the south Texas present. As Tyler notes:

> Every ethnographer is a child of her time and comes to the field
> informed by contemporary significances; the meaningful events of
> her generation and the consensus of theory and practice are the land-
> marks and boundaries of her imagination. This guarantees that what
> she sees and writes is not likely to be what Haddon or Rivers or
> Evans-Pritchard or even Levi-Strauss would have seen or written,
> and this difference has nothing to do with anything that may have
> happened to the people ethnographers study, though that too is part
> of the historical context, but is simply the result of all these other
> ethnographers having written before, of their having contributed to a
> discourse which is always emergent, always being interpreted, which
> the ethnographer enters at a unique point, and which is as much the
> object of her enterprise as the natives themselves. (1987:101)

In the shadow and light of those who have written before me, I have
entered Mexican-American south Texas at my own unique point and moment in the 1970s and in Part II. Therein I have critiqued what I have
termed an emergent subaltern postmodernity experienced in race and

class terms but having its most telling impact on the lives of working-class women. As in the past, today's Mexican-Americans are not wholly without shared democratic expressive resources—folklore—to respond with critical difference to this postmodern negation, though these practices are themselves marked by contradiction and repression. In this regard I side with my cross-campus colleague and friend, Doug Foley, in his debate with Paul Willis and the notion of popular culture as "resistance." Foley's own study of south Texas high school popular culture tells us of culture "in capitalist societies as a 'popular culture' of power relations filled with contradiction and struggle" (1990:199). I have traced this popular cultural response in various performances salient in south Texas.

Yet though I critique and respond to late-capitalist postmodernity in these terms, my own textual rendering—my past and present ethnography of Parts I and II—is itself at least partially participant in a postmodern intellectual culture, the work of Clifford, Marcus, Tyler, Rosaldo, Taussig, and Jameson, among others. The critical reader might well wonder if there is not a contradiction, a repression, or at least a paradox here, and she might be right. One possible response may be to say, again with Tyler, that because "[postmodern] life in the field is itself fragmentary," as I have suggested it is, "a postmodern ethnography is [therefore] fragmentary," which is to say essayistic, "because it cannot be otherwise" (1987:208). But this response—this odd form of representational mimesis—will not fully do for me. I have tried to critically address this potential contradiction by attempting to account for postmodernity's social origins and specificity in neo-Marxian terms, a manifestation of late capitalism. As such it is not simply our latest given "culture" but a specific form of the continuing warfare against which my people take up expressive arms, arms actually fundamentally *modernist* in character. Yet, as Fredric Jameson has said, we *live* in the postmodern, and our participation in it to some considerable degree is inevitable, for notwithstanding its social origins, its form is, at our intellectual class level, powerful, flexible, attractive (Jameson 1992:47–54). Conscious of its power of form, I take it up—or so I would persuade myself—less as a fated condition and more as a controlled tactical weapon.[6] The idea is to dance with the devil.

Notes
Glossary
References
Index

Notes

INTRODUCTION

1. It is instructive to note that in his recent *War without Mercy: Race and Power in the Pacific War,* John Dower points to widespread notions of Japanese passivity and incompetence among the U.S. military and civilian populace in the days just prior to December 7, 1941 (1986:94–108).

2. I chose these figures as my major predecessors on several criteria: (1) the synoptic character of their work in terms of genres and the south Texas region; (2) their well articulated representation of a particular theoretical/historical context; (3) their own "presence" in the academic, public sphere; and finally (4) the extended, expressive character of their writing.

3. James Clifford suggests that academic minorities might be less inclined to experiment formally out of a concern for their academic self-interest, particularly in matters of tenure and promotion (1986:21n). In the current postmodern moment, my concern is quite the opposite: that some such folks, particularly graduate students, are *too* inclined to what Clifford refers to "a preoccupation with self-reflexivity and style" and that it indeed might be "an index of privileged estheticism" (1986:21n), or, perhaps, a form of postmodern "hyper-correction," emulating the current dominant practice in the academy. My struggling sense of the essay form with its resonance with oral tradition is both my engagement with and refusal of this "preoccupation."

4. It is instructive and supportive of my argument here that two other south Texas native intellectual/scholars have independently turned to war as an organizing metaphorical concept for their studies of south Texas (Montejano 1987; Saldívar 1990).

5. Ironically, it has often been the case that having left the social warfare of south Texas and other parts of Mexican America, Mexican-American boys (this is the precise age/gender term I want) have often found themselves dying on battlefields far from home, at Belleau Wood, Omaha Beach, Khe Sanh, and, of course, under General Walker's enlightened leadership in Korea.

211

CHAPTER 1. JOHN GREGORY BOURKE

1. In Mexican Spanish, a *cabrón* is literally a grown male goat and a *cabrito* with its diminutive form is a small kid goat. However, in general usage, *cabrón* is a general curse, sometimes an honorific, depending on context.

2. To be sure, in this kind of popular cultural construction of Mexican-Americans, there is, of course, also a cultural poetics that will precede Bourke, Dobie, Gonzalez, and Paredes. Because this kind of informal stereotyping cultural poetics is so well known in the literature, I have chosen not to dwell on it here (Robinson 1977; Pettit 1980; de Leon 1983). Rather, my analysis of past cultural poetics will focus on those who professionally and consciously engaged in ethnographic practice, and, of these, Bourke is the first for the south Texas area.

3. It should be noted that Bourke's "The American Congo" is, in part, also a response to critical and sometimes unfair attacks made upon him in local Mexican-American newspapers (Porter 1986:288–89).

4. Bourke was, of course, preceded in his identification with the south Texas border Mexicans by those Irish-American soldiers who deserted from Zachary Taylor's army in 1846–47 and went over to the Mexican side to a large extent on the basis of common Catholicism and a common experience of Anglo-American prejudice (Miller 1989).

5. In later commentary Bourke's biographer, Joseph Porter, reinforces my reading of Bourke's Irish-Mexican identification and displacement. In a personal communication, he says: "You make an excellent point about his ambivalence about his own Irish background and his inconsistent attitudes about Mexican-Americans. It explains, to my mind, some of the contradictions in Bourke's attitudes and behavior. Bourke was extremely proud of his Irish background, and along with his friends and contemporary ethnologists Washington Matthews and James Mooney (both of Irish background), Bourke shared a strong interest in Gaelic language and Celtic history and folklore. He also regarded the Irish as an important component in the culture of Mexico.

"Bourke's parents were immigrants, and they were firmly middle-class, both economically and in attitudes, in Ireland and in the United States. I think that their middle class beliefs and aspirations remained with Bourke for life. After the Civil War he detested the new super rich of the Gilded Age with its industrialization and urbanization.

"I think that his middle class bias allowed him to remain proud of his Irish heritage while simultaneously despairing of and rejecting what he perceived as the poverty and hopelessness of Ireland itself. This can be seen in the fact that Bourke, the son of immigrants, was very suspicious of the massive immigration during the Gilded Age. If you carefully read his remarks about Mexican-Americans in San Antoñio, Rio Grande City, Brownsville, and in Northern Mexico, his positive comments are about shopkeepers, middling ranchers, tradesmen, teachers, priests, and others that he regarded as "middle class" (or aspiring middle class) Hispanics" (Porter 1990).

CHAPTER 2. FRANK DOBIE

1. J. Frank Dobie published a number of books and edited several collections on Southwestern Americana. See McVicker (1968). I have selected only those extended writings of the greatest relevance for south Texas. In addition to McNutt's fine assessment, other important statements on Dobie's life are Mc-Murtry (1968), Owens (1967), and Tinkle (1978).

2. While we're on the subject of folklorists going to war, we take note of Dobie's great admiration for Captain Bourke (Dobie 1958).

3. Dobie published a preliminary version of this article in the *Journal of American Folklore* edited by Franz Boas (1923).

4. Notwithstanding his repeated claims to be able "to speak Mexican," Dobie's slipshod Spanish is clearly evident in this article and throughout his corpus.

CHAPTER 3. JOVITA GONZALEZ

1. *Dew on the Thorn,* a novel about the period 1826–48 in south Texas, was submitted to Macmillan and rejected. It remained unpublished, and as this book goes to press I have found the novel under the title *Caballero* in the E. E. Mireles & Jovita Gonzalez Mireles Papers, Special Collections and Archives Department, Corpus Christi State University. I am very grateful to Dr. Thomas Kreneck, archivist, for making this collection available, hereafter referred to as the Mireles-Gonzalez Papers. The Gonzalez-Dobie correspondence (1926–46) is to be found in the J. Frank Dobie Collection housed in the Harry Ranson Humanities Research Center at the University of Texas at Austin. Most of this correspondence is undated, although internal evidence in the letter permits some close approximation.

2. In the introduction to *Man, Bird, and Beast,* Dobie formulates again his ethnographic approach to folklore and associates Jovita Gonzalez with it: "I look for two things in folk-lore. I look for flavor and I look for a revelation of the folk who nourished the lore. If the lore interests me, I want to know its history; unless it has something of flavor and fancy and smacks of the folk, then it is not likely to interest me. If a thing is interesting, that is all the excuse it needs for being. Some day, it is quite likely, Miss Jovita Gonzalez will plunge in and trace her charming stores of the red bird, the paisano, the woodpecker, the cenizo bush and other objects back to the Middle Ages; but I hope she will not take time to do this until she has extracted all the dewey freshness that the Mexican folk of the Texas border put in their tales" (1930:6).

3. A *San Antonio Express* newspaper account on Gonzalez (August 27,

1934) reports that Dr. George Lyman Kittridge "known as the Dean of American folklore considers her work the best of its kind in the southwest and has used her articles in his English classes." Among the laudatory letters of recommendation on her behalf may be found those from H. Y. Benedict, then president of the University of Texas, and Paul S. Taylor who would become a distinguished economist specializing in Mexican labor in the United States. She also receives high praise in the *New York Times Book Review* for her contribution to one of Dobie's books, *Texas and Southwestern Lore*. The reviewer, Stanley Walker, identifies her as a "descendant of a family of wealthy Spanish landowners" (November 13, 1927). All of these sources are in the Mireles-Gonzalez Papers.

4. These mostly undated and unidentified newspaper clippings are to be found in the Mireles-Gonzalez Papers.

5. James McNutt interviewed Jovita Gonzalez in 1981, two years before her death.

6. The Mexican American Library Project of the Benson Latin American Collection at the University of Texas at Austin houses a small collection of Jovita Gonzalez de Mireles manuscripts. In it can be found what appears to be an undated recollective sketch from youth called "Comenzamos con Problemas—Un Incidente Feo" (Problems Begin—An Ugly Incident), where the author at an unspecified time later in her life recalls how she cried to her grandmother when Anglo-American little girls refused to play with her, saying she was bad and should go back to Mexico. "I shall go see the Mother Superior," the grandmother is quoted as saying; "my granddaughter shall not be insulted and humiliated."

7. Américo Paredes tells us that Gonzalez is mistaken in identifying this song as a true *corrido;* the song is actually "in garbled *decimas* (ten-line, internally rhyming stanzas) rather than in *corrido* form." The earliest true *corridos,* he says, are those he has identified as such, particularly "El Corrido de Kiansis" about south Texas Mexican *vaqueros* driving cattle up to Kansas and pitting their skills against those of the Anglo Cowboys. He is, of course, technically correct. One suspects, however, that the nonscholarly folk often use the emic genre *corrido* to refer to a variety of songs, and this is probably how they identified it to Gonzalez. More important, and technical definitions notwithstanding, has not Jovita Gonzalez early on identified the Texan-Mexican resistance fighter confronting the Anglos "with his pistol in his hand"? But Professor Paredes says that Remigio Treviño "most probably . . . was a Pro-Union guerrilla" and therefore not a true forerunner of the Kansas *vaqueros* or Gregorio Cortez. He provides no evidence on the point (Paredes 1976:25).

8. The sharp knife of irony is, perhaps, driven home yet again when, in 1940, Gonzalez makes her final ethnographic contribution in an essay published in a Dobie collection, *Mustangs and Cow Horses,* a book of horse stories. First, however, it is worth noting one of Dobie's own contributions to his collection, called "As Smart as a Cutting Horse." His opening paragraph reads: "In the language of the range, to say that somebody is 'as smart as a cutting horse' is to say that he is

smarter than a Philadelphia lawyer, smarter than a coyote, smarter than a Harvard graduate—all combined. There just can't be anything smarter than a smart cutting horse. He can do everything but talk Meskin' and he understands that" (Gonzalez de Mireles 1940:403). Next to Dobie's essay we find Jovita's contribution, "The Mescal-Drinking Horse," the story of "El Pajaro," a lowly scrub horse in southern Texas who liked to drink El Pajaro mescal and acquired fame for his ability to smell oncoming Texas Rangers and thereby to save his master's life. Alas, in his later years, El Pajaro got religion, became a priest's horse, and was renamed Morning Star (1940:396–402). Even here we find an anticipation of the smart little horse that Gregorio Cortez rode to escape the Rangers (Paredes 1958:42–47). Her 1940 story on "The Mescal Drinking Horse" is the last of Gonzalez: published cultural studies, although she presented two more papers in 1947 and 1948 before the Texas Folklore Society. They remained unpublished. After 1940 she dedicated herself largely to the teaching of secondary school Spanish and with her husband, E. E. Mireles, co-authored a series of Spanish language textbooks. I am currently at work on a book on this couple's full intellectual career.

CHAPTER 4. AMÉRICO PAREDES

1. Professor Paredes once told me that there was no direct communication between Webb and/or Dobie and himself throughout their careers in Austin. However, it may interest the reader to know that Dobie did comment on *With His Pistol in His Hand*. On the facing page of Dobie's personal copy in the Dobie Collection at Austin, Dobie writes: "Paredes knows more about *corridos* than about *hombres del campo*." He also underlines, without comment, almost every Paredes reference to the Texas Rangers in the text. Finally, he comments on this paragraph in *With His Pistol . . .* : "The picture of the Mexican as an inveterate thief, especially of horses and cattle, is of interest to the psychologist as well as to the folklorist. The cattle industry of the southwest had its origins in he Nueces-Rio Grande area, with the stock and the ranches of the Rio Grande rancheros. The "cattle barons" built up their fortunes at the expense of the Border Mexican by means which were far from ethical. One notes that the white Southerner took his slave women as concubines and then created an image of the male Negro as a sex fiend. In the same way he appears to have taken the Mexican's property and then made him out a thief" (1971:20). In the margin of this paragraph Dobie writes: "Just about the truth."
Elsewhere, Paredes writes the following assessment of Dobie's work: Classifying Dobie as a "romantic regionalist," he says: "Most 'regionalists,' moreover, have been romantics through and through. The romantic point of view deals not with living things but with idealizations of them, in a world where there are no contemporary problems. This romantic attitude very often follows the conquest of new territory. In the history of Spanish folklore, the vogue for everything *morisco*

(Moorish) after the fall of Granada is well known. It is this tendency to sentimen-
talize a conquered people, within its elements of condescension, which directs the
efforts of the majority of 'regionalists.' They have focused their energies on the
regional groups, that is to say on the 'Romantic Southwest.' They look for local
color, for the rare, the archaic, the bizarre, and as a result the sort of folklore with
which we are concerned has small place in their collections.

"Combine this with lack of personal communication between collector and
informant, and you have the regionalists' most serious flaw. This is why J. Frank
Dobie, for example, could spend his life among Mexican informants in Mexico as
well as in the United States without ever really getting to know them; why John A.
Lomax and others collected Mexican songs in South Texas without being aware of
the existence of a whole tradition of Border *corridos* dealing with cultural conflict.
They collected variants of the "Corrido de los Sediciosos" ("Corrido of the Seditionists") which related the uprising in 1915 of a group of Texas Mexicans com-
manded by Aniceto Pizaña, but they were variants which ridicule the "sediciosos"
and give the role of hero to the Texas Rangers, hated so strongly by the regional
folk groups!

"A certain mistaken delicacy, of the desire not to offend, not to bring up pain-
ful matters which we all know have existed and which we all want to remedy, has
convinced some folklorists that it would be in poor taste to expose the conflict
between the Mexican and North American cultures" (1977:16–17).

It should also be noted that in his recently published novel, *George Washington
Gomez* (1990), Professor Paredes offers a caustic, almost savage satirical sketch of
an eminent Anglo-Texas folklorist in the 1930s whom he dubs "K. Hank Harvey"
(1990:270–75).

2. Yet I am well aware that Professor Paredes has constantly attacked Octavio Paz for his hyperbolic vision of urban *pachucos* and Mexican-Americans in
general, most recently in a public address at the University of Texas at Austin
when he received the Order of the Aztec Eagle Medal from the Republic of Mexico (November 20, 1990). Never one to kowtow to hegemonic power, in his acceptance speech Professor Paredes "thanked" the Mexican government by attacking
most of its conformist intellectuals such as Paz for their disparagement of
Mexican-Americans.

CHAPTER 5. EMERGENT POSTMODERN MEXICANO

1. As I write these words in summer 1992, the Limonada area, for example, is
reporting temperatures of 105 degrees, an unemployment rate of 21.5 percent,
and an increasing homicide rate attributed by the authorities to gangs and an
increasing drug traffic. Further downriver in the Lower Rio Grande Valley, the
same conditions prevail, although there the accumulated pollution of the Rio
Grande by the *maquiladora* industry is suspected as the cause of a range of increasing health problems including childbirth brain disorders. The war continues.

2. As with all Americans, the divorce rate is increasing dramatically in this population.

3. Here we must note the independent though related use of *difference* by Ramón Saldívar (1990:6–9). My *difference*, of course, is my focus on the more everyday, working-class expressive practices of difference rather than a socially distanced literary production.

CHAPTER 6. CARNE, CARNALES, AND THE CARNIVALESQUE

1. Based on field research carried out, at various moments, during 1981 and 1982 under the partial auspices of a grant from the National Research Council and the Ford Foundation. All personal names, including nicknames, as well as place names (except for Hidalgo County), are fictitious.

2. For a masterful descriptive and analytical account of working-class Mexican-American food culture in south Texas see Montaño (1992).

CHAPTER 7. THE NATIVE DANCES

1. Almost all personal as well as nicknames and place names, other than San Antoñio and Alamo Heights, are fictitious. Based on friendships developed between 1975 and 1978 while residing in San Antoñio.

2. As Peña speaks of the degradation of musical culture from the high resistively pure moment of the heroic *conjunto,* it is as if he is rhetorically constructing a new Gregorio Cortez, this one with his accordion in his hand. And were this particular influence not enough, and, oddly enough for a Marxist, Peña also seems concerned about *fuereños,* the new *fuereños:* "contributing to the decline of the conjunto in Texas has been the heavy influx of undocumented Mexican workers . . . ," an influx which, citing Vernon Briggs, he tells us, has "assumed epidemic proportions." The tone of alarm and the metaphor of illness continue. Since these new *fuereños* favor a more "tropical" musical style, they "pose a substantial threat to the economic health of conjunto by encroaching deeply into the crucial public-ballroom dance circuit"(1985:160).

CHAPTER 8. THE DEVIL DANCES

1. Based on field research carried out, intermittently, between 1979 and 1981 under the partial auspices of a National Chicano Council for Higher Education grant from the Ford Foundation. All names are fictitious.

2. See Motif. No. G 303.10.4.0.1 (Devil Haunts Dance halls) and variants in Stith Thompson's *Motif Index of Folk Literature,* as well as Motif No. G 303.6.2.1

(Devil Appears at a Dance) in Baughman's *Type and Motif Index of the Folktales of England and North America*.

See John O. West's descriptive *Mexican American Folklore* for a summary of such brief descriptive reports (1988:73–74 and 271 n. 14). Also, and more important, de Leon reports the devil in his account of nineteenth-century Texas-Mexican folklore (1982:160, 164, 166). See also Perez (1951) for reports of sightings in Austin, Texas.

Professor Yolanda Broyles-Gonzalez of the University of California at Santa Barbara reports retrospectively on the devil's appearance at dances in San Antoñio in a popular article in a local newspaper (1985). She was then teaching at the University of Texas at San Antoñio.

3. What did appear to be relatively new was the relative *intensification* of such appearances and sightings beginning in south Texas in the 1970s and then gradually spreading to other parts of greater Mexico in a seeming new wave of "popularity." My principal way of verifying this intensification was through the reports of student collectors who took my class in Mexican-American folklore first as teaching assistant at the University of Texas at Austin and later at the University of Texas at San Antoñio throughout the 1970s. This reportage together with my own awareness of ongoing experience in the Mexican-American community of south and central Texas persuaded me that this traditional legend experienced a resurgence and wide dissemination in this period by comparison with preceding decades and our own time.

Then, of course, I began to hear of him in a more direct manner when I went dancing in San Antoñio between 1975 and 1978. Yet initially my reaction was to ignore him as I was coming to my interpretation of dancing. Retrospectively, I now suspect that then I could not make interpretive sense of the figure of evil that I had known in my childhood amidst a performance which seemed to me to be one of creative, assertive critical difference as I have suggested. But his quite evident presence in the dancing culture of south Texas at this time could not be ignored, or so I decided just as I was leaving San Antoñio to accept a postdoctoral fellowship at UCLA where I would spend the academic year 1978–79. I spent the fall of that year working through the student-collected data I had received, reflecting on the conversation I had had in San Antoñio dance halls and reading a great deal of theoretical literature. But I had yet to meet the devil in the field myself. During the Christmas season of 1978 the devil appeared as in one of Bourke's nativity plays. I had briefly returned to south Texas to visit my parents in Corpus Christi, Texas, and while eating Christmas *tamales,* a female relative told me about such a recent appearance at a dance hall, El Cielito Lindo in Limonada. I returned to UCLA for the rest of the academic year and applied for and received a Ford Foundation summer fellowship to track down the devil that coming summer. I thank the Foundation, Rolando Hinojosa, and Arturo Madrid for their support. That same spring, I was also invited to rejoin the anthropology department at the University of Texas at Austin where I had done my graduate work, this time as an assistant professor alongside my mentor, Professor Américo Paredes. I moved to Austin in May. Then, following roughly the same path that John Bourke and Gregorio Cortez had taken in their respective journeys to south Texas, and with my cousin's information in hand, I arrived at Mendieta's place in the summer of 1979.

CHAPTER 9. CULTURE AND BEDEVILMENT

1. Cf. Macklin and Crumrine (1973) for an example of a partial effort to historicize the activities of three folk saints operating in northern Mexico about this same time.

2. Yet see my discussion in Chapter 6. Is it the case that the carnivalesque frees men from this fate, a fate also conditioned by poverty in a capitalist social order?

3. Sometimes, those who are severely ill are brought to the chapel by their families who collectively engage in a ritual prayer of supplication for a miraculous cure (Romano 1964:114–17).

4. Tomás Rivera's novel appeared in its first 1971 edition with Quinto Sol Publications. Written originally in Spanish, it has since been reissued in a new translation by Arte Publico Press under a new title, *And the Earth Did Not Devour Him* (1987). I am using this latter text.

5. But here one must make note of two *Latina compañeras* whose projects, coincident with my own writing, pursue these same issues in compelling terms. Behar (1993) writes evocatively of Esperanza and also Chencha, Mexican working-class women and sometime *curanderas*, and their relationship to race, class, and gender domination in Mexico and across the border. Drawing on her growing-up experiences in south Texas, Anzaldua (1987) explores literal and metaphorical "borders" in relation to these same sources of domination again, in evocative form. Through their writing they seem to become literary *curanderas*, attempting to heal what Anzaldua calls "la herida abíerta" (the open wound" of the U.S.-Mexico border. See also the fine literary evocation of supplications to Don Pedrito Jaramillo by Sandra Cisneros in her "Little Miracles, Kept Promises" in *Woman Hollering Creek* (1991). Yet, the *curandera is* a figure of paradox. As we go to press, a *curandera* has been co-indicted in a murder-for-hire scheme within the postmodern upper-middle-class Mexican culture of Brownsville, Texas. The devil comes in many forms (Brenner 1993).

6. Yet, long before I knew Tyler's work and the postmodern school of critical ethnography, I met my wife, Marianna Adler, who in the 1970s offered a compelling model of this kind of ethnography, married to feminism and Marxism, at a moment when I was beginning my writing dance with the devil and was in dire need of such (Adler 1980).

Glossary

A toda madre   Fine, terrific, great. *Madre* (mother) is a near-sacred role and symbol in *mexicano* culture, so that it has great potency for use as an expression of extreme approval, as in a *toda madre* (literally, "it's very mother"), or as an ultimate curse, as in *chinga tu madre* (fuck your mother).

agabachada   From *gabacho,* one of several *mexicano* slur words for Anglos. Used here in the feminine, an *agabachada* is an Anglicized woman.

bato   Guy, dude.

bro   Short for "brother." As with so much *mexicano* English slang, this one is borrowed from blacks, with whom *mexicanos* often have contiguous neighborhoods and shared occupations.

centavo   Literally, a cent or penny. Hence, in south Texas, J. C. Penney is sometimes called *el centavo.*

chingao   Local pronunciation of *chingado,* from *chingar* (to sexually violate). Can be used as an all-purpose curse, the way "fuck" is in English.

compa   Short either for *compañero* (companion) or *compadre* (coparent). Something like "good buddy" in English.

conjunto   A musical ensemble consisting of a lead accordion, guitars, rhythm section, and vocalization.

ese   Guy, dude.

hondo   Money.

la brack   Slang *mexicano* expression for Brackenridge High School in San Antoñio.

menudo   Mexican beef tripe soup. Consumed ritually after a night out on the town or on Saturday or Sunday mornings.

puta(o)   A promiscuous individual, but also used as a general all-purpose curse.

ruca   Literally, an old hag, but used more often as a slang term for woman, perhaps something like "broad" or "chick."

telenovelas   Latin American soap operas.

watchate   A Hispanicized version of "Watch it!"

References

Adler, Marianna. 1980. Women, Class, and Patriarchy: The Reproduction of an Ideology in Everyday Life. MA thesis. University of Texas at Austin.

Alarcón, Justo. 1980. Las metamorfosis del diablo en El Diablo en Texas de Aristeo Brito. De colores 5:30–44.

Anzaldua, Gloria. 1987. Borderlands/La Frontera: The New Mestiza. San Francisco: Spinsters/Aunt Lute Books.

Appadurai, Arjun. 1981. Gastro-politics in Hindu South Asia. American Ethnologist 18:494–511.

Arce, Carlos H.; Edward Murguia; and W. Parker Frisbie. 1987. Phenotype and Life Changes of Chicanos. Hispanic Journal of Behavioral Sciences. 9:19–32.

Arnold, Matthew. 1962 (1867). On the Study of Celtic Literature. In Lectures and Essays in Criticism, ed. R. H. Super. Ann Arbor: University of Michigan Press. 291–386.

Bakhtin, Mikhail. 1984. Rabelais and His World. Bloomington: Indiana University Press.

Barrera, Mario. 1979. Race and Class in the Southwest: A Theory of Racial Inequality. Notre Dame: Notre Dame University Press.

Bateson, Gregory. 1972. A Theory of Play and Fantasy. In Steps to an Ecology of Mind. New York: Random House. 177–193.

Bauman, Richard. 1975. Verbal Art as Performance. American Anthropologist 77:290–312.

Bean, Frank D.; Elizabeth H. Stephen; and Wolfgang Opitz. 1985. The Mexican Original Population in the United States: A Demographic Overview. In The Mexican American Experience: An Interdisciplinary Anthology, eds. Rudolfo O. de la Garza, Frank D. Bean, Charles M. Bonjean, Ricardo Romo, and Rodolfo Alvarez. Austin: University of Texas Press. 57–78.

Behar, Ruth. 1993. Translated Woman: Crossing the Border with Esperanza's Story. Boston: Beacon Press.

Berman, Marshall. 1982. All That Is Solid Melts into Air. New York: Simon and Schuster.

Berman, Russell. 1986. The Rise of the German Novel: Crisis and Charisma. Cambridge: Harvard University Press.

Bloch, Maurice. 1974. Symbols, Song, Dance and Features of Articulation: Is Religion an Extreme Form of Traditional Authority? Archives européennes de Sociologie 15:51–81.

Bloom, Harold. 1973. The Anxiety of Influence. New Haven: Yale University Press.

Bourke, John G. 1893. The Miracle Play of the Rio Grande. Journal of American Folklore 6:89–95.

Bourke, John G. 1894a. The American Congo. Scribner's Magazine 15:590–610.

Bourke, John G. 1894b. Popular Medicine, Customs, and Superstitions of the Rio Grande. Journal of American Folklore 7:119–46.

Bourke, John G. 1895. The Folk-Foods of the Rio Grande Valley and of Northern Mexico. Journal of American Folklore 8:41–71.

Bourke, John G. 1896. Notes on the Language and Folk-Usage of the Rio Grande Valley (with Especial Regard to Survivals of Arabic Custom). Journal of American Folklore 9:81–116.

Bovenschen, Silvia. 1978. The Contemporary Witch, the Historical Witch and the Witch Myth: The Witch Subject of the Appropriation of Nature and Object of the Domination of Nature. New German Critique 15:83–119.

Brenner, Marie. 1993. Murder on the Border. New Yorker (Sept 13), 52–75.

Briggs, Charles L. 1988. Competence in Performance: The Creativity of Tradition in Mexicano Verbal Art. Philadelphia: University of Pennsylvania Press.

Brito, Aristeo. 1990 (1976). The Devil in Texas/El Diablo en Texas. Tempe, AZ: Bilingual Press.

Brown, Norman O. 1959. Life against Death: The Psychoanalytical Meaning of History. New York: Random House.

Broyles-Gonzales, Yolanda. 1985. Even the Devil Dances at El Camaroncito. San Antonio Light (May 27), E1–E5.

Bruner, Edward M. 1986. Ethnography as Narrative. In The Anthropology of Experience, eds. Victor W. Turner and Edward M. Bruner. Urbana: University of Illinois Press. 139–55.

Calderon, Hector, and José David Saldívar, eds. 1991. Criticism in the Borderlands: Studies in Chicano Literature, Culture, and Ideology. Durham: Duke University Press.

Cisneros, Sandra. 1991. Woman Hollering Creek and Other Stories. New York: Random House.

Clifford, James, and George E. Marcus, eds. 1986. Writing Culture: The Poetics and Politics of Ethnography. Berkeley: University of California Press.

Clifford, James. 1986. Introduction. Writing Culture: The Poetics and Politics of Ethnography, ed. James Clifford and George Marcus. Berkeley: University of California Press.

Clifford, James. 1988a. On Ethnographic Authority. *In* The Predicament of Culture: Twentieth-Century Ethnography, Literature, and Art. Cambridge: Harvard University Press. 21–54.

Clifford, James. 1988b. The Predicament of Culture: Twentieth-Century Ethnography, Literature, and Art. Cambridge: Harvard University Press.

Crain, Mary M. 1991. Poetics and Politics in the Ecuadorean Andes: Women's Narratives of Death and Devil Possession. American Ethnologist 18:67–89.

Cummings, Laura. 1991. Carne con Limón: Reflections on the Construction of Social Harmlessness. American Ethnologist 18:370–372.

de la Fuente, Patricia. 1986. Invisible Women in the Narrative of Tomás Rivera. Revista Chicano-Riqueña 13:81–89.

de Leon, Arnoldo. 1982. The Tejano Community, 1836–1900. Albuquerque: University of New Mexico Press.

de Leon, Arnoldo. 1983. They Called Them Greasers: Anglo Attitudes toward Mexicans in Texas, 1821–1900. Austin: University of Texas Press.

Dobie, J. Frank. 1923. El Cancion del Rancho de Los Olmos. Journal of American Folklore 36:192–96.

Dobie, J. Frank. 1925. Versos of the Texas Vaqueros. Publications of the Texas Folklore Society, ed., J. Frank Dobie. 4:30–43.

Dobie, J. Frank. 1930. Coronado's Children: Tales of Lost Mines and Buried Treasures of the Southwest. Austin: Southwest Press. Reprinted by the University of Texas Press (1978).

Dobie, J. Frank. 1958. John G. Bourke as Soldier, Writer, and Man. Arizona Quarterly 14:226–33.

Dobie, J. Frank. 1980a (1964). Some Part of Myself. Austin: University of Texas Press.

Dobie, J. Frank. 1980b (1935). Tongues of the Monte. Austin: University of Texas Press.

Dobie, J. Frank. 1981 (1929). A Vaquero of the Brush Country. Austin: University of Texas Press.

Dodson, Ruth. 1951. The Curandero of Los Olmos. *In* The Healer of Los Olmos and Other Mexican Lore, ed. Wilson M. Hudson. Dallas: Southern Methodist University Press. 9–70.

Dorson, Richard M. 1971. Is There a Folk in the City? *In* The Urban Experience and Folk Tradition, ed. Américo Paredes and Ellen J. Stekert. Austin: University of Texas Press. 21–52.

Douglas, Mary. 1968. The Social Control of Cognition: Some Factors in Joke Perception. Man: The Journal of the Royal Anthropological Institute 3:361–76.

Douglas, Mary. 1971. Deciphering a Meal. *In* Myth, Symbol, and Culture, ed. Clifford Geertz. New York: W. W. Norton. 61–81.

Douglas, Mary. 1978 (1966). Purity and Danger: An Analysis of the Concepts of Pollution and Taboo. London: Routledge & Kegan Paul.

Dower, John W. 1986. War without Mercy: Race and Power in the Pacific. New York: Pantheon.

Dufour, Charles L. 1968. The Mexican War: A Compact History, 1846–48. New York: Hawthorn Books. 98–99.

Ellman, Richard, and Charles Feidelson, Jr., eds. 1965. The Modern Tradition: Backgrounds of Literature. New York: Oxford University Press.

Fanon, Frantz. 1963. The Wretched of the Earth. New York: Grove Press.

Fernandez, James. 1986. Persuasions and Performances: The Play of Tropes in Culture. Bloomington: Indiana University Press.

Fischer, Michael M. J. 1986. Ethnicity and the Post-Modern Arts of Memory. In Writing Culture: The Poetics and Politics of Ethnography, ed. James Clifford and George E. Marcus. Berkeley: University of California Press. 194–223.

Foley, Douglas. 1977. From Peones to Politicos: Ethnic Relations in a South Texas Town. Austin: University of Texas, Center for Mexican American Studies.

Foley, Douglas. 1990. Learning Capitalist Culture: Deep in the Heart of Tejas. Philadelphia: University of Pennsylvania Press.

Foster, Hal. 1983. The Anti-Aesthetic: Essays on Postmodern Culture. Port Townsend, WA: Bay Press.

Foster, Susan L. 1992. Dancing Culture. American Ethnologist 19:362–66.

Frisbie, W. Parker; Wolfgang Opitz; and Frank D. Bean. 1987. Cultural Attachment and Marital Instability among Hispanics. Texas Population Research Center Papers, Series 9.

Garcia, John. 1981. "Yo Soy Mexicano . . .": Self-Identity and Sociodemographic Correlates. Social Science Quarterly 62:88–98.

Garcia, Richard A. 1978. Class, Consciousness and Ideology—The Mexican Community of San Antonio, Texas: 1930–1940. Aztlán 9:23–70.

Geertz, Clifford. 1973a. Deep Play: Notes on the Balinese Cockfight. In The Interpretation of Cultures. New York: Basic Books.

Geertz, Clifford. 1973b. Thick Description: Toward an Interpretive Theory of Culture. In The Interpretation of Cultures. New York: Basic Books.

Geertz, Clifford. 1980. Blurred Genres: The Refiguration of Social Thought. American Scholar 29:165–79.

Gilroy, Paul. 1991. "There Ain't No Black in the Union Jack": The Cultural Politics of Race and Nation. Chicago: University of Chicago Press.

Glazer, Mark. 1984. Continuity and Change in Legends: Two Mexican American Examples. In Perspectives on Contemporary Legend: Proceedings of the Conference on Contemporary Legend, ed. Paul Smith. Sheffield: CECTAL. 108–27.

Gomez-Quiñones, Juan. 1974. 5th and Grande Vista (Poems, 1960–1973). New York: Coliccion.

Gonzalez, Jovita. 1927. The Folklore of the Texas-Mexican Vaquero. Publications of the Texas Folklore Society, ed. J. Frank Dobie. 4:7–22.

Gonzalez, Jovita. 1930a. America Invades the Border Towns. Southwest Review 15:469–477.

Gonzalez, Jovita. 1930b. Social Life in Cameron, Starr, and Zapata Counties. MA thesis. University of Texas at Austin.

Gonzalez, Jovita. 1930c. Tales and Songs of the Texas-Mexicans. Publications of the Texas Folklore Society, ed. J. Frank Dobie. 8:86–116.

Gonzalez, Jovita. 1932. Among My People. Publications of the Texas Folklore Society, ed. J. Frank Dobie. 10:99–108.

Gonzalez, Jovita. 1935. The Bullet-Swallower. Publications of the Texas Folklore Society, ed. J. Frank Dobie. 10:107–14.

Gonzalez de Mireles, Jovita. 1940. The Mescal-Drinking Horse. Publications of the Texas Folklore Society, ed. J. Frank Dobie, Modz C. Boatright, and Harry C. Ransom. 16:396–402.

Graham, Joe Stanley. 1981. The Caso: A Study of an Emic Genre of Folk Narrative among Mexican-Americans of West Texas. Ph.D. dissertation. University of Texas at Austin.

Gramsci, Antonio. 1971. Selections from the Prison Notebooks of Antonio Gramsci. 2d ed. Ed. & trans. Quintin Hoare and Geoffrey Nowell Smith. London: Laurence and Wishart.

Gramsci, Antonio. 1988. An Antonio Gramsci Reader: Selected Writings, 1916–1935. Ed. David Forgacs. New York: Schocken Books.

Greenblatt, Stephen. 1980. Renaissance Self-Fashioning: From More to Shakespeare. Chicago: University of Chicago Press.

Greenblatt, Stephen. 1988. Shakespearean Negotiations: The Circulation of Social Energy in Renaissance England. Berkeley and Los Angeles: University of California Press.

Grenier, Gilles. 1985. Shifts to English as Usual Language by Americans of Spanish Mother Tongue. In The Mexican-American Experience: An Interdisciplinary Anthology, ed. Rudolfo O. de la Garza, Frank D. Bean, Charles M. Bonjean, Ricardo Romo, and Rodolfo Alvarez. Austin: University of Texas Press. 346–358.

Hanna, Judith Lynne. 1979. To Dance Is Human: A Theory of Nonverbal Communication. Austin: University of Texas Press.

Hansen, Niles. 1981. The Border Economy: Regional Development in the Southwest. Austin: University of Texas Press.

Harrigan, Stephen. 1987. Cisneros at Forty: the Hopes, Haunts and Heartaches of Texas' Political Superstar. Texas Monthly (September issue), 83–91, 134–41.

Harris, Charles H., and Louis R. Sadler. 1978. The Plan of San Diego and the Mexico United States Crisis of 1916: A Reexamination. Hispanic American Historical Review 58:381–408.

Harvey, David. 1989. The Condition of Post-Modernity. Cambridge: Blackwell.

Hastings, Max. 1987. The Korean War. New York: Simon and Schuster.

Hearn Francis. 1976–77. Toward a Critical Theory of Play. Telos 30:145–60.

Heath, Shirley Brice. 1990. Introductory Comments. Seminar Series. Reversibility and Majority/Minority Discourse. University of Virginia. Unpublished.

Herrera-Sobek, Maria. 1988. The Devil in the Discotheque: A Semiotic Analysis of a Contemporary Legend. In Monsters with Iron Teeth: Perspectives on

Contemporary Legend, ed. Gillian Bennett and Paul Smith. Sheffield: Sheffield Academic Press. 147–58.

Herzog, Lawrence A. 1990. Where North Meets South: Cities, Space, and Politics on the U.S.-Mexico Border. Austin: University of Texas Press.

Hinojosa, Gilberto. 1983. A Borderlands Town in Transition: Laredo, 1755–1870. College Station: Texas A & M University Press.

Jameson, Fredric. 1981. The Political Unconscious: Narrative as a Socially Symbolic Act. Ithaca: Cornell University Press.

Jameson, Fredric. 1984. Postmodernism, or, The Cultural Logic of Late Capitalism. New Left Review, no. 146 (July–August), 59–92.

Jameson, Fredric. 1992. Postmodernism, or the Cultural Logic of Late Capitalism. Durham: Duke University Press.

Johannsen, Robert W. 1985. To the Halls of the Montezumas: The Mexican War in the American Imagination. New York: Oxford University Press.

Lauria, Anthony, Jr. 1964. Respeto, Relajo, and Interpersonal Relations in Puerto Rico. Anthropological Quarterly 3:53–67.

Lavender, David. 1966. Climax at Buena Vista: The American Campaigns in Northeastern Mexico, 1846–47. New York: J. B. Lippincott Co.

Limón, José E. 1973. Stereotyping and Chicano Resistance: An Historical Dimension. Aztlán 4:257–70.

Limón, José E. 1974. El Primer Congreso Mexicanista de 1911: A Precursor to Contemporary Chicanismo. Aztlán 5:85–117.

Limón, José E. 1981. The Folk Performance of Chicano and the Cultural Limits of Political Ideology. In ". . . And Other Neighborly Names": Social Process and Cultural Image in Texas Folklore, ed. Richard Bauman and Roger D. Abrahams. Austin: University of Texas Press. 197–225.

Limón, José E. 1983. Texas-Mexican Popular Music and Dancing: Some Notes on History and Symbolic Process. Latin American Music Review 4:229–246.

Limón, José E. 1987. Mexican Speech Play: History and the Psychological Discourses of Power. Texas Papers on Latin America, no. 87-06. Austin: University of Texas Institute of Latin American Studies.

Limón, José E. 1989. Carne, Carnales and the Carnivalesque: Bakhtinian Batos, Disorder and Narrative Discourse. American Ethnologist 16:471–86.

Limón, José E. 1992. Mexican Ballads, Chicano Poems: History and Influence in Mexican-American Social Poetry. Berkeley: University of California Press.

Lloyd, David. 1987. Nationalism and Minor Literature: James Clarence Mangan and the Emergence of Irish Cultural Nationalism. Berkeley: University of California Press.

Lyndon B. Johnson School of Public Affair. 1979. The Health of Mexican Americans in South Texas. Policy Research Project No. 32. University of Texas at Austin.

Macklin, Barbara June, and N. Ross Crumríne. 1973. Three Northern Mexican Folk Saint Movements. Comparative Studies in Society and History 15:89–105.

Macklin, June. 1980. "All the Good and Bad in This World." *In* Women, Traditional Medicine, and Mexican American Culture, ed. Margarita Melville. St. Louis: C. V. Moseby. 127–54.

Madsen, William. 1964. The Mexican-Americans of South Texas. New York: Holt, Rinehart, and Winston.

Malinowski, Bronislaw. 1961 (1922). Argonauts of the Western Pacific. New York: E. P. Dutton.

Manganaro, Marc, ed. 1990. Modernist Anthropology: From Fieldwork to Texts. Princeton: Princeton University Press.

Marcus, George E. 1986. Contemporary Problems of Ethnography in the Modern World System. *In* Writing Culture: The Poetics and Politics of Ethnography, ed. James Clifford and George E. Marcus. Berkeley: University of California Press.

Marcus, George E., and Dick Cushman. 1982. Ethnographies as Texts. Annual Review of Anthropology 11:25–69.

Marcus, George E., and Michael M. J. Fischer. 1986. Anthropology as Cultural Critique: an Experimental Moment in the Human Sciences. Chicago: University of Chicago Press.

Maril, Robert Lee. 1989. Poorest of Americans: The Mexican-Americans of the Lower Rio Grande Valley of Texas. Notre Dame: Notre Dame University Press.

Markides, Kyriakos S., and Thomas Cole. 1985. Change and Continuity in Mexican American Religious Behavior: A Three Generational Study. *In* The Mexican American Experience: An Interdisciplinary Anthology, ed. Rudolfo O. de la Garza, Frank D. Bean, Charles M. Bonjean, Ricardo Romo, and Rodolfo Alvarez. Austin: University of Texas Press. 402–9.

Martin, Randy. 1985. Dance as a Social Movement. Social Text 12:54–70.

McMurtry, Larry. 1968. In a Narrow Grave: Essays on Texas. New York: Simon and Schuster.

McNutt, James Charles. 1982. Beyond Regionalism: Texas Folklorists and the Emergence of a Post-Regional Identity. Ph.D. dissertation. University of Texas at Austin.

McVicker, Mary Louise. 1968. The Writings of J. Frank Dobie: A Bibliography. Lawton, OK: Museum of the Great Plains.

Miller, Michael V., and Robert Lee Maril. 1979. Poverty in the Lower Rio Grande Valley of Texas: Historical and Contemporary Dimensions. Department of Rural Sociology Technical Report No. 78-2. College Station, TX: Texas A & M University.

Miller, Robert Ryal. 1989. Shamrock and Sword: The Saint Patrick's Battalion in the U.S.–Mexican War. Norman: University of Oklahoma Press.

Minh-ha, Trinh T. 1989. Woman, Native, Other: Writing Postcoloniality and Feminism. Bloomington: Indiana University Press.

Montaño, Mario. 1992. The History of Mexican Food Folkways of South Texas: Street Vendors, Offal Foods and Barbacoa de Cabeza. Ph.D. dissertation. University of Pennsylvania.

Montejano, David. 1987. Anglos and Mexicans in the Making of Texas, 1836–1936. Austin: University of Texas Press.

Nelson-Cisneros, Victor. 1975. La Clase Trabajadora in Tejas, 1920–1940. Aztlán 6:239–65.

Noriega, Chon, ed. 1992. Chicanos and Film. Representation and Resistance. Minneapolis: University of Minnesota Press.

Nun, José. 1969. Superproblacíon relativa ejerto industrial de reírva y masa marginal. Revista Latinoamericana de Sociologia. (July), 178–236.

Oates, Stephen B. 1973. Los Diablos Tejanos: The Texas Rangers. *In* The Mexican War: Changing Interpretations, ed. Odie B. Faulk and Joseph A. Stout, Jr. Chicago: Swallow Press. 120–36.

Olivares, Julian, ed. 1986. International Studies in Honor of Tomás Rivera. Houston: Arte Publico Press.

Ortner, Sherry B. 1984. Theory in Anthropology since the Sixties. Comparative Studies in Society and History 26:126–66.

Ostriker, Alicia. 1987. Dancing at the Devil's Party: Some Notes on Politics and Poetry. *In* Politics and Poetic Value, ed. Robert Van Hallberg. Chicago: University of Chicago Press. 207–24.

Owens, Williams A. 1967. Three Friends: Roy Bedichek, J. Frank Dobie, and Walter Prescott Webb. Austin: University of Texas Press.

Paredes, Américo. 1958. The Mexican Corrido: Its Rise and Fall. *In* Madstones and Twisters, ed. Mody C. Boatright, Wilson M. Hudson, and Allen Maxwell. Dallas: Southern Methodist University Press. 91–105.

Paredes, Américo. 1966. The Anglo-American in Mexican Folklore. *In* New Voices in American Studies, ed. Ray B. Browne, Donald M. Winkelman, and Allen Hayman. Lafayette, IN.: Purdue University Studies. 113–28.

Paredes, Américo. 1968. Folk Medicine and the Intercultural Jest. *In* Spanish-Speaking in the United States: Proceedings of the American Ethnological Society, ed. June Helm. Seattle: University of Washington Press. 104–19.

Paredes, Américo. 1971 (1958). With His Pistol in His Hand: A Border Ballad and Its Hero. Austin: University of Texas Press.

Paredes, Américo. 1976. A Texas-Mexican Cancionero. Urbana: University of Illinois Press.

Paredes, Américo. 1977 (1966). El Folklore de los Grupos de Origin Mexicano in Estados Unides. Folklore Americano 14:146–63. Reprinted as The Folk Base of Chicano Literature *in* Modern Chicano Writers, ed. Joseph Sommers and Tomás Ybarra-Frausto. (Englewoods Cliffs, N.J.: Prentice-Hall, 1977), 4–17. I translate the original title in my text, but I cite from this latter version as a matter of scholarly convenience.

Paredes, Américo. 1978. On Ethnographic Fieldwork among Minority Groups: A

Folklorist's Perspective. *In* New Directions in Chicano Scholarship, ed. Ricardo Romo and Raymund Paredes. La Jolla: Chicano Studies Center, University of California at San Diego. 1–32.

Paredes, Américo. 1986. Thoughts on Tomás Rivera. *In* International Studies in Honor of Tomás Rivera. Houston: Arte Publico Press. 24–25.

Paredes, Américo. 1990. George Washington Gomez. Houston: Arte Publico Press.

Paz, Octavio. 1961 (1951). The Labyrinth of Solitude: Life and Thought in Mexico. New York: Grove Press.

Peacock, James. 1968. Rites of Modernization: Symbolic and Social Aspects of Indonesian Proletarian Drama. Chicago: University of Chicago Press.

Peña, Manuel. 1980. Ritual Structure in a Chicano Dance. Latin American Music Review 1:47–73.

Peña, Manuel. 1985. The Texas-Mexican Conjunto: History of a Working Class Music. Austin: University of Texas Press.

Perez, Soledad. 1951. Mexican Folklore from Austin, Texas. *In* The Healer of Los Olmos and Other Mexican Lore, ed., Wilson M. Hudson. Dallas: Southern Methodist University Press. 71–125.

Pettit, Arthur G. 1980. Images of the Mexican American in Fiction and Film. College Station: Texas A&M University Press.

Porter, Joseph C. 1986. Paper Medicine Man: John Gregory Bourke and His American West. Norman: University of Oklahoma Press.

Porter, Joseph C. 1990. Personal letter to the author.

Rabinow, Paul. 1986. Representations Are Social Facts: Modernity and Post-Modernity in Anthropology. *In* Writing Culture: The Poetics and Politics of Ethnography, ed. James Clifford and George E. Marcus. Berkeley: University of California Press. 234–61.

Ramos, Samuel. 1962 (1934). Profile of Man and Culture in Mexico. Austin: University of Texas Press.

Reimers, Cordelia W. 1985. The Wage Structure of Hispanic Men. *In* The Mexican American Experience: An Interdisciplinary Anthology, ed. Rudolfo O. de la Garza, Frank D. Bean, Charles M. Bonjean, Ricardo Romo, and Rodolfo Alvarez. Austin: University of Texas Press. 118–32.

Relethford, J. H.; M. P. Stern; S. P. Gaskell; and H. P. Hazuda. 1983. Social Class, Admixture and Skin Color Variation in Mexican-Americans and Anglo Americans Living in San Antonio, Texas. American Journal of Physical Anthropology 61:97–102.

Rivera, Tomas. 1987. And the Earth Did Not Devour Him. Houston: Arte Publico Press.

Robinson, Cecil. 1977. Mexico and the Hispanic Southwest in American Literature. Tucson: University of Arizona Press.

Romano V., Octavio Ignacio. 1964. Don Pedrito Jaramillo: The emergence of a Mexican American Folk Saint. Ph.D. dissertation. University of California at Berkeley.

Romano V., Octavio Ignacio. 1965. Charismatic Medicine, Folk-Healing and
Folk-Sainthood. American Anthropologist 67:1151–73.
Romo, Ricardo. 1977. The Urbanization of Southwestern Chicanos in the Early
Twentieth Century. *In* New Directions in Chicano Scholarship, ed. Ricardo
Romo and Raymond Paredes. La Jolla: Chicano Studies Center, University
of California at San Diego.
Rosaldo, Renato. 1980. Ilongot Headhunting, 1883–1974: A Study in Society and
History. Stanford: Stanford University Press.
Rosaldo, Renato. 1985. Chicano Studies. Annual Review of Anthropology
13:405–27.
Rosaldo, Renato. 1987. Politics, Patriarchs, and Laughter. Cultural Critique
6:65–86.
Rosaldo, Renato. 1988. Fables of the Fallen Guy. Working Paper No. 21. Stan-
ford: Stanford University Chicano Research Center.
Rosaldo, Renato. 1989. Culture and Truth: The Remaking of Social Analysis.
Boston: Beacon Press.
Rosenbaum, David E. 1988. A Candidate Who Is More like Bush: Lloyd Millard
Bentsen, Jr. New York Times (July 13), 1.
Rubel, Arthur. 1966. Across the Tracks: Mexican Americans in a South Texas
Town. Austin: University of Texas Press.
Russell, Jeffrey Burton. 1986. Mephistopheles: The Devil in the Modern World.
Ithaca: Cornell University Press.
Said, Edward W. 1979 (1978). Orientalism. New York: Random House.
Saldívar, José D. 1991. Chicano Border Narratives as Cultural Critique. *In* Criti-
cism in the Borderlands: Studies in Chicano Literature, Culture, and Ideology,
ed. Hector Calderon and José David Saldívar. Durham: Duke University
Press. 167–87.
Saldívar, Ramón. 1990. Chicano Narrative: The Dialectics of Difference. Madi-
son: University of Wisconsin Press.
Saragoza, Alex. 1990. Recent Chicano Historiography: An Interpretive Essay.
Azltán 19:1–177.
Shannon, Kelley. 1993. Housing for Poor Criticized: San Antoñio Ranks among
Worst in National Study of Housing Quality. Associated Press. Austin
American-Statesman (Nov. 10, 1993), B-4.
Siegel, Bernard J. 1970. Defensive Structuring and Environmental Stress. Ameri-
can Journal of Sociology 76:11–32.
Sommers, Joseph. 1977. From the Cultural Premise to the Product: Critical Modes
and Their Application to a Chicano Literary Text. New Scholar 5:51–80.
Spielberg, Joseph. 1974. Humor in Mexican-American Palomilla: Some His-
torical, Social, and Psychological Implications. Revista Chicano-Requeña
2:41–50.
Stocking, George. 1987. Victorian Anthropology. New York: Free Press.
Strathern, Marilyn. 1987. An Awkward Relationship: The Case of Feminism and
Anthropology. Signs 12:276–92.

Taussig, Michael. 1980. The Devil and Commodity Fetishism in Latin America. Chapel Hill: University of North Carolina Press.

Taussig, Michael. 1984. History as Sorcery. Representations, no. 7:87–109.

Telles, Edward E., and Edward Murguia. 1990. Phenotypic Discrimination and Income Differences among Mexican Americans. Social Science Quarterly 71:682–96.

Tienda, Marta, and Lisa J. Neidert. 1985. Language, Education, and the Socioeconomic Achievement of Hispanic Origin Men. In The Mexican American Experience: An Interdisciplinary Anthology, ed. Rudolfo O. de la Garza, Frank D. Bean, Charles M. Bonjean, Ricardo Romo, and Rodolfo Alvarez. Austin: University of Texas Press. 359–76.

Tinkle, Lon. 1978. An American Original: The Life of J. Frank Dobie. New York: Little, Brown & Co.

Trotter, Robert T., and Juan Antonio Chavira. 1981. Curanderismo: Mexican American Folk Healing. Athens: University of Georgia Press.

Turner, Victor. 1974. Victorian Anthropology. New York: Free Press.

Tyler, Stephen A. 1986. Post-Modern Ethnography: From Document of the Occult to Occult Document. In Writing Culture: The Poetics and Politics of Ethnography, ed. James Clifford and George E. Marcus. Berkeley: University of California Press. 122–40.

Tyler, Stephen A. 1987. The Unspeakable: Discourse, Dialogue, and Rhetoric in the Postmodern World. Madison: University of Wisconsin Press.

Van Maanen, John. 1988. Tales of the Field: On Writing Ethnography. Chicago: University of Chicago Press.

Velasquez-Trevino, Gloria. 1985. Cultural Ambivalence in Early Chicana Prose Fiction. Ph.D. dissertation. Stanford University.

Viramontes, Helena Maria. 1988. Miss Clairol. In Chicana Creativity and Criticism: Charting New Frontiers in American Literature, ed. María Herrera-Sobek and Helena María Viramontes. Houston: Arte Publico Press. 101–5.

Waldman, Elizabeth. 1980. Profile of the Chicana: A Statistical Fact Sheet. In Mexican Women in the United States, ed. Adelaída del Castillo and Magdalena Mora. Los Angeles: UCLA Chicano Studies Center. 195–204.

Webb, Walter Prescott. 1931. The Great Plains. Boston: Ginn.

Webb, Walter Prescott. 1935. The Texas Rangers. Cambridge: Houghton Mifflin.

Weems, John Edward. 1974. To Conquer a Peace: The War between the United States and Mexico. Garden City, NY: Doubleday.

West, Cornel. 1993. Race Matters. Boston: Beacon Press.

West, John O. 1988. Mexican American Folklore. Little Rock: August House.

West, Richard. 1980. An American Family—Roots: The Mexican Version. Texas Monthly (March 1980), 108–19, 166–81.

White, Hayden. 1973. Metahistory: The Historical Imagination in Nineteenth-Century Europe. Baltimore: Johns Hopkins University Press.

Whiteford, Linda. 1977. Family Relations in Seco County: A Case Study of Social Change. Ph.D. dissertation. University of Wisconsin–Milwaukee.

Williams, Norma. 1990. The Mexican American Family: Tradition and Change. Dix Hills, NY: General Hall.

Williams, Raymond. 1977. Marxism and Literature. Oxford: Oxford University Press.

Williams, Raymond. 1989. The Future of Cultural Studies. *In* The Politics of Modernism: Against the New Conformists. London: Verso Books. 151–62.

Willis, Paul. 1981. Learning to Labour: How Working Class Kids Get Working Class Jobs. New York: Columbia University Press.

Young, Robert. 1985–86. Back to Bakhtin. Cultural Critique 1:71–92.

Zamora, Emilio. 1992. The World of the Mexican Worker in Texas. College Station: Texas A&M University Press.

Zavella, Patricia. 1987. Women's Work and Chicano Families: Cannery Workers of the Santa Clara Valley. Ithaca: Cornell University Press.

Index

New Directions in Anthropological Writing
History, Poetics, Cultural Criticism

GEORGE E. MARCUS
Rice University

JAMES CLIFFORD
University of California, Santa Cruz

GENERAL EDITORS

Nationalism and the Politics of Culture in Quebec
Richard Handler

*The Pastoral Son and the Spirit of Patriarchy: Religion, Society, and
Person among East African Stock Keepers*
Michael E. Meeker

Belonging in America: Reading Between the Lines
Constance Perin

Himalayan Dialogue: Tibetan Lamas and Gurung Shamans in Nepal
Stan Royal Mumford

Wombs and Alien Spirits: Women, Men, and the Zār *Cult in
Northern Sudan*
Janice Boddy

*People as Subject, People as Object: Selfhood and Peoplehood in
Contemporary Israel*
Virginia R. Domínguez

Sharing the Dance: Contact Improvisation and American Culture
Cynthia J. Novack

Debating Muslims: Cultural Dialogues in Postmodernity and Tradition
Michael M. J. Fischer and Medhi Abedi

Power and Performance: Ethnographic Explorations though Proverbial Wisdom and Theater in Shaba, Zaire
Johannes Fabian

Dialogue at the Margins: Whorf, Bakhtin, and Linguistic Relativity
Emily A. Schultz

Magical Arrows: The Maori, the Greeks, and the Folklore of the Universe
Gregory Schrempp

After Freedom: A Cultural Study in the Deep South
Hortense Powdermaker
With an Introductory essay by
Brackette F. Williams and Drexel G. Woodson

Dancing with the Devil: Society and Cultural Poetics in Mexican-American South Texas
José E. Limón